Part O

Everything in nature is connected; if you harm one thing, you harm everything.

– Cherokee Proverb

It's not uncommon for temperatures in the North Carolina mountains to creep into the seventies during the month of March. It's called Fool's Spring, the first warm spell each year that lulls creatures – human beings included – into thinking that winter is over, and spring has arrived. Inevitably, Fool's Spring is followed by Second Winter, a sudden cold snap where the temperatures drop below freezing, the wind blows cold, and some snowflakes might fall.

The mountains normally experience six pseudo seasons between the end of the real winter and the beginning of the actual spring. The cycle begins with Fool's Spring, which is followed by Second Winter. Then comes the Spring of Deception; a second warm spell where you're lulled into believing it's the no kidding, honest-to-~~god~~God arrival of spring since mother nature has already fooled you once. You realize you've been tricked again when Third Winter rolls through with chilly, gusty winds and frost. Then comes The Pollening, a period that lasts a few weeks where every flat surface is blanketed in a gritty yellow film of pollen from the trees, bushes, and weeds as they spring back to life. And then along comes Mud Season, days and days of rain – often pouring down in biblical proportions – that washes away the pollen, turns the creeks and the rivers a rusty brown, makes the red Appalachian clay slick to walk on, and nourishes the plants enabling them to pop when Actual Spring finally arrives. As the saying goes, if you don't like the weather now, wait an hour.

1

The bear was four years old. She gave birth to her first cub the year before, a healthy and rambunctious male that was now approaching a hundred pounds. She would keep him under her watch for several more months before kicking him out in late summer and forcing him to make his own way in the world. She had kept him close by her side when he was a wee cub oblivious to danger and in need of her constant attention in order to survive in the rugged mountain wilderness. As he grew, she afforded him a wider berth to explore and to begin honing the skills he would need when he had to live on his own, but she made sure he stayed close enough that she could summon him with a loud grunt when she sensed it was necessary for his own good.

The black bears that inhabit the North Carolina mountains don't hibernate like the grizzlies and brown bears hibernate in other parts of North America. That's due primarily to winters in North Carolina not being as cold and prolonged as in the chillier climes where other varieties of bears reside. While some bears hibernate for the winter – falling into a state of unconsciousness and sharply reducing their metabolism to conserve energy – black bears sleep in their dens for extended periods and then venture out in search of food during warm spells.

Mom and the yearling had established a den that kept them safe and dry. It was inside a crevice on the south side of Brushy Mountain, just a few miles outside of where the city of Asheville is situated today. Unless you saw them coming or going from the den, or you happened to spot strands of coarse black hair stuck in the bark of the sourwood tree near the entrance where mom and the yearling paused to scratch their backs when they emerged from the den, you weren't likely to notice it. The entrance was an opening between two boulders that was just wide enough for mom to squeeze through. Long before the yearling would mature and reach his full adult weight of nearly five hundred pounds, his girth would expand, and it would prevent him from entering the den where he was raised.

Fool's Spring arrived on time in March of 1784. The yearling awoke first and began to rustle, which nudged mom and brought her out of her weeks long slumber. Her first sensation was a sense of melancholy because she hadn't given birth to more cubs over the winter. She mated with two male bears the prior summer and she carried two embryos through the fall and into winter, but neither of the embryos attached to her uterine wall to develop into bear cubs. Female black bears often mate with more than one male and give birth to cubs with different fathers and with noticeable differences in their features. One cub might have a black snout, for instance, while his or her sibling has a brown snout because they had different fathers and inherited their different traits. Nature doesn't allow the embryos to attach to the mother's uterine wall if it senses that the mother lacks the weight and the stamina required to get her and her infant cubs through the winter and safely on to spring. The mother bear didn't know why nature decided she shouldn't give birth to any cubs that year and she hoped it wasn't a harbinger of things to come. She realized that before long, when she forced the yearling to go out and start a life of his own, she'd be left all alone on Brushy Mountain.

The two bears stretched the muscles they hadn't used in weeks and then shook off the dust that had accumulated on their fur. Mom walked slowly out of the den through the gap between the boulders. The warm sunlight felt especially pleasing after weeks spent in the cold, damp den. A few seconds later, the yearling appeared. He immediately eyed the sourwood tree just a few feet away, walked over to it, stood up on his hind legs, turned around, and vigorously rubbed his back against the rough sourwood bark. The sensation felt so good that he couldn't help but utter a low, rumbling moan of sheer delight.

Mom raised her head and stuck her snout up into the gentle breeze. Bears have a keen sense of smell that's estimated to be three thousand times more sensitive than the human nose. Some folks say that a black bear can smell a ripe apple from twenty miles away. Mom inhaled deeply and held it in for several seconds. She detected acorns that had fallen from the oak trees and beech nuts that had dropped from the beech trees last fall. Oak trees and beech trees produce more acorns and nuts once every third year in what is called a "mast" year, a term derived from the Old English word "mæst," meaning nuts accumulated on the ground from the trees in the forest. An adult black bear consumes about five thousand calories a day during the spring and summer, but it takes in nearly twenty thousand calories a day during the fall when it forages eighteen to twenty hours a day to bulk up in preparation for the arrival of winter. Mom recalled the prior year had been a mast year, which had made it easy for her and the yearling to fill their bellies and bulk up.

The rhetorical question asks, "does a bear shit in the woods?" The answer is yes ... but bears don't poop or pee in their dens while they're sleeping. It had been several weeks since the bears had set foot outside their den, so both mom and the yearling paused to relieve themselves before heading off in search of food.

Mom began the slow, meandering descent down Brushy Mountain heading in an easterly direction towards Bee Tree Creek where they could stop for a drink of clear, cold mountain stream water. Her route was in the same general direction as the smoke she smelled, which emanating from a cabin about a mile away.

The two bears used their claws to dig into rotting trees and to flip over large rocks and tree stumps to look for grubs and insects. They munched on leaves, grass, and acorns as they plodded along on what they thought was their first of many spring journeys to come. They

4

stopped at Bee Tree Creek, bent down, and drank. Mom paused for a moment, raised her snout into the air again, and sniffed. The smell of the smoke from the cabin was stronger and the scent told mom that something delicious was at the other end. She decided it warranted a closer look.

The cabin was on the east side of the creek on a slight rise not far from the creekbank. It was a single-pen cabin – a cabin consisting of a single room with a fireplace situated at one end – which was a common cabin style for those who wanted to build quickly in order to have shelter in place to protect them from winter's cold. Those with enough time and enough help might erect a saddlebag or a dogtrot cabin. A saddlebag consists of two pens built around a chimney located in the center of the structure and a dogtrot has a room on both ends, each with its own fireplace, with the area in between the two referred to as the dogtrot. The little cabin was made of roughhewn oak, pine, and tulip poplar trees. An ax was used to cut a saddle notch near the ends of each log so they could be joined together to secure the corners of the cabin. A mixture of straw and clay sealed the seams between the logs to keep out the cold. The roof was made of overlapping rough-cut boards. The chimney was crafted from stacked stones that were held in place with clay that had been excavated from the creekbank. There were no windows, just solid walls on all four sides. The door had a wooden latch and was held in place by leather hinges.

Mom and the yearling walked down the mountain behind the tree line on the west side of the creek and stopped about fifty yards from the cabin, which was a little further below them and over on the other side of the creek. A large scruffy dog was curled up asleep next to the front door. A thin stream of grey smoke rose from the chimney and wandered off in the southerly breeze where it slowly dissipated and then vanished all together. Even though mom and the yearling were upwind, and the smoke was blowing the other way, they noted the warm, earthy smell from the oak wood burning in the fireplace. They detected a sweeter smell too, although they weren't sure exactly what it was. It was the aroma wafting up from an iron pot hanging over the flames in the fireplace that contained chunks of rabbit and venison mixed with corn and potatoes to concoct a thick and hearty stew.

The yearling was intrigued by the interesting smells and walked out from the tree line and over to the top of the creekbank to a better vantage point. The gentle rustling of the stream provided enough ambient noise that the sound of his movements went undetected on the other side of the creek. Mom and the yearling were upwind of the cabin, so the breeze carried their scents in its direction. A dog's sense of smell isn't as keen as a bear's, but it's far more sensitive than the human nose. The dog opened his eyes and sniffed. He smelled something, but he didn't know what it was. He raised his head, sniffed again, and scanned the other side of the creek. He saw the yearling first near the creekbank and then he spotted mom a few yards away over by the tree line. The dog leapt to his feet, started barking, and ran over to the edge of the creek. Mom and the yearling froze. A moment later, the cabin door swung open, and a man walked out carrying a gun. "What's all the ruckus about?" The man looked to see where the dog was focused, and then he cast his gaze in that direction. As he did, he saw two bears on the opposite side of the creek as they turned and started to run up the hill. He raised his musket, took aim, and squeezed the trigger. The sound of the musket firing echoed across the valley. The bears kept running up the hill, turned left, receded into the brush, and disappeared into the forest. As they did, the dog stopped barking and walked over to the man. "Good boy," the man said as he reached down, rubbed the dog's head, turned, and walked back inside the cabin.

Joseph and Sarah Williams settled in Augusta County in Virginia's Shenandoah Valley in 1747, just a few years after the county was carved out from the western part of Orange County. They established a farm on a tract of land they acquired from William Beverley that was a small piece of the one-hundred and nineteen-thousand acres Governor William Gooch granted to Beverley in 1736. That's where Joseph and Sarah Williams chose to put down roots and raise their family.

Thomas was the youngest of Joseph and Sarah's five children. He was born in the summer of 1758. As soon as he was old enough to be of help, he joined his parents, his brother, and his three sisters in tending to the farm where they grew corn and beans and grain and kept a small herd of cattle and a flock of chickens. When his chores were done, Thomas ventured into the forest to explore and when it was warm, he waded in the creek looking for salamanders and crawdads under the rocks. He liked to play with his older siblings, but he was just as happy to go off alone and trek through the woods around the farm. By the time he was in his teens, Thomas was a skilled hunter and woodsman. He'd head out with the musket his father bought for him, and he'd return with a rabbit, a squirrel, a deer, or a turkey that he would skin and dress, and his mother would cook.

In 1778, at the age of twenty, Thomas decided to venture south into the Carolinas. His mother Sarah had died a few years earlier during an influenza epidemic, and he could see that his father wasn't as vigorous as he'd once been. Thomas had stayed there on the farm out of loyalty to his family. His older brother Martin had just returned home after attending the College of

William & Mary, where he was a classmate of James Monroe. Now that Martin was back at home, Martin could take on the duties Thomas performed and help his father manage the farm. Joseph had encouraged Thomas to go to college like his older brother, but Thomas preferred to be outdoors rather than stuck inside a stuffy classroom. Thomas knew that his brother's ambition was to be a farmer and perhaps later a politician, and the plan was for him to inherit the family farm when their father passed away, so rather than waiting around until that happened to decide what he was going to do with the rest of his life, Thomas chose to get an early start. He saddled up his horse, said his goodbyes, and headed south.

Thomas made his way to Davidson's Fort – which is now called Old Fort – at the base of the Blue Ridge Mountains in North Carolina about twenty miles east of present-day Asheville. Samuel Davidson acquired a little over a square mile – six hundred and forty-four acres of land – in 1770 and later built a stockade to protect what was then the western most colonial outpost from attacks by the Cherokee who inhabited the region. It became known as Davidson's Fort.

In the summer of 1776, General Griffith Rutherford left three hundred troops to guard Davidson's Fort as he and twenty-four hundred men moved up into the mountains through the Swannanoa Gap and over into what is now western North Carolina and eastern Tennessee. During "Rutherford's Trace," they burned three dozen Cherokee villages, destroyed hundreds of acres of corn, and slaughtered herds of cattle in their part of the Cherokee Expedition, a coordinated simultaneous attack on the Cherokee in South Carolina, North Carolina, and Virginia. General Rutherford and his troops returned to Davidson's Fort in the fall of 1776 and the fort continued to serve as a base of operations for periodic military campaigns against the Cherokee for the next decade.

Thomas and General Rutherford had something in common; they both learned surveying and mapping skills at an early age. General Rutherford was taught how to survey while working on a relative's farm soon after he arrived in America from Ireland. He would put those skills to use again when his military service was done and he was appointed by North Carolina Governor Alexander Martin to survey and map land west of the mountains that had been set aside to satisfy the claims of the men who served North Carolina in the war for independence. Starting around the age of thirteen, Thomas worked from time to time as an aide to Daniel Kennedy, a surveyor employed by William Beverley to survey and map the vast western part of Augusta County that at the time was uncharted territory. In fact, until 1790, Augusta County had no defined western boundary and extended indefinitely into what is now West Virginia and Kentucky. Over the years, Thomas became quite skilled as a surveyor and when he moved south to Davidson's Fort, he intended to put those skills to use to earn a living.

The British and the Cherokee negotiated a treaty in 1763 in which the British agreed that they would not settle west of the Blue Ridge Mountains along what today is the Eastern Continental Divide. As a result, when Thomas arrived in North Carolina, there were few maps or records documenting the territory to the west of Davidson's Fort.

Governor Josiah Martin fled from Tryon Palace in New Bern in May 1776 as revolutionary fervor began to boil, and from then until 1792 when Raleigh was officially designated as the state capital, the seat of North Carolina's government was wherever the legislature was able to meet. Nonetheless, the government continued to function ... more or less. Thomas secured employment as a surveyor for the state accompanying military expeditions up into the mountains where he was tasked with mapping the rivers, streams, peaks, and valleys. He made numerous trips, some lasting for just a few days and others for several weeks, and he

9

became well-acquainted with the land between Davidson's Fort and what most of the Cherokee called "Tah-kee-os-tee" (meaning "racing waters") and now known as the French Broad River.

Thomas was a striking man. He stood just over six feet tall, had broad shoulders, long brown hair, and was fit from years of hard work on the family farm in Virginia. His good looks, coupled with his reputation as a hard-worker and a skilled surveyor, made him the frequent topic of conversation amongst men and women in and around Davidson's Fort who had daughters of marrying age. When he was back in Davidson's Fort after a trip into the mountains, he received frequent invitations from local farmers and merchants to come over for Sunday dinner. It didn't take him long to realize that the invitations were not entirely altruistic and over time he became quite adept at making excuses to avoid becoming ensnared in another matrimonial scheme.

Thomas wasn't particularly religious, but he believed in a higher power and attended services at the church in Davidson's Fort on most Sundays when he wasn't up in the mountains. As the area grew, local folks decided they needed a full-time pastor rather than a rotating roster of lay preachers who had varying levels of oratory skills and bible knowledge. Reverend George Edwards accepted the offer and moved his family to Davidson's Fort in the summer of 1781.

Reverend Edwards and his wife Grace had a daughter, Emma. Emma was twenty, had wavy reddish-brown hair, a pale complexion, exquisite features, and a gracious and endearing demeanor. She was a voracious reader and could hold her own in any conversation on the topics of the day. She was the object of much attention from the young men around Hillsborough where she and her parents lived before moving to Davidson's Fort, but she never gave much thought to marriage, even though the subtle hints her parents dropped suggested they thought about it often.

The church in Davidson's Fort was packed the Sunday Reverend Edwards delivered his first sermon. Thomas arrived just as the service was about to begin and he had to stand near the back of the room since every seat on the rows of benches was full, a first as best he could recall. After a hymn and a prayer, Reverend Edwards introduced himself and thanked those in attendance for the warm welcome and the gracious hospitality he and his family had received in the few days since they arrived in Davidson's Fort. He asked his wife and daughter to stand up so he could introduce them. As they turned and faced the audience, Thomas looked in their direction; and whatever happened after that was a blur. Thomas had to steady himself as he felt his knees begin to buckle. It was summer and warm, but that didn't explain the perspiration that had suddenly formed on his brow or the thump-thump-thump in his chest that he thought he could literally hear out loud. When Emma smiled and nodded towards the audience, he thought it was the most glorious thing he had ever seen, and it was an image that would remain etched into his memory for the remainder of his days. Thomas couldn't tell you the topic of Reverend Edwards's sermon or whether he shut his eyes and bowed his head during the closing prayer. Emma Edwards made a profound impression, and now Thomas Williams was totally smitten.

Several of the ladies from the local area organized a social gathering following the service to permit Reverend Edwards and his family to get acquainted with their new congregants. Reverend Edwards, his wife Grace, and Emma stood beneath an oak tree next to a table that was loaded with slices of cakes, cookies, and cups of apple cider. A line formed to shake their hands and exchange pleasantries before moving along to the refreshments. Thomas took his place in line and when the time came, he shook the hands of Reverend Edwards and his wife. "I'm Thomas Williams. Welcome to Davidson's Fort." Reverend Edwards smiled and thanked him, and his wife nodded in agreement. Thomas moved a few steps further down the receiving

11

line and extended his hand to Emma. She took it and he noticed how warm and tender it felt and how perfectly it fit in his grasp.

"I'm Thomas Williams, and I want to …" and at that moment, his mind went blank, and he searched frantically for the words that were supposed to follow.

Emma waited a few seconds and smiled. "Well, hello, Thomas Williams. I'm Emma Edwards and I'm pleased to make your acquaintance. Do you live here in Davidson's Fort?"

Thomas's mind was still spinning and trying to catch up. "I … I … I …" he stammered, and then, as he attempted to gesture with his left hand, he knocked a cup of cider off the table next to him and onto the grass, earning him a sour look from Anne Davidson who was tending the refreshment table. Emma raised her hand to her lips to cover a chuckle at Thomas's clumsy, bumbling introduction.

"I'm so sorry," he said as he bent over, retrieved the cup, and handed it to an annoyed Anne Davidson.

The receiving line was beginning to stack up with those who had greeted the Reverend and his wife and were waiting to say hello to Emma so they could move on to the refreshments. Emma smiled at Thomas. "I look forward to seeing you again, Thomas Williams." He smiled back, looked into her eyes, and said, "Aye, as do I."

Trips up into the mountains to survey the terrain lost much of its appeal after Emma Edwards arrived in Davidson's Fort. Most of Thomas's hours were spent thinking of her and contriving excuses that would require him to be in her presence. His attendance at church services increased exponentially and he was always among the first to volunteer when Reverend Edwards asked for help with repairs and improvements to the church. Emma seemed to develop a sudden interest in carpentry and in helping her father at the church, something she hadn't done when they were back in Hillsborough. It seemed clear to those who saw Thomas and Emma together that she was just as taken with him as he was with her. You could almost see the glow around them, and it couldn't help but make you smile.

That fall, Thomas walked over to the church on a Saturday afternoon where Reverend Edwards was deep in thought as he worked on his Sunday sermon. Thomas had paced back and forth all morning and had finally worked up the nerve to ask Reverend Edwards for Emma's hand in marriage. Thomas paused for a moment at the door of the church, drew in a deep breath to steady himself, and then he removed his hat and went inside.

"Reverend Edwards, I'm not a rich man, but I work hard, I've saved most of what I've earned, and I know that I can be a good provider. Sir, I'm in love with your daughter, and I promise you that I will love her every minute of every day until the day I die. Sir, I'm here to beg of you, may I please have your permission to marry Emma?"

Reverend Edwards was no fool. He had seen the two of them together and noticed how they seemed radiant in each other's presence. "Son, I'm not a rich man either, so I hope you aren't doing this because you're expecting a big dowery." The Reverend drew in a deep breath, exhaled, and smiled. "I've seen the happiness you two bring each other and I've suspected for some time that this day was going to come. I've already discussed it with my wife, and I've discussed it with the Lord, because I wanted to be ready when you eventually came to see me. So, my answer is yes, you have my blessing and my permission to marry Emma."

Thomas extended his hand, and Reverend Edwards took it and then pulled him in for a hug. "I'm entrusting her to you son, and I expect you to take good care of her." Thomas looked him in the eye and said, "I will, sir. I promise you, I will."

Just before Christmas in 1871, Reverend Edwards officiated the ceremony uniting Thomas Williams and his daughter, Emma Edwards. It was the best Christmas Thomas Williams had experienced in his twenty-three years on this earth. It would prove to be the best Christmas he would ever experience.

Thomas, with the help of some friends, built a small, but comfortable, one room cottage on a bank next to Mill Creek with a perfect view from the front porch of the sun setting behind the mountains off to the west in the evenings. Not long after they moved in, a skinny puppy showed up on their doorstep one morning. Despite repeated efforts to shoo him away, the pup refused to leave. By dinnertime, Emma had named him Bill.

Thomas continued to make trips up through the Swannanoa Gap and out into the Blue Ridge Mountains to survey and map the wilderness, but he always longed to get back home to Emma. On chilly fall nights, as he lay awake next to a campfire trying to stave off the cold, he pictured himself in bed back at home, entwined in Emma's warm embrace, and engulfed in the fire of the passion they felt when they were alone together. When they were apart, Thomas felt as if a piece of him had been ripped out, and he knew the only way to fill that void was to finish his work as quickly as he could and race back down the mountain to the cottage by the stream and the woman he loved with every ounce of his being.

Once Bill had aged a bit and fattened up, he began accompanying Thomas on some of his trips up into the mountains. Bill was no substitute for Emma, but Thomas appreciated his companionship. When Thomas was away, Emma spent time with her parents and assisted her father as he tended to his pastoral duties. It helped to keep her busy and her mind occupied rather than pining for Thomas constantly. She never knew exactly when he would return home from one of his trips up into the mountains, and each time he came back and walked through the door,

14

she experienced an overwhelming wave of euphoria. She wished there was some way she could grab hold of that sensation and shove it into a jar so she could crack open the lid and breathe in the warm, intoxicating feeling whenever she needed it.

Thomas wrote to his father shortly after he married Emma and told him the good news. His father wrote back, expressed his congratulations, and said he hoped he would have the pleasure of meeting his new daughter-in-law someday. Thomas's brother Martin had gotten married not long after Thomas left. He and his wife Mary and their young children moved in with Thomas's father and helped take care of him and run the farm. His three sisters were all married too. The oldest, Bess, lived on the farm with her husband John who helped Joseph and Martin tend to the farm. The middle sister, Annie, lived a short distance away on a farm with her husband, Stewart, and their infant daughter. The youngest sister, Clara, moved to Richmond where her husband Ben – who had been one of Martin's classmates at William & Mary – and his father owned and operated the tobacco exchange and several tobacco and cotton warehouses. Joseph Williams knew that his wife Sarah was smiling down from heaven, happy in the knowledge that her five children were alive and well and married and creating families of their own.

It took eight days for Thomas and Emma to travel by horseback to the farm in Augusta County, Virginia, from their home in Davidson's Fort, when they made the journey as summer drew to an end in 1782. It was the first time since he left four years earlier that Thomas had been back home. His father was in his early sixties, and he was frailer than Thomas remembered when he last saw him. Joseph was thrilled to see his youngest son and even more thrilled to meet his new daughter-in-law. He gave Emma a hug and said, "you've got to tell me what Thomas did to trick you into marrying the sorry likes of him," and he laughed so hard that he started to cough and had to sit back down on his chair on the front porch.

Martin and Mary and their two children – a son who was three and a daughter who was not quite two – came out to greet Thomas and Emma, and a few minutes later Bess and John came over from their house a few hundred yards away. Bess was carrying an infant who was wrapped snuggly in a blanket. Thomas was unaware until that moment that he had a new niece who was just two months old. Annie and Stewart and their two-year-old son arrived the next day in a wagon that carried them the five miles from their farm. Clara and Ben couldn't make the journey from Richmond because Clara was just a couple of weeks away from giving birth to their first child and she couldn't handle traveling over a hundred miles in a wagon on the rough and rutty trail.

That evening, they set up a long table under the oak trees behind the house. They lit a fire using hickory logs stacked in the stone firepit and the men cooked a pork shoulder that came from a hog John had slaughtered a few days earlier and venison steaks from a deer Stewart shot and killed the day before he and Annie arrived. The women gathered in the kitchen and cooked corn and beans that were grown there on the farm. Mary, Bess, and Annie peppered Emma with questions about her family and what life was like in Davidson's Fort, and Emma asked them about their experiences growing up with Thomas there on the farm. When the cooking was done and they sat down at the table to eat, they drank wine that Clara and Ben had sent over from Richmond with a note saying that the wine came from grapes grown on vines in Mr. Jefferson's vineyard at Monticello just outside of Charlottesville.

There was much laughter as the Williams siblings regaled their respective spouses with stories about growing up together. Some of the stories were true and all of them contained at least a grain of truth. Thomas had never given it much thought before, but as he sat there it occurred to him how lucky he had been to be one of the children of Joseph and Sarah Williams. There were certainly some annoyances and conflicts amongst the five children when they were young, but those memories had receded into the background and were displaced by the good memories of the time they had spent together. Emma enjoyed hearing stories about Thomas growing up and it gave her a feeling of contentment, but it also caused her to feel some envy because as an only child, she had missed out on similar experiences, and she lacked those kinds of warm sibling memories.

Towards the end of the evening, Joseph raised his glass. "A toast,' he said. "As we sit here tonight, I know that I've been very fortunate, and that God has blessed me more than I ever deserved. I'm so proud of each of you and of Clara, and I wish she could have been here with us too. But as proud as I am, the person who would have been even prouder than me would be your mother. I've been sitting here listening to the stories and enjoying the laughter, and at times I swear I could almost see your mother's smiling face as I looked around the table. Nothing in this world would have made her happier than to be here right now to see her children and her grandchildren, and I know that she's looking down on us right now with great pride. So, here's a toast to my most precious memory, the memory of your mother. Here's to my dear Sarah." As the wine glasses clinked, tears trickled down Joseph's cheeks. He truly was proud of his family, but he was lonely, and he pined for his sweet Sarah.

Thomas and Emma stayed at the farm for two weeks, and then it was time to make the trek back to Davidson's Fort. After a big breakfast of pork, eggs, and corn muffins, they said their goodbyes, mounted up, and rode off. As the farmhouse was almost out of sight, Thomas looked back and felt a knot tighten in his throat as he fought to hold back tears. He didn't know

17

when or if he'd see the place again or whether his father would still be alive if he ever managed to make the journey back. He wasn't sure why, but when he rode off that day to return to North Carolina, it was a lot harder than it had been when he'd left four years earlier.

The long ride home was monotonous, but Thomas and Emma enjoyed their time together. They talked almost all day as they rode along and then they snuggled by the campfire at night until they fell asleep. Thomas was weighing an idea that would have a major impact on the couple, and he considered bringing it up to hear what Emma thought about it as they made their way to Davidson's Fort, but he decided to keep it to himself a little longer. Emma had something major to discuss too, and she considered sharing it with Thomas as they rode along, but she didn't. Both thought they'd break their big news soon, but not right now.

The day before they reached Davidson's Fort, they stopped to rest next to the Catawba River. They led their horses down to the riverbank for a drink of water and then they both laid down in the shade of a maple tree to stretch their sore backs and give their sore butts a break. After ten minutes or so had passed, Emma stood up and said she was going to go over behind a mountain laurel to relieve herself, and Thomas said when she was done, they'd mount up and be on their way. Emma walked behind the mountain laurel and next to a big log, pulled down her pants, and peed. She pulled her pants up and turned to walk back over to Thomas when nestled a few feet away she saw a fat copperhead coiled up in the brush and looking right at her. She screamed and fell backwards over the log. Thomas jumped to his feet and ran in her direction.

"Are you okay? What happened?" He looked to his right and on the other side of the log he saw the snake coiled and ready to defend its ground. He stomped the log with his boot and the snake slithered away and disappeared into the brush.

"Can you get up?" Thomas asked.

"I don't know. I twisted my back, and I've hurt my ankle."

Thomas put his hands under Emma's arms and slowly lifted her up. She tried to take a step and winced in pain, and Thomas caught her as she stumbled. He put her arm over his shoulder and helped her hobble back over to the maple tree where he slowly lowered her to the ground. Emma pulled up the leg of her pants and pulled off her boot and groaned. Her ankle was swollen, and it was starting to turn purple.

Thomas asked, "Can I feel it to see if anything is broken?" and Emma nodded in agreement. She flinched when he mashed on her swollen ankle and probed around her foot. "I don't think you've broken anything, but it's going to be sore for a while. How's your back?"

Emma stretched and grimaced. "I've pulled something, but I think I'll be okay. Help me up." Thomas took both of her hands and pulled Emma up on her feet.

"We've got a few more hours to go today," he said, "and we'll make it to Davidson's Fort tomorrow. Are you able to ride or do we need to stay here overnight?"

"I think I can ride a little while longer," she responded, "and I don't want to stay here with that damned snake around. Help me up onto my saddle and let's get out of here." Thomas assisted Emma over to her horse, helped her get her good foot in the stirrup, and gave her a big boost up. "Thanks. Let's go. I'm ready to get home."

Reverend Edwards and Grace were glad to see Thomas and Emma return home after a month away, but they weren't nearly as excited to see them as Bill was. As soon as Thomas and Emma rode up in front of the Edwards's house and Thomas helped Emma down from her horse, Bill bolted out the door, jumped up on Thomas, spun around, jumped up on Emma, and then ran in circles around them as fast as he could until he finally fell over on his back panting in exhaustion and waiting on someone to scratch his belly.

"Calm down pal," Thomas said as he reached down and rubbed Bill's belly, which caused Bill's back legs to kick like he was running in place. Thomas laughed. "You're going to keel over dead, you fool, and I don't have the strength right now to dig a hole to bury you."

"What happened," Reverend Edwards asked when he saw Emma hobble towards the house.

"I had a run-in with a copperhead, and he fared better than I did. He scared me and I fell backwards over a log, twisted my back, and sprained my ankle. I suppose the only good thing about it is that it happened yesterday near the end of our journey, so I didn't have to put up with the discomfort for too long."

"Well, let's get you inside and off your feet," Reverend Edwards said as he took Emma by the arm and helped her walk towards the house. "I'm thankful you didn't get snakebit and I'm glad you made it back home. You're going to need to rest for a few days and let things heal up."

Emma was happy to be back in Davidson's Fort. She was an only child and had never been away from her parents for more than a day or two at a time before she and Thomas set out for Virginia. She enjoyed visiting Thomas's family and discovering more about the life he lived before they met, but she was exhausted from the long journey and thankful to be able to sleep in her own bed again. Thomas was leaving in a few weeks to go back up into the mountains and, while she missed him mightily whenever he was away, she was looking forward to some peace and quiet and rest. She was tired and she hadn't felt completely well in a couple of weeks. She thought she knew why, but she wanted to be certain before she said anything to Thomas or to her parents. She thought she would know for sure by the time he returned from his expedition.

Thomas made his final trip of the season up into the mountains hoping to reach a settlement along the Watauga River that had been annexed into North Carolina five years earlier. He had heard about the settlement and how it was flourishing, and he thought that maybe he and Emma might leave Davidson's Fort and move north to the Watauga River. Davidson's Fort had grown considerably since Thomas got there, and it was beginning to get too crowded and busy for his taste. He hadn't mentioned the potential of moving to Emma, and he knew how much she enjoyed being near her parents, so he thought he should check it out first before he said anything to her.

Thomas rode up through Swannanoa Gap to the North Fork of the Swannanoa River where he turned north. He followed the river up to its headwaters about three miles west of Mount Mitchell, which the Cherokee called "Attakulla," the highest peak in North America east of the Mississippi River at an elevation of six-thousand six-hundred and eighty-four feet. He continued north until he reached the North Toe River, and he followed the river west until it merged with the Cane River to form the Nolichucky River. The weather suddenly turned cold, and even though he hadn't reached the Watauga River, Thomas knew he needed to head back home before snow began to fall. Thomas rode south through Green Mountain Gap, to the west of Mount Mitchell, and back down through the Swannanoa Gap to Davidson's Fort and home to Emma. When the weather warmed up in the spring, he told himself, he would try again to reach the settlement on the Watauga River.

The Appalachian Mountains are the oldest mountains in the world dating back four-hundred and eighty-million years and extend all the way from central Alabama up into Newfoundland in southern Canada. The Appalachians are believed to have soared to a height of twenty-five thousand feet at their birth when the North American and African plates collided, but millions and millions of years of erosion slowly wore them down over time.

The Blue Ridge Mountains are part of the Appalachian Mountain range and extend from northern Georgia to southern Pennsylvania and includes two National Parks: the Shenandoah National Park and the Great Smoky Mountains National Park, which are connected by the Blue Ridge Parkway. The Blue Ridge Mountains got their name from the distinctive blue haze that hovers over the mountains most days. The blue haze is the result of isoprene, a chemical emitted by trees to protect themselves from excessive heat, particularly in the hot summer months. Among the most prolific emitters of isoprene are oak trees, which are abundant in the Blue Ridge Mountains. The earliest known inhabitants of the Blue Ridge – the Cherokee – referred to these mountains as "Sa-koh-na-gas," which not surprisingly means blue.

Native American tribes made their homes in the Blue Ridge Mountains for centuries before their first encounter with Europeans. In 1540, a Spanish expedition led by Hernando de Soto reached western North Carolina and the thriving Native American town of Joara situated along the Catawba River just north of what is now Morganton in Burke County. De Soto and his men camped at Joara for several days to allow their horses to rest and to give the men a chance to search for gold, and then they packed up and moved on.

In January 1567, Spanish explorer Juan Pardo and over a hundred Spanish soldiers arrived at Joara where they built a settlement that they called Fort San Juan de Joara. Fort San Juan was built eighteen years before the English tried to establish a settlement on Roanoke Island on the coast of North Carolina that today is known as the ill-fated "Lost Colony." Fort San Juan predates the English settlement at Jamestown, Virginia, by forty years and the Mayflower's landing at Plymouth Rock in Massachusetts by fifty-three years. Joara is believed to have been in existence since about 1000 A.D. and it was a regional capital with authority over other native towns in the upper Catawba River region.

Pardo continued moving west and built five more forts along what he thought would be a land route to silver and gold in Mexico. Pardo left Spanish soldiers behind at Fort San Juan when he and the rest of his troops returned to Santa Elena, a Spanish settlement on what is now Parris Island, South Carolina, to repel an expected invasion by the French to reclaim what had previously been a French fort.

Initially, the Spanish soldiers and the native people lived together in relative harmony at Joara. The soldiers even partnered with Joaran warriors to conquer rival chiefdoms in the region. After about eighteen months, however, the peace was broken, perhaps because native men were angered by soldiers developing relationships with native women, placing increasing demands on the native population for food and resources, and spreading European diseases amongst them. In the spring of 1568, native warriors attacked and killed the Spanish soldiers and burned Fort San Juan and the five other forts that Pardo had built. Only one Spanish soldier survived the massacre, Juan Martin de Badajoz, who managed to escape thanks to the help of his Native American wife Teresa. Juan Martin and Teresa eventually made their way to Santa Elena on the coast of South Carolina where they raised two daughters before Juan Martin was killed in July 1576 during a Spanish military campaign to quell a native uprising.

Spain abandoned Santa Elena in 1587, and the remaining Spanish settlers relocated to St. Augustine in Florida. Joara is believed to have continued to exist until the late sixteen hundreds

23

when it was abandoned for reasons that to this day remain a mystery. Both present day Catawba and Cheraw people are believed to be descendants of the Joarans.

Captain William Bean and his wife and four children settled along the Watauga River in 1769 in an area that is now in the northeast corner of Tennessee. As "Bean's Station" prospered, more families followed and in 1772 the community formed the Watauga Association and established rules to govern themselves after negotiating a lease with the Cherokee for land along the Watauga River. President Teddy Roosevelt later said that the Watauga Association represented the "first men of American birth to establish a free and independent community on the continent." The Association petitioned the Colony of Virginia in 1776 to annex the district, but Virginia declined. Their petition to North Carolina, however, got a more favorable reception and the Watauga Association area was annexed into North Carolina as Washington County in November 1777.

The Cherokee, who aligned with the British rather than the colonists, attacked the Watauga settlement in July 1776, but they were defeated. On July 20, 1777, the Long Island of the Holston Treaty between North Carolina and the Cherokee put an end to hostilities and settled the territorial boundaries. The Cherokee may have resolved their dispute with the settlers who had moved in and occupied their lands along the Watauga River, but there was no such resolution with the settlers who were beginning to creep into the area a little further south.

At birth, he cried so hard that he could be heard throughout the village, and he kicked and squirmed as if he had emerged ready to do battle. He was named Danuwoa, which means "the warrior." His father was killed in the attack on the Watauga Association when Danuwoa was ten years old. As is often the case with young sons, Danuwoa looked up to his father and thought that he was the bravest warrior, most skilled hunter, and wisest member of the tribe. News of his father's death at the hands of the white European settlers hit Danuwoa hard. He put on a brave face in the presence of others, but when he was alone in the woods and away from the village, he cried as hard as he had cried at his birth. The white settlers had moved into the area to the north along the Watauga River uninvited and continued to encroach further and further south into tribal lands as if it belonged to them and not the native people who had occupied it for generations. Danuwoa knew that he was only ten years old and powerless to do anything to avenge his father's death and the afront to his people, but he made a promise to himself that when the time was right and he was able, he would do his part to balance the ledger.

Adahy was born several months after Danuwoa. His father spent a lot of time away from the village hunting and exploring, so as a baby he was named Adahy, which means "lives in the woods." His name was aptly chosen as there was nothing Adahy enjoyed more than venturing out into the forest, at first to play with his friends and then to hunt and explore as he got older. There were others of his age in the village, but he was closest to Danuwoa and the two spent most of their days together as they grew up. His father had returned home from the attack on the Watauga Association and told the story of the failed attempt to drive the white settlers back across the river and off the land they stole. Adahy wasn't as passionate about avenging the tribe's defeat as Danuwoa who talked about it incessantly, but he knew that one day he too would do his part to restore the tribe's honor and evict the intruders.

Degataga was the grandson of Attakullakulla, one of the preeminent Cherokee leaders of the seventeen hundreds. Attakullakulla – which means "little carpenter" – was one of six

Cherokee leaders who traveled to England in 1730 to make a treaty of trade and alliance between the British and the Cherokee people. He was captured by the Caughnawaga – Canadian Iroquois natives – in 1739 and didn't return to Cherokee country until 1742 when the Cherokee and Iroquois made peace. Attakullakulla was an advocate for peace and for trade, and over the years he was instrumental in negotiating agreements intended to prevent conflicts, limit territorial encroachment, and facilitate the exchange of goods. Those agreements included the treaty that leased land along the Watauga River to the settlers from the Watauga Association and a treaty in 1777 that agreed to neutrality in the war between the British and the American colonists.

Attakullakulla's son, Tsiyu Gansini – meaning "dragging canoe" – didn't inherit his father's dedication to avoiding conflict. He chose to ally with the British at the beginning of the Revolutionary War and was assigned to lead one part of a three-pronged attack against American settlers, which included the attack on the Watauga Association in July of 1776. Tsiyu Gansini was injured in the attack on the Watauga Association and barely escaped with his life. Following a counterattack by colonial militias against native villages, his father Attakullakulla sued for peace. Tsiyu Gansini opposed his father initiative and refused to admit defeat. He led a group of Cherokee people further south and west where they established new villages and continued to attack settlements throughout the region.

That's the lineage Degataga – which means "standing together" – was born into; a grandfather legendary for his commitment to peace and diplomacy and a father legendary for his commitment to battle and to war. Degataga was a little over a year younger than Danuwoa and Adahy and was closer to Uguku – meaning "hooting owl" – who was his own age and his cousin.

In the latter part of 1783, John McDonald – a Scotsman who oversaw British concerns in the region where the new native villages sprang up – told Tsiyu Gansini that white settlers were migrating from the foothills up into the Blue Ridge Mountains where they were clearing land, building farms, and creating settlements. As soon as winter started to fade, Tsiyu Gansini summoned Danuwoa, Adahy, Degataga, and Uguku. He told them white settlers near the Tahkee-os-tee (the French Broad River) were encroaching on native land and putting down roots, and he was sending them to scout the area and report back. He warned them to avoid the militias they might encounter, and he instructed them, "you are to observe and not to engage. If the stories of settlements prove to be true, we will go back there in sufficient numbers when the time is right to drive the trespassers off our land and send a message that they are not welcome here. But for now, your task is to go there, gather information, and to return safely. Do you understand?" They all nodded their heads and answered in the affirmative.

The next morning, the four young warriors left the village and proceeded east, following the path of the Hiawassee River. When they reached a point where the Hiawassee turned south, they veered off and followed Tusquittee Creek to the east, then Clear Creek to the north to the Nanthahala River. By the time they reached the Tuckasegee River near the current site of Bryson City, daytime temperatures were beginning to warm. They discovered what was left of a cornfield near an abandoned village that had been burned to the ground by General Rutherford and his troops several years earlier during the Rutherford's Trace campaign. They took ears of corn that had dried down on the stalk over the winter, ground it into corn meal, and poured it into deerskin pouches. The corn had been a welcome find and replenished the dwindling stock of cornmeal they brought with them on their journey.

Tsiyu Gansini designated his son Degataga to lead the group, but within days it was clear that Danuwoa was the leader, not through a coup or some deliberate effort to usurp Degataga, but simply by virtue of his natural leadership abilities. Danuwoa was the most skilled at navigating the unfamiliar terrain and the others were content to follow his lead. Danuwoa decided when the group would stop to rest and when they would set up camp for the night. By the time the group reached the French Broad River just east of present-day Brevard, Danuwoa was clearly the group's de facto leader.

The French Broad River is believed to be the third oldest river in the world. It has cut through the ancient stones of the southern Appalachian Mountains for eons, by some estimates, for three-hundred and twenty-five million years. It is one of the few rivers in North America that flows north rather than south. While the river is relatively wide, it isn't very deep. In the late eighteen hundreds, Colonel S.V. Pickens launched an ill-fated steamboat service on a seventeen-mile stretch of the river using a ninety-foot-long double-decker steamboat named the Mountain Lily. Colonel Pickens was successful in getting Congress to appropriate funds for dredging to support his enterprise, but some were skeptical of his venture. A Senator from Ohio observed that the river was so shallow that "a catfish couldn't even navigate the French Broad." Between 1881 and 1885, the Mountain Lily only managed to make a couple of trips up and down the river and a flashflood in 1885 caused it to run aground where it was abandoned. Wood from its hull was later salvaged and used to build Riverside Baptist Church and the ship's bell was hoisted up into the church's belfry.

The young warriors followed the west bank of the French Broad River north to a point where the Swannanoa River joins it near the location of what would become George Vanderbilt's Biltmore Estate, which was completed in 1895 on the south side of Asheville. It had once been the site of a thriving native town, but the town was destroyed during the Rutherford's Trace campaign. The young warriors walked across the French Broad River in water that was knee-deep over to its eastern shore, and then they followed the Swannanoa River off to the east. When they reached the point where Bull Creek merges with the Swannanoa River, they turned north and followed the creek until they reached Shope Creek where they turned east. They followed Shope Creek until the creek ended at its source, a spring situated at the base of Lane Pinnacle.

They made the climb up to the top of Lane Pinnacle, which rises to an elevation of five-thousand-two-hundred-and-thirty feet. Except for some scattered pines and hemlocks, the trees were mostly bare, so they could see most of the Swannanoa Valley. Uguku spotted a thin plume of gray smoke rising into the blue sky from somewhere on the other side of Brushy Mountain off in the distance, and he pointed it out to the others. Danuwoa said they would camp at the base of Lane Pinnacle for the night, and they would check on the source of the smoke the next morning if it was still there. Up to that point in their journey, they had observed a few trappers and hunters who were transiting through the area, but they hadn't come across any permanent homes or settlements. Maybe the smoke was just a hunter's campfire and whoever lit it would be packed up and gone by morning … or maybe not.

Bill was the first to spot Thomas off in the distance as he rode towards the house. Thomas didn't take Bill with him on this trip because he hoped to cover a lot of ground each day in his quest to get to the Watauga River and back before cold weather set in, and Bill would have had a hard time keeping up with the brisk pace. Bill began to bark and ran off in Thomas's direction to welcome him home. Emma heard the commotion, walked out onto the porch, and saw Thomas approaching from the west as the sun was beginning to set behind the mountains. It was October, and the days were growing progressively shorter, and the nights were getting colder.

As soon as Thomas climbed down off his horse and planted both feet on the ground, Bill jumped up and hit him in the belly with both of his front paws, nearly knocking Thomas down.

"Damn, Bill! Calm down. I'm happy to see you too," he said as he rubbed Bill's head. Emma moved in for a three-way hug with Thomas and Bill. She put her arms around Thomas's neck, leaned in, and planted her lips firmly against his for a long kiss. "I've missed you," she said as she stood in his grasp with their foreheads touching. "I'm glad you're back home safe and sound. Put the horse away and come inside and get cleaned up. I was about to walk over to my father and mother's house for dinner, and I know they'll be thrilled to see that you've returned."

"Welcome home, son!" Reverend Edwards said as he embraced Thomas at the doorway. "Come in." Grace walked over, gave Thomas a hug, and said, "I'm glad you're back home, Thomas. I always worry about you when you're away and I'm always thankful when you get home safely." Thomas was grateful that Emma's family had taken him in wholeheartedly like he was one of their own. He knew their love for him was genuine, and he felt the same way about them.

Since they arrived in Davidson's Fort, Reverend Edwards and Grace had become beloved members of the community. They tended to the sick, did their best to feed those who were hungry, and provided shelter to those who were in need. Thomas had never heard them utter a bad word about anyone, including those who deserved a slew of bad words. It seemed their faith in the Lord was as genuine as their affection for Thomas. Thomas knew that not all spouses have such warm relationships with their in-laws, and he considered himself very fortunate indeed.

When they sat down at the table for dinner, Reverend Edwards offered a prayer. It included thanks for Thomas's safe return and for Thomas and Emma to continue enjoying good health and happiness.

A few minutes into the meal, Emma said, "I have some news I want to share with you." As all three looked her way, she smiled and said, "I'm pregnant."

Reverend Edwards reached over, placed his hand on Emma's right hand, and gave it a long squeeze, and Grace did the same to Emma's left hand. Tears of joy rolled down Grace's cheeks. Reverend Edwards beamed. "Oh darling, that's wonderful!"

Thomas stood up and walked around the table. Emma stood up too, and Thomas took her in his arms. "I love you so much. You're going to be the best mother the world has ever known," and then Thomas looked over at Grace and added, "no offense, Missus Edwards." "None taken, Thomas," she replied. "How long have you known?" Thomas asked.

"I had my suspicions before we left for Virginia, and those suspicions grew stronger while we were there, but I wasn't sure until just recently. Congratulations, my dear husband. You're going to be a father."

The dinner with his family up in Virginia had a short run at the top of Thomas's list of the most enjoyable meals he ever had. This one knocked it down a peg … or at least it did for a time.

After dinner, Emma and Grace talked and as best they could calculate, the baby would arrive sometime in the month of April. Grace said she was going to start working on a little quilt for the baby. Reverend Edwards and Thomas made plans to take some oak and hickory slabs to Charlie Walker's sawmill over on Mill Creek to get them cut into boards they would use to build a crib. As Thomas and Emma walked home in the light of a full moon that night, with his arm around her shoulder and her arm around his waist, it seemed that everything was right with the world. A baby was coming, and they couldn't wait for it to arrive.

It was a cold winter that year in Davidson's Fort. The first snow flurry came in mid-October and the first substantial snow – nearly a foot – fell on the ninth of November and lingered on the ground for the better part of a week. It took Grace nearly two weeks to finish the baby's quilt, and it was truly a work of art. You could see that a lot of time and much love went into it. Emma and Grace sewed baby clothes and made blankets. Thomas and Reverend Edwards were meticulous in their work on the baby's crib, and it was something to behold when they were done. The quality of their craftsmanship would have rivaled what most furnituremakers in a woodshop could have achieved. No detail was left undone and now it was just a matter of waiting for the baby to arrive.

Thomas received a letter from his brother Martin in mid-January of 1783. It said that his father, Joseph, had fallen ill right before Christmas and passed away. Martin said they buried him next to their mother, beneath the oak trees behind the house. He said that in his final days, Joseph had fallen into a coma, and when he passed it appeared he went peacefully and without suffering any pain. Thomas found some comfort in that. He could see that his father's health was declining when he and Emma visited him the prior summer, and he knew that inevitably he'd be getting the letter that arrived that day. Still, he wept, and his heart ached.

By the middle of February, Emma was spending most of the day in bed. Her back hurt and no matter how long and lovingly Thomas rubbed it, the pain just wouldn't go away. By March, she rarely got out of bed, even when nature called, and Thomas took care of that too.

Grace spent most of her days at Emma's side and did her best to tend to Emma's every need and to make her as comfortable as possible. Grace thought back to how hard it had been when she gave birth to Emma and how close they'd both come to death. She remembered that the intensity of the pain was so severe that at some point she lost consciousness. The ladies who attended to her said that when Emma finally emerged, she was tiny, and it appeared as though she had arrived stillborn, but after a few seconds passed, she gasped, drew in a breath, and started to cry. Grace lost a lot of blood during the delivery and Reverend Edwards thought he was going to lose her. He stayed by her side and prayed, and miraculously she hung on and eventually pulled through. It had been a grueling ordeal, and the complications Grace suffered meant Emma would be an only child. Grace sat at Emma's bedside, held her hand, and prayed her daughter wouldn't suffer through what she had experienced twenty-two years earlier.

March 23, 1783, was a Sunday. It was cold and cloudy, and the wind howled. Thomas and Grace had taken turns sitting by Emma's side throughout the night, and Reverend Edwards came over at first light. It was obvious that Emma was in distress, which meant the baby was in distress too. There was no doctor in Davidson's Fort and when a baby was born the local women attended to the birth. Grace could see that Emma was in trouble. She sent Reverend Edwards over to the Davidson's house to fetch Anne Davidson to come and help. Reverend Edwards, Anne, and Anne's adult daughter Ruth arrived a short time later. Grace wasn't certain, but she suspected the baby was going to make an early arrival.

Thomas held onto Emma's hand like he was clinging to her to keep her from being swept over the top of a waterfall. "I love you Emma, I love you so much. You're going to get through this, I know you will. And you, and me, and the baby, we're going to be fine. Hold on to me Emma. Hold on to me and don't let go." Emma managed a weak smile, but she couldn't speak. Soon, she began to moan.

"You and the Reverend move away, Thomas," Anne Davidson said as she stepped in.

"Grace and Ruth and I will take it from here. The best thing you can do for Emma right now is to pray. You pray as hard as you can." Thomas and Reverend Edwards prayed. They both prayed as hard as they could pray.

"Please, God. If you've got to take someone, take me. Please don't take Emma or the baby. Please, God, let them live," Thomas prayed silently as he sat there with tears rolling down his cheeks. "Please don't take my Emma."

Just past noon on Sunday, March 23, 1783, Emma Williams drew in her final breath, slowly exhaled, and slipped away from life here on this earth. She had screamed and convulsed for several hours and then in the final moments it seemed as if she was at peace. Anne and Grace did their best to get the baby out, but it wouldn't come, so the baby was lost too. Thomas dropped to his knees next to Emma, wrapped his arms around her, pulled her lifeless body up to his chest, and cried unconsolably. "Why, God? Why? Why did you take her and not me," he said over and over as he held her tight and rocked back and forth in agony.

Reverend Edwards stood on the other side of the bed, tears pouring down like rain. A moment later, his body shook like he was having a violent seizure. He didn't say anything for what seemed like the longest time, and when he spoke, Grace wished that he hadn't. "You promised me you'd take care of her and look what you've done. Look what you've done to my sweet Emma!" he yelled as he lunged towards Thomas.

Grace, managed to compose herself quickly and grabbed Reverend Edwards by the arm to stop him. "You don't mean that George. You're upset."

"No! Emma would be alive and well if she hadn't met this son-of-a-bitch! She and the baby would be alive right now if he hadn't made her ride all the way up to Virginia and back while she was pregnant. She wouldn't have hurt herself and the baby if she had stayed right here where she belonged. It's his fault! He's the one who killed her! He lied to me when he said he'd take care of her," Reverend Edwards said as he broke free of Grace's grasp, turned away, and stormed out the door.

Grace followed after him, calling his name and begging him to stop, but he just kept going until he reached his house, opened the door, and went inside where he screamed and cried as he cursed both Thomas and God. He was a father who had lost a child he loved more than he loved life itself. He was hurting and broken, and he needed someone to blame. Unfortunately, the someone he chose was Thomas Williams.

It took Anne and Ruth several minutes to get Thomas to let go of Emma. When he did, he grabbed his coat and hat, took down his musket and a bag of black powder, went outside and saddled up his horse, loaded some supplies on the back of Emma's horse, and rode away with Bill trailing along behind him. Thomas never looked back as he rode west towards the mountains and away from Davidson's Fort.

Anne and Ruth cleaned Emma up and prepared her body for burial. Even though life had passed out of her, she was still just as pretty as the day she stood up in church and melted Thomas's heart with her radiant smile. Charlie Walker built a casket using some of the oak boards he had milled for Thomas and Reverend Edwards to construct the crib that would never be used.

It took a week for the ground to thaw enough for the men to dig a grave next to the church to bury Emma. Reverend Edwards was able to hold himself together long enough to say a few words before they lowered Emma into the ground and covered her casket with dirt. He ended his remarks by saying, "I was torn to pieces when Emma died, and I said some things that day that I wish I hadn't said and that I'll regret forever. I blamed God and I blamed Thomas, and I was wrong on both counts and I'm so sorry. Thomas Williams is a good man. He promised me he'd love Emma until the day he died, and I know he meant it and he'll keep his promise. I shouldn't have blamed him for what happened to Emma. It wasn't his fault. I hope that someday he'll forgive me for the way I acted that day."

By the time they lowered Emma into the ground, Thomas was camped beside Bee Tree Creek not far from Brushy Mountain. He cut down some skinny pines and made a lean-to to provide some temporary shelter for himself and Bill. Then he started chopping down more substantial trees – oaks, pines, and tulip poplars – so he could build a cabin where he planned to stay until he could sort out where he'd go and what he'd do now that Emma had been ripped away from him forever. He knew he'd never go back to Davidson's Fort. There were too many memories there and there was too much pain. In an instant, what had been a seemingly perfect world had turned into an intolerable purgatory. He knew in his heart that Reverend Davidson had lashed out at him in grief and didn't really blame him for Emma's death … or at least that was the thought he chose to cling to. Reverend Edwards never knew it, but Thomas Williams forgave him.

It took him several months, but by summer, Thomas had finished the cabin. He'd used a horse and a rope to hoist the logs into place since he worked alone and couldn't lift them by himself. Bill was no help, but he was a good companion. Thomas talked to him often even though he never got a response other than a tail wag or a wet lick. At first, not a minute went by that he didn't think about Emma, but by the time the first snow fell that winter, he only thought of her every hour or so. It was worse at night when the ache in his chest kept him awake, and no matter how hard he tried not to think about Emma, he couldn't keep her out of his ming. He and Bill would venture off into the forest to hunt or go down to the Swannanoa River to catch fish.

By the beginning of 1784, Thomas was pretty much settled and had gotten himself into a tolerable if not outright comfortable routine. He still didn't know what he was going to do with the rest of his life, but he was content to remain there at Bee Tree Creek until he could figure it out.

And that comfortable routine continued until one morning in March when a mother bear and her yearling showed up on the other side of Bee Tree Creek.

Danuwoa told Uguku to climb back up to the top of Lane Pinnacle to see if smoke was still visible down by Brushy Mountain while he and Degataga and Adahy prepared breakfast and packed up. Uguku returned a short time later and said smoke was still coming from the same spot where they had seen it the afternoon before. They ate, gathered up their gear, and began their trek to investigate the source of the smoke. They headed east until they reached Bee Tree Creek. They turned south and followed the creek down the east side of Brushy Mountain. There was a small clearing at a bend in the creek, and from there they could see a thin plume of smoke about a quarter of a mile away where it rose up and drifted off in the breeze. They retreated into the protection of the tree line and moved cautiously down towards the smoke. About halfway there, they heard a loud boom and a few seconds later they saw two bears – one an adult and the other a juvenile – running west through the woods about twenty-five yards below them. The bears were in such a rush that they didn't even notice the four young warriors. Danuwoa looked over to the other side of the creek and saw a small cabin about a hundred yards away. Smoke rose from its chimney and floated away and disappeared.

Thomas thought his shot had missed its mark, but he went back inside his cabin to get his coat and hat and a pouch of black powder and some musket balls before venturing over to the other side of the creek to make sure. He repacked his musket, walked outside, and said "come on boy" as he and Bill headed to the other side of the creek and up the hill to where the bears had disappeared into the trees.

Thomas saw a small pool of fresh blood on the ground. Apparently, his shot had found its mark after all, although judging from the speed at which the bear ran away, it hadn't been a clean shot that would have taken the bear down right there by the creek. It was a middling size bear, and Thomas thought to himself that he could put the meat and the hide to good use if he could find it. He headed off into the woods hoping that his shot had been good enough to bring the bear down somewhere nearby and that it hadn't wandered off into a thicket to die and never to be seen again. The trail wasn't too hard to follow at first. The bears had taken off running at full speed, and rather than picking their way through the brush and the bramble, they had plowed directly ahead and blazed an obvious trail in the process.

The bears ran as hard as they could for several minutes. It wasn't until they slowed their pace that the mother bear felt a sharp pain near her right shoulder. At first, she thought she must have jabbed herself on something as she ran away from the sound of the gunshot in a panic, but soon she noticed that the pain went deep and was intensifying. She had an inkling that she was in trouble and her immediate concern was to make sure the yearling was safe. The den was too close to the cabin where the gunshot had occurred, and it was too dangerous to go back there. She had to get the yearling further away to a place where he'd be out of harm's way.

The bears were just south of Watch Knob. They walked in a southwesterly direction towards the Swannanoa River. The further they walked, the worse the pain grew, but the mother bear was determined to keep going for as long as she could to get her cub to safety. They turned west once they reached the river and continued on until they came to Bull Creek. The mother bear could barely walk at that point. The pain was excruciating and the fur around the site of the wound was matted thick with blood. Her breathing was heavy, and her mind was growing foggy. She knew her time was growing short, and she intended to use all of it to protect her cub. She had planned to force him out on his own in a few months, but it seemed that time was arriving sooner than she'd expected. She had thought that she was the one who was going to be left all alone, but now she knew it would be the young cub who we have to make a go of it by himself.

They stopped for a minute to get a drink of water, and then they continued north up Bull Creek. The mother bear hobbled along, dragging her right front leg as best she could. She uttered a low rumble every step or two from the pain that burned inside her like a fire that grew hotter by the minute. The yearling was scared. His mother had always been strong and decisive – his protector – but now she was weak and in distress. He wanted to help her, but there was nothing he could do.

They made it about eight hundred yards before the mother bear couldn't go any further. They were on the east bank of Bull Creek on what is now called the Bull Creek Trail, part of the present-day Warren Wilson College trail system. The mother bear saw an old oak tree on the other side of the creek about fifty feet from the bank. She was exhausted, in pain, and needed to rest. She walked the yearling across the creek and forced him to go up into the oak tree's branches. She stretched out at the base of the tree. She needed to rest, but she was afraid that if she closed her eyes and drifted off, she might not wake up again. For the moment, the yearling was safe in the tree above her, and he couldn't come down and wander off without rousting her. She was going to lay there, praying that some rest would cause the pain to subside and hopefully go away. She had done all that she could do for the moment. She just had to rest.

The four young warriors stayed about a hundred yards above Thomas and Bill on the ridgeline and trailed behind them a bit so that the southerly breeze wouldn't carry their scent down below and attract Bill's attention. Thomas was focused on tracking the bears and he spotted enough broken tree branches, trampled vegetation, paw prints, and occasional blood spots to follow the path they'd taken. He was going to keep following them until the sun was directly overhead and if he hadn't caught up with them by then, he was going to turn back since he wasn't equipped to stay out in the woods overnight.

It was late morning when Thomas reached the intersection of the Swannanoa River and Bull Creek. There were a lot of bear tracks along the sandy shoal where the two streams merged, and it was apparent that the bears had stopped there for a bit. The tracks turned north and followed the creek. Bill went down to the water's edge to get a drink. He suddenly stopped lapping at the water, raised his head, and sniffed the air. He smelled something. Mostly what he smelled was the scent of the black bears that had just passed through, but there was something else in the air too, but he couldn't identify it. He ran and caught up with Thomas who had moved on ahead.

Danuwoa raised his hand to signal the others to stop. The four froze in place when they saw Bill raise his head and sniff, and they were relieved when he ran off to catch up with the man he was accompanying and ignored them. Tsiyu Gansini had instructed them to observe and not to engage, and they intended to obey his edict.

Thomas hadn't walked very far when he saw bear tracks leading down into Bull Creek. He followed the tracks with his eyes to the other side. A short distance away, he saw the mother bear laying at the base of an oak tree. But where was the other one? He looked to the left and right thinking it might be hiding in the rhododendrons or the mountain laurels, but then he looked up and saw the yearling stretched out on a large oak branch about twenty feet above the mother bear. He knew that he shot at the larger of the two and he didn't want or need to shoot a second bear. It appeared that the larger of the two bears was dead, but he couldn't be sure from that distance. Since his musket only afforded him one shot before he had to stop for thirty seconds or so to load another round, he didn't want to tangle with two bears at once. As he paused to weigh his options, he thought to himself that he hoped Bill would stay quiet and not startle the bears.

Thomas decided to cross the creek to take a closer look at the bear spread out at the base of the tree. He thought the sound of the rushing water cascading over the rocks would conceal his approach and he could slip over to the other side without arousing the bear sleeping up in the tree. He moved slowly down the bank, eased into the water, and then moved cautiously up the gentle slope. Bill followed him and Thomas held his hand out to try and get Bill to keep behind him and stay quiet. The two bears were about fifty feet away. Thomas scanned back and forth between the two and it appeared that neither one had detected his approach. He raised his musket to a ready position and took a few steps forward to get a better look.

Once Thomas and Bill were on the other side of the creek, the four young warriors moved down the hill and hid behind a thick stand of rhododendrons several yards above the creek. Each one removed an arrow from his quill and placed it on the bowstring. Danuwoa motioned for

41

Degataga and Uguku to move a little farther up the creek and for Adahy to move a little farther down the creek. He wanted to be sure that at least one of them would have an unobstructed shot at Thomas if for some reason it became necessary. He knew that Thomas wouldn't be able to haul the entire bear back to the cabin on his own in one trip, so if they waited patiently, they could help themselves to the meat that he left behind. Danuwoa knew they could remain hidden and not attract the man's attention, but he worried about the dog.

Thomas was about thirty feet from the mother bear when he stepped on a twig. The mother bear heard it snap, and it instantly jolted her from her rest. There's nothing more determined than a mother bear who's forced to defend her cub. A wave of adrenalin overpowered the mother bear's pain and weakness, and for a moment she forgot all about her wound. She rose to her feet prepared to do all that she could do to protect the cub. She growled as loud as she could, stood up on her hind legs, and raised her left arm displaying the long sharp claws protruding from her paw. Thomas could see that her right arm was hanging down and limp, and the fur around it was wet and matted. The sound of her growl woke the yearling. He looked down from his perch on the limb and saw his mother standing up and moving forward towards a man holding a gun. He sank his claws into the bark of the tree and started to climb down as fast as he could.

The mother bear was about twenty feet away and coming towards Thomas. He pressed the musket against his shoulder, squeezed the trigger, and fired a shot into the chest of the mother bear. She groaned and fell to the ground with a thud. Thomas tried to reload his musket as quickly as he could in case the second bear charged him. The yearling stopped coming down the tree a few feet short of the ground when he heard the gunshot. He looked at his mother stretched out flat, paused for a second, jumped down, and ran north up Bull Creek. The last thing the mother bear saw as she labored to draw in the final breath she'd ever take was the yearling disappear into the forest. She had done all that she could do for her cub. She had given him her last full measure. He was on his own now.

His musket reloaded and the second bear long gone, Thomas walked over to the bear he had killed. She was a beauty. Thomas paused for a moment to ponder how he would get the hide and the meat back to his cabin, which was a couple of miles away as the crow flies. As he stood there over the bear, Bill started barking. Thomas turned to see what had attracted Bill's attention, and on the other side of the creek he saw Adahy partially concealed behind the rhododendrons. Thomas started to raise his musket, but then he heard a zing and felt a sharp pain in his abdomen as Danuwoa's arrow pieced his skin. A second later, he heard another zing as Uguku's arrow zipped past him just a few inches from his head. And then he heard a third and final zing. Thomas looked down to see Degataga's arrow buried deep in the left side of his chest. The musket fell from his hands, he dropped to his knees, and then he collapsed over onto his side next to the bear.

Thomas knew immediately that he was dying. In his final seconds, he thought to himself that death wasn't nearly as traumatic as he always thought it would be. There was pain of course, but there was no panic or fear. Instead, he felt a sense of peace and calm, like everything was somehow going to be alright. He thought of Emma, and he remembered the glorious vision of her the first time he saw her standing in the front of the church when she turned and smiled. He imagined Emma opening her arms to hug him and welcome him back like she had done so many times before when he returned home to her from his trips into the mountains. The image of her grew more sharp in his mind and he sensed her presence. He saw her smile at him, and he smiled back at her, comforted by knowing that they would be together again soon. Emma extended her hand, and he reached out and took it. "Welcome home, Thomas. I've missed you." "I've missed you too," he said as his heart beat one last time, and then they turned and walked away.

Thomas Williams kept the promise he made to Reverend Edwards that Saturday afternoon in the little church in Davidson's Fort … he had loved Emma with all of his heart until the day he died.

By the time the four warriors crossed the creek, Thomas was gone, and his lifeless body was slumped over against the bear. Bill stood guard over Thomas and snarled at the warriors as they approached, but Uguku was able to toss a rope around his neck, pull him away, and tie him to a tree. Danuwoa took his foot and pushed Thomas's body over so that he was flat on his back. His eyes were open, but they were fixed and dead. It seemed odd to Danuwoa that Thomas appeared to be smiling. How could someone be joyful as he crossed over death's door? He broke the arrows off near where they had entered Thomas's body and then he rolled Thomas over on his stomach. Danuwoa pulled out his knife, grabbed Thomas by the hair, and removed his scalp. The others pulled out their knives and went to work on the bear, carving off pieces of hide and hunks of meat. When they were done, Danuwoa said, "leave them be. We'll go back to the cabin, and we'll burn it down, and then we'll move on before night falls." Uguku asked, "what about the dog?" "Bring him," Danuwoa responded. Uguku untied Bill from the tree, and the four young warriors and the dog crossed back over Bull Creek and walked off into the forest.

Bill looked back at Thomas for as long as he could as Uguku pulled him along. His heart ached.

It was the middle of the afternoon by the time the four young warriors and Bill reached Thomas's cabin. They went inside and found the stew that Thomas had been cooking over the fire in the fireplace. They ate it and then they went through his few belongings and took what they could use and could carry with them. Uguku asked Danuwoa what they were going to do with Bill. Danuwoa said he had an idea. He took Thomas's scalp, poked a hole through it with his knife, put a strip of cloth through the hole, and tied it around Bill's neck. "Hopefully he'll make his way back to wherever he came from and take a message to the white intruders that they're not welcome here on our land." Danuwoa led Bill outside, untied the rope that was around Bill's neck, smacked him on the butt with it, and yelled at him to scare him away. Bill ran south down Bee Tree Creek at full speed and didn't look back.

Adahy and Degataga took embers from the fireplace, spread them around the cabin, and fanned them. It didn't take long for the fire to ignite and spread throughout the cabin. The four young warriors stood beside the creek for several minutes and watched the cabin as it went up in flames. They collected their gear, headed north up Bee Tree Creek, and continued their journey.

Blood from the mother bear trickled slowly into a shallow trench that had been created by rainwater as it carved a path down towards Bull Creek. Thomas's blood trickled towards the creek in a parallel trench, and the two trenches eventually merged, and the blood of the bear and the blood of Thomas Williams mixed into a single scarlet ribbon that snaked its way slowly towards the creek. A little further down, about twenty-five feet from the edge of Bull Creek, an acorn from the big oak tree sat at the bottom of the trench and soon it was covered by the stream of blood. It was March of 1784, and Actual Spring was just around the corner, that day beside Bull Creek when the acorn began its transformation into a mighty oak.

Fool's Spring lasted just long enough to lull creatures – human beings included – into thinking winter had gone and spring was here, but the wind turned crisp as Second Winter approached. Reverend Edwards was chopping wood to keep the fire in the fireplace burning and the house warm through the night. He still thought of Emma every day, and of Thomas too. It had been a year since they both departed, and his heart had started to mend, but it still had a long way to go, and he knew that it would never heal completely. He placed another log on the stump by the woodpile and he was about to raise his ax to split it when out of the corner of his eye he detected motion, looked over, and saw Bill running towards him. His immediate thought was that meant Thomas was close behind, so he looked off to the west expecting to see Thomas on horseback riding in his direction, but all he saw was the sun about to set behind the mountains.

When Bill reached him, Reverend Edwards saw that something was tied around Bill's neck, so he bent down, untied the piece of cloth, and held the object up to take a closer look at it in the fading light. He dropped it, walked slowly over to the porch, sat down on a step, and cried.

Every day from then until the day he died, Reverend Edwards prayed for Emma and for Thomas. He prayed they were both at peace, and he prayed for Thomas's forgiveness. Reverend Edwards blamed himself for driving Thomas away from Davidson's Fort and to his death. It was a guilt he carried with him to his grave.

Part Two – James Craig and Henry West

The morning after Bill wandered back into Davidson's Fort and Reverend Edwards made the grisly discovery that Thomas Williams had been killed, a dozen troops headed up into the mountains to search for Thomas's body hoping to bring it back for burial next to Emma. They also hoped to find who killed Thomas and exact revenge for his brutal death. No one knew exactly where Thomas went after Emma died, so they didn't know where to look for him. Reverend Edwards said that on Thomas's last trip before Emma's death, he had intended to reach the settlement on the Watauga River, but he turned back before he got there because of the weather, and he said Thomas had talked about the settlement before, so if he was to venture a guess where to look for him, he would start there.

The troops rode west until they got to the French Broad River, and then they headed north up to the Watauga River where they found the settlement. No one there had seen Thomas or even heard anything about him from the trappers and hunters who passed through regularly. The troops left the next day and began making their way back towards Davidson's Fort. They passed within two miles of Bull Creek where Thomas's body lay next to the mother bear beside the oak tree, and within three miles of the burnt remains of his cabin next to Bee Tree Creek.

No one ever solved the mystery of where Thomas went after he left Davidson's Fort, what he did in the last year of his life, or exactly how he died – except for Bill, and Bill kept the secret. Thomas was the first non-native person to settle in what is now Buncombe County, but since no one other than the four young warriors knew about it, history would award that distinction to someone else.

After they left Thomas's cabin, the four young warriors continued east through Black Mountain and over to what is now called Point Lookout. From there, they could see Davidson's Fort in the distance at the base of the mountains. They couldn't tell how many people lived there, but they could see that it was a sizeable settlement with several solid and substantial structures in place. They agreed amongst themselves that it would be difficult for them to attack it and drive out the settlers unless they had a massive force and the element of surprise on their side.

Tsiyu Gansini sent them to look for settlement activity in the French Broad River region, and they completed their mission, so they began their journey home. They chose a looping route that took them northwest through what is now Madison County and then southwest through Haywood, Swain, Graham, and Cherokee counties, and finally home to their village. As was the case on the eastward leg of their journey, they observed a few hunters and trappers along the way who were transiting through the area, but they saw no further evidence of efforts to establish permanent settlements. They crossed the French Broad River late one morning at a spot several miles north of where the town of Marshall is located today. They never knew that the troops from Davidson's Fort who were looking for Thomas's body and for them crossed their path a few hours later as the troops made their way north up to the Watauga River settlement. They didn't know that their paths would eventually cross again.

When the four young warriors reached their village, Tsiyu Gansini was pleased to hear that the proliferation of settlements was not as extensive as John McDonald believed. He was familiar with the settlement to the north along the Watauga River from the failed attack a few years earlier, and he suspected that since then, the settlement had expanded and the population had grown, and it had crept further south. The effort to drive those settlers out failed, and with several years of additional growth, it would be even more challenging to oust them now. Tsiyu

Gansini was more interested in Davidson's Fort and encroachment on Cherokee land from the east. The encounter with Thomas and the discovery of his cabin on Bee Tree Creek indicated that white settlers had indeed made their way up into the mountains and onto native land, and it was clear that their path flowed through Davidson's Fort and the Swannanoa Gap. He decided that in a few weeks he would lead a bigger group back to the area equipped for battle, if it appeared to him that they could oust the settlers. The four young warriors warned Tsiyu Gansini that Davidson's Fort was substantial and well-fortified, and it would be difficult to attack, but he knew they had never experienced battle before and he was skeptical whether their dire assessment was indeed accurate. He considered what they had to say, but Tsiyu Gansini wanted to see the settlement and decide for himself.

John Davidson and his wife Jane immigrated to America from Ireland along with their four sons – George, Thomas, and twins William and Samuel – and their daughter Rachel in 1740. They arrived in Philadelphia and made their way to Virginia and settled in Augusta County just a few miles from where Thomas Williams was born and raised. After they settled in Virigina, they had a fifth son, John, who was known as "One-Eyed John" because he lost an eye when a musket misfired and injured him when he was a young man, and they had two more daughters, Elizabeth and Margaret. They ventured further south to North Carolina in 1748 where they built a farm in an area that includes parts of Iredell and Mecklenburg counties today, including land that now lies beneath the waters of Lake Norman, the largest man-made lake in North Carolina, constructed by Duke Power in 1962 when they damned up the Catawba River and built a hydroelectric plant.

In 1770, four of the brothers – all but Thomas – migrated from Iredell County, which is just north of Charlotte and east of Hickory, to what is now Burke County and the area around present-day Old Fort. One-Eyed John, his wife Nancy, and all but one of their children were killed by Cherokee warriors who attacked their farm not long after they arrived. Some say the massacre of One-Eyed John and his family led his brother, Captain Samuel Davidson, to build a blockhouse to provide settlers with refuge from attacks by native warriors. It became known as Davidson's Fort and later evolved into the town of Old Fort.

Captain Samuel Davidson received a land grant in an area that today includes Buncombe County in payment for his military service in the Revolutionary War. In May of 1784, not long after Thomas Williams was killed, Samuel rode up through the Swannanoa Gap and into the mountains equipped with a musket, an ax, a skinning knife, and enough supplies to sustain him and his horse for a couple of weeks. He knew the fate of his brother One-Eyed John and Thomas Williams, at the hands of the Cherokee, so he kept close watch on his surroundings and avoided spots that could provide cover for a Cherokee ambush. His aim was to find a suitable patch of land, build a temporary cabin, go back to Davidson's Fort for his family, bring them up, and then construct a permanent home and start a farm.

Samuel found a spot he liked in a valley about a mile south of the Swannanoa River on Christian Creek not far from the current site of Warren Wilson College and less than five miles from where Thomas Williams built his cabin. It was surrounded by a thick forest of evergreen and hardwood trees, had a good source of drinking water, and offered abundant natural resources, like deer, elk, buffalo, and turkeys. Just as Thomas had done the previous year,

Samuel went to work clearing an area for a cabin, cutting down and honing trees to construct it, and collecting stones to build a chimney for a fireplace. It was hard work, particularly since he worked alone, but in a couple of weeks, the cabin and a lean-to for the slave woman they would bring with them were finished. Samuel cleared a small patch for a garden and cobbled together some rough-hewn furniture to outfit the cabin. When his work was done, he rode back to Davidson's Fort to fetch his family.

Samuel's wife Mary was not keen on leaving Davidson's Fort and heading off into the mountain wilderness, particularly since she had given birth to a baby girl just a few months earlier. But it was Samuel's dream, and so she relented without making a fuss about it, just as she had done when they'd left Iredell County for Davidson's Fort not long after they got married. They helped build Davidson's Fort out of nothing, and it quickly became a robust community. She hoped the same would happen again in this next new place that Samuel chose.

Two days after he came back to Davidson's Fort, Samuel, his wife Mary, their infant daughter Ruth, and a young slave woman named Liza, headed up into the mountains to begin a new chapter. They brought a plow blade to turn the soil, seed corn to plant in the spring, seedlings for a garden, a grindstone for sharpening knives and implements, and pots and pans for cooking. They arrived at the little cabin late in the afternoon just as the sun was about to set.

Mary's heart sank as she surveyed her new home. It was rough, it was remote, and it lacked the hustle and bustle of Davidson's Fort. She had friends there and a sense of security. Now, she felt lonely as a dense fog of dread crept over her like the darks clouds that roll down and swamp the Swannanoa Valley from time to time.

That wasn't the case for Samuel. For him, this new place was a marvelous adventure and a tremendous opportunity. He knew there were dangers and that it would be lonely living isolated

51

out in the wild, but this was a beautiful and bountiful place, and inevitably more people would follow them up through the Swannanoa Gap and join them in raising up a new community. That evening, as they gathered around the table for their first meal in their new home, Samuel offered a prayer.

"Dear Lord, we're grateful to you for a safe journey and thankful that you have led us to this place where we'll make our home. We pray that you'll watch over us and look favorably upon our efforts. Thank you for this food that you've provided to sustain us. Keep us safe now and in the days ahead. Amen." Mary and Liza joined in, "amen."

The next morning, Samuel showed Mary and Liza around the area. "I've cleared a little patch over here where we can plant a garden, and over the winter, I'm going to keep clearing back that way so we can plant more crops come spring," he said as he gestured towards the tree line. "The water in the creek is cold and clear. When I was here before, not a day went by I didn't see a deer or a turkey strolling through, and occasionally an elk or a bear, and there are rabbits and squirrels everywhere, and herds of buffalo. I can ride down to Davidson's Fort and back in a day's time if we need anything to get us through the winter, but I think we've got most everything we'll need right here," he said as he smiled and reached over and took Mary's hand.

"It's beautiful, Samuel, it truly is." Mary tried her best to work up what might pass as an approving smile. "You've picked a wonderful spot, and I know our family will grow and prosper here. But I implore you to be mindful of the dangers, and particularly the dangers that could find our Ruth. There're bears and natives and other things out there that could do her harm, and we're all counting on you to protect us and keep us safe."

Samuel leaned in and kissed her. "Don't you worry, Mary. God will protect us. And I'll always have one eye on my work and the other one looking out for trouble. We'll be fine here; we'll be just fine. Trust me."

Later, Samuel hitched the plow to one of the horses and tilled the area he had cleared for the garden. Liza planted potatoes, collard greens, string beans, and squash, and she brought buckets of water up from the creek to moisten the ground to get the seedlings started. Mary tended to Ruth and did what she could with the few possessions they'd brought to try and make the tiny cabin feel more like a home. As she worked, Mary thought about Davidson's Fort. She enjoyed the company of other women her age and, even though it had only been a few days, she missed her friends and their conversations about what was going on in their day-to-day lives. And she missed the gossip; Lordy, how she missed the gossip! Catherine Alexander was always on the lookout for a whiff of impropriety or rumor of some scandalous intrigue, and she shared it freely, often sprinkled liberally with embellishments for good measure, with Mary and the other ladies in their little group. Mary was lonely, just as she had been when they first arrived in Davidson's Fort, and she hoped that this new place would soon take root and grow like Davidson's Fort had grown. It couldn't happen soon enough for her.

Liza's parents were slaves who were sold at auction on the dock in Wilmington minutes after they were led off the slave ship that brought them to America after they were kidnapped from their homes in West Africa. It had been a horrible journey; cramped and hot, with little food or water, and no privacy. Some of the others in the cargo hold perished along the way and their bodies were tossed overboard just like the human waste was tossed into the ocean from the ship's slop buckets, with no prayers, no pause, and no concern. Her parents were thankful when they were led up from the ship's hold to the main deck, where they breathed in fresh air and saw sunlight for the first time in days. They were both in their late teens and were kidnapped and led away from their village, shackled, and forced onto the ship for the voyage across the Atlantic. There were others already on board abducted from other villages the ship visited as it made its way up the coast of West Africa. Her parents knew each other well, but they never had a romantic relationship. Still, when they were sold off on the Wilmington dock in a lot with six others – a total of six men and two women – and began the journey to John Davidson's farm in Iredell County, they took some comfort from the fact that they were together and not totally alone amongst a group of strangers.

Liza wasn't sure exactly when she was born or how old she was. Samuel seemed to recall that she was born in 1768, the year before he married Mary and two years before he left the farm and moved to what became Davidson's Fort. That made her about sixteen years old when they made their way up through the Swannanoa Gap to the cabin on Christian Creek. White mothers were prone to brag about their children: "John is so strong!" "Catherine is so industrious!" "Martin is so clever!" Enslaved black mothers downplayed their children's positive attributes. Liza's mother learned that lesson from older female slaves who were mothers and passed down the lessons they'd learned the hard way. So, when one of the Davidsons would say what a fine-looking young girl Liza was, her mother would respond, "Well now, she's a bit sickly and a little slow, but I'm going to keep my eye on her, and I think she'll be able to make do when she gets a little older." A slave child who was strong, industrious, or clever was a valuable commodity, and a slaveowner might snatch the child away and sell him or her to someone else to earn a profit. Liza's mother mastered the art of making sure the Davidsons perceived Liza as being not too worthless and not too valuable so that they would keep her around. And her plan worked just fine … for a time.

54

Liza helped her mother with chores around the Davidson's house. Over time, she learned to cook, to gut and clean fish and game, to dress and quarter farm animals, and to sew. In 1783, when Samuel sent word to his mother that Mary was pregnant, Jane Davidson – who had been a widow since John Davidson died a few years earlier – wrote back and offered to send Liza to Davidson's Fort to help tend to the house and take care of the baby. Jane said Liza was quiet, dependable, and a good cook and housekeeper. Samuel discussed it with Mary and wrote back to his mother accepting her gracious offer. A couple of weeks later, Liza, along with a young male slave that Jane sent to help Samuel's twin brother William at his gristmill, arrived in Davidson's Fort in the back of a wagon with the rest of the cargo.

Since the day she was born, Liza had never been away from her mother for more than two or three hours at a time. Now, separated from the woman who had cared for her and nurtured her every day of her life, she was scared and lonely. Her mother knew Samuel and she was acquainted with Mary, and she told Liza that she believed they would treat her well, but she warned her not to cause any trouble and to do exactly as she was told. For several weeks after she arrived in Davidson's Fort, Liza cried every night and sometimes when she was alone and knew that no one could hear her. What her mother had told her proved true. Samuel and Mary treated her well, and she knew she was far more fortunate than some others in her situation who had to endure physical and mental abuse in addition to doing back-breaking work for long hours in the hot sun, but it wasn't enough to fill the hole in her heart left after she was ripped away from the only person who had every truly loved her.

Liza was small, standing just under five feet tall and weighing less than a hundred pounds, but she was stronger than her diminutive appearance might suggest. She had mostly worked in the house at John Davidson's Iredell farm, and she often overheard the family's conversations about local and world events, religion, medicine, and science. In the evenings, when the work was done and dinner was over, an older enslaved man who helped the Davidson's keep the farm's ledgers taught her to read, write, and do math. In truth, Liza was far more capable and much cleverer than the Davidsons were led to believe, and her talents would later prove invaluable to the family she was forced to serve.

Over the summer, Samuel chopped down trees and used the horses to pull the stumps out of the ground to clear a larger area for planting in the spring. He used some of the wood to reinforce the cabin in preparation for winter and with some of the rest he and Liza built a pole barn where they could store feed and shelter the horses during bad weather. They built a small shed where they could cure the meat and tan the hides from the deer, bears, and rabbits Samuel killed when he went hunting. Once a week or so, Samuel would walk up to the Swannanoa River and return hours later with a stringer of fish. Liza helped Mary tend to the cabin, cook the meals, and take care of Ruth. Liza didn't say much the first few weeks they lived on Christian Creek, but over time, as she and Mary got better acquainted, they spent hours talking. Liza wasn't as entertaining as Davidson's Fort preeminent gossip Catherine Alexander, but Mary had to make do and Liza was all she had.

Mary hadn't traveled much, but she had been to the ocean and visited the Governor's family at Tryon Palace, and she'd seen a lot of other places and things Liza never had and never would see with her own eyes. Liza liked hearing about what seemed to her to be interesting people and exotic places. Mary was surprised at the breadth and depth of Liza's knowledge. She knew details about the Declaration of Independence, the reasons the colonies went to war with Britian, and the nature of the conflicts between the European settlers and the Native American tribes on whose land the settlers intruded. In many respects, Mary found her conversations with

Liza to be more deep and profound and less petty than the conversations she had with the women she considered her peers back in Davidson's Fort, even if her conversations with Liza were not nearly as titillating.

By the middle of October, the summer heat faded away and the night air turned crisp. Samuel stood outside the cabin just before sunset, looked out towards the ridgeline, and admired the vibrant fall colors: the orange of the maples, the red of the oaks and the sourwoods, the bronze of the hickories and the chestnuts, the yellow of the poplars and the beeches, intermixed with the green of the pines, the hemlocks, and the rhododendrons. It was if God had put nature's entire color palate on display right there, and it was stunning. Samuel smiled. He felt that they were truly blessed to live in a place of such incredible beauty.

Samuel thought back, and he was pleased at how much they had accomplished in the few months since they arrived at Christian Creek. They were in good shape to get through the winter, and they were ready to hit the ground running when spring came. That night at dinner, he told Mary and Liza that he planned to ride down to Davidson's Fort the next morning to get supplies. He had used up most of his stock of gunpowder and musket balls, and he needed to replace a plow blade that broke when it struck a rock. Mary said she could use some thread to stitch buckskin clothing from the hides drying in the shed and Liza said they needed salt to cure meat to help get them get through the winter. Samuel hadn't left them alone for more than a couple of hours at a time when he went off to hunt or fish, and he told them not to worry, he would leave early the next morning, and he would be back before dark. It was only a fifteen mile ride each way, so if he didn't dawdle too long in Davidson's Fort, he'd be home in time for dinner.

Everyone arose early the next morning. Samuel found duck eggs the last time he went fishing in the Swannanoa River, and Liza scrambled them over the fire in a cast iron skillet. She made home fries from leftover potatoes and warmed up some corn pone she'd cooked the day before. Samuel had let the horses wander free so they could graze in the meadows near the cabin and save the straw stored in the pole barn for when they needed it over the winter. He'd tied a cowbell around the neck of one of the horses so he could hear them when he needed to find them and bring them back to the cabin.

After breakfast, Samuel got up from the table and headed towards the door. "I'm going to go round up the horses, bring them back here, and get them fitted for the trip. I want to get going soon to make sure I'm back here by dinnertime."

"Do you want me to pack you something to eat, Mister Samuel?" Liza asked.

"Thank you, Liza, but I'll get something to eat when I'm in Davidson's Fort. But I hope you and Mary have something good planned for dinner. I'll be hungry by the time I get back."

A week earlier, Tsiyu Gansini and thirty warriors left their village and set out on a mission to surveil Davidson's Fort. The four young warriors were part of the group and Tsiyu Gansini tasked Danuwoa with leading the way. Cold weather and snow would arrive before long, and Tsiyu Gansini intended to make this a short trip so they would be back home before cold weather settled in for the season, but he wanted a chance to assess Davidson's Fort with his own eyes. If the conditions were right, they might try and drive the settlers out this time, but if not, seeing what they'd be up against would enable him to prepare for a return trip to finish the task in the spring. Since they might launch an attack, Tsiyu Gansini had the warriors draw muskets from the village armory along with black powder and musket balls. Thoughts of the failed attack on the Watauga River settlement lingered in his mind, and he wanted to make sure the mistakes they made there were not repeated at Davidson's Fort.

The warriors crossed the French Broad River just below the point where the Swannanoa River merges into it and then they followed the Swannanoa River to the east. A short time later, one of the warriors saw smoke rising above the tree tops off in the distance almost directly in line with the path they were on. It was late in the afternoon and Tsiyu Gansini thought it would be a good time to stop for the night. He told his warriors to backtrack a mile or two to make sure whoever was in the path ahead of them wouldn't see the smoke from their campfires. He told Degataga and Uguku to go ahead on foot, find the source of the smoke, and report back to him on what they found.

The other warriors retraced their steps and then stopped and set up camp. Danuwoa told Tsiyu Gansini that it was about a day's ride from where they were to Point Lookout and then less than day's ride from there down to Davidson's Fort. "We'll pass close to the cabin we destroyed when we were here before, if you want to see it. It's north of the river and it would add several hours to our journey, but it's in the same general direction we're headed."

"That's not necessary," Tsiyu Gansini responded. "After we take care of the trespassers ahead of us, I want to proceed directly to the spot you described where I can see the outpost at the base of the mountains. I want to determine the safest route for us to approach it so I can get a good look and decide whether we'll attack it now or wait until spring."

When Degataga and Uguku reached an opening, they saw that the smoke was coming from a location south of the Swannanoa River, and they went down to the water's edge, found a shallow spot, and crossed over to the other side. There wasn't much of a breeze, but what little there was blew in a southeasterly direction. They decided on a path that would take them to the

59

south and east of the source of the smoke so they would be downwind where their scents wouldn't be detected if a dog was present like there had been when they encountered Thomas Williams. When they reached Christian Creek, they turned east and moved along beside the stream. Soon, they spotted a cabin. It was on the north side of the creek, so they crossed over the creek and moved ahead concealed by the tree line until they were a short distance to the east of the cabin where they stopped and hid behind a stand of mountain laurels.

The cabin was slightly larger and appeared to be better constructed than the cabin they burned down on their earlier trip. They saw a pole barn, a curing shed, and a cleared patch where a garden was planted. Two horses were grazing a short distance from the house. A couple of minutes later, a man came out of the cabin and walked over to the horses. He took something off of a post and tied it around the neck of one of the horses, and then he shooed the horses away. As the horses plodded along, a bell clanged. Before long, the horses disappeared over a slight ridge. A woman with dark skin came out of the cabin carrying a bucket a few minutes later. She walked over to the garden, bent over, and appeared to pick something off a vine and place it in the bucket. After several minutes of picking from the garden, she lifted the bucket and walked back to the cabin.

Degataga and Uguku made their way back to the camp and arrived there just after sunset. The warriors gathered around as Degataga and Uguku described what they had observed to Tsiyu Gansini. They said the cabin and the outbuildings showed that this was a more established homesite than the cabin they burned down in the spring. They hadn't ventured as far south as Christian Creek on their last trip, so they didn't know if the cabin was there back then or if it had been built more recently, but it appeared that it was fairly new. They described the fair-skinned man and the dark-skinned woman, and how the man tied a bell around the neck of one of the horses and then shooed them away. Tsiyu Gansini wasn't sure if they would attack Davidson's Fort on this trip, but he was certain they would evict these trespassers and drive them off of Cherokee land.

The warriors were up before the sun the next morning. Tsiyu Gansini thought that a large group was more likely to be detected, and besides, he didn't need many warriors to dispatch a pair of intruders, so he assembled a small group that included Degataga, Uguku, Danuwoa, Adahy, and two older and more seasoned warriors to accompany him to the cabin. He instructed the others to break down the camp and get ready to move on to Lookout Point after they took care of the trespassers.

Degataga and Uguku led the group and soon they spotted smoke above the trees up ahead of them. It showed that the wind was blowing out of the west, so this time they decided to approach the cabin from the north, on the same side of Christian Creek as the cabin. When the group was about a quarter of a mile away, they heard a bell clanging nearby. Tsiyu Gansini signaled for three of the warriors to move around to the right and for the other three to move around to the left of where they heard the bell. They moved up over a ridge and saw two horses grazing in a clearing about fifty yards away. They encircled the horses and slipped ropes around their necks. They led the horses into the forest and tied them to a tree. Tsiyu Gansini removed the bell from around the horse's neck and handed it to Danuwoa.

"Danuwoa, I want you to creep up behind the ridge above the cabin and wait there. When someone comes out, ring the bell. If they take notice, start walking back in this direction. We'll form two lines behind those trees in a V-shaped formation. When you've lured one of the trespassers out into the clearing, we'll open fire on my command." The warriors all nodded their heads in agreement. Danuwoa took the bell, walked across the clearing, and disappeared into the forest.

Danuwoa didn't have to wait long. Soon after he took his position on the ridge, Samuel Davidson opened the cabin door and walked outside. Danuwoa paused a moment and then rang the bell. Samuel stopped and looked in his direction. Danuwoa walked back through the forest towards the clearing where the others had taken their places. He hadn't gone far when he heard Samuel whistle and then shout, "come on now. We need to get going." Danuwoa rang the bell every few seconds as he continued to make his way back towards the clearing. Samuel was about seventy-five yards behind him as they made their way through the forest. Samuel yelled, "come on, we need to go." Seconds later, as Samuel stepped into the clearing, he stopped and looked around. "Where are those damned horses," he muttered to himself. Danuwoa rang the bell one last time and then Tsiyu Gansini yelled "fire!" as he squeezed the trigger of his musket. A fusillade of musket balls struck Samuel in the stomach, the chest, and the face, and he was dead before his body hit the ground.

Mary and Liza heard the muskets boom, and they looked at each other in silence. Mary glanced over next to the door and saw that Samuel's musket was still hanging on the wall. She knew that he wasn't coming home. She dropped to her knees and cried.

Liza knew that Samuel was dead too. She ran over to Mary and grabbed her by the shoulders. "Get up, Miss Mary! We got to get out of here. Come on now, we can't just sit here. Whoever's out there will be coming for us too. We got to take Ruth and we got to run. Get up now! Come on, get up! Now, damn it! Now!"

Liza forced Mary to stand up. She grabbed their coats off the pegs on the wall, tossed one to Mary, and the two women put them on quickly. Liza lifted Ruth from her crib and wrapped her in a blanket. "Come on! Let's go!" Liza said as she opened the door, looked outside, and then ran towards the woods over by the creek with Ruth cradled tightly in her arms. Mary followed close behind her. They ran for several minutes and then Liza said, "they'll be looking for us and we don't need to help them find us. Let's get down in the creek and walk on the rocks so we don't leave footprints for them to follow." They walked in the creek bed for nearly half an hour, and then they climbed up the bank and headed off through the forest.

It was fifteen miles down to Davidson's Fort, and Liza was determined to get there as quickly as she could. They paused to rest at the top of the Swannanoa Gap. It was the first time Mary had a chance to stop and think about anything other than their escape, and as she thought of Samuel lying somewhere out in the woods, she started to cry.

"I can't go on!" she wailed. "I've got to go back and find Samuel. He might be hurt and laying out there somewhere wondering why I haven't come to help him," she said as she stood up. "Miss Mary, you know good and well that Mister Samuel is gone," Liza replied as she grabbed Mary by the arm. "And he'd want you to take care of yourself and Ruth rather than worrying over him. We got a long way to go, and we won't be safe until we get to Davidson's Fort. We'll mourn Mister Samuel when we get Ruth to safety, but for right now, we got to keep moving." Liza let go of Mary's arm, bent down, picked up Ruth, and then led them home to Davidson's Fort.

When the shooting stopped, Tsiyu Gansini walked over to Samuel's lifeless body, pulled out his knife, and removed Samuel's scalp. He held it up over his head as the other warriors raised their guns and whooped in celebration. They walked down to the cabin, took what they could use, and then set the cabin ablaze. The warriors that hadn't accompanied Tsiyu Gansini saw the thick smoke billowing up over the tops of the trees and rode in that direction.

"The dark-skinned woman Uguku saw yesterday. Are we going to look for her?" Danuwoa asked Tsiyu Gansini.

"No," Tsiyu Gansini responded. He knew that some of the pale-skinned intruders kept African slaves in bondage and forced them to toil in their fields. He figured the dark-skinned woman had suffered enough, and besides, she wouldn't be coming back and trying to steal their land. He thought that by killing the white man who held her captive they might have given her the freedom that he denied her. "She's no threat to our people. Let her go."

Mary, Liza, and Ruth walked all day and into the night. They reached Davidson's Fort just as most folks were getting ready for bed. Liza led them to the home of Major William Davidson, Samuel's twin brother. When he came to the door, Mary threw herself into William's arms and cried. "Samuel's dead. Somebody shot him," she said as broke down in tears, slipped from William's grasp, and fell to her knees on the front porch. Liza was holding Ruth in her arms. William's wife Margaret walked over and said she'd take the child. Liza handed Ruth over and then helped Mary up on her feet, led her inside, and sat her down in a chair.

William asked Liza what happened. "Mister Samuel was going to ride down here today to get supplies. He went out early this morning to get the horses and a few minutes later Miss Mary and I heard guns firing. Mister Samuel's gun was still hanging on the wall in the cabin, so we knew it wasn't him doing the shooting. I got Miss Mary and Miss Ruth out of there as quick as I could, and we walked all day and all night to get here. I'm real sorry about Mr. Samuel."

"Thank you, Liza," William replied. "And thank you for getting Mary and the baby back here where they're safe. You've done a good thing and I'm grateful. I'll head back up there in the morning and find out what happened, and I'll take care of whoever's responsible."

William went from house to house that night, spreading the word about Samuel, Mary, and the baby. He told the men to meet up at first light, and they would go find Samuel and whoever shot him. In the morning, William, other members of the Davidson family, and a group of soldiers and townsmen mounted up and headed for the Swannanoa Gap. Before they left, William promised Mary that they would find Samuel and give him a proper Christian burial. And he promised her that they would find whoever was responsible for killing him and they'd settle the score. Mary considered herself a good Christian woman, but in her heart, she hoped whoever killed her husband suffered greatly before they died.

Danuwoa led the warriors to Lookout Point. Tsiyu Gansini could see Davidson's Fort down below in the distance. He saw that the trail leading down the mountains through the Swannanoa Gap appeared to be well-traveled and he worried that they would be too exposed if they followed it down to Davidson's Fort. He decided it was just too risky. Even though it was going to add a day or two to their journey, he decided they would head further north and approach Davidson's Fort from that direction.

They rode east of Mount Mitchell and camped near Setrock Falls along the South Toe River. The next day, they rode on to Rockhouse Creek, which runs a few miles south of where the town of Spruce Pine sits today. They camped there for the night and planned to head east the next morning, pass near Linville Gorge, and then turn south towards Davidson's Fort.

William Davidson and the militia reached the burnt remnants of Samuel's cabin next to Christian Creek late in the morning. The way Liza described the sound of the gunfire, William knew it had to have come from close by, so he sent men off in groups of two into the forest to look for Samuel and it only took a few minutes for them to find his body in the opening just over the ridge from what remained of the cabin. The men dug a grave and buried Samuel right where he died. They took two posts and lashed them together to form a crude wooden cross and they shoved it into the loose soil at the head of his grave. Now, more than two centuries later, a stone marker sits atop Samuel's resting place on Jones Mountain near Warren Wilson College. After the last shovel of dirt was tossed, the men assembled around the grave in a circle and removed their hats. William offered a prayer for Samuel's soul and for God's mercy on Mary and Ruth. William put his hat back on his head and said, "alright gentlemen. Let's go find the sons of bitches who did this."

As they were preparing to leave, William bent down, picked up a handful of dirt from next to the grave, rubbed it together between his fingers, and let it spill back down to the ground. "That's some mighty fine soil," he said to his teenage son, George, who was standing nearby.

"Aye. 'Tis indeed," George responded.

John Greer was a hunter and trapper who had spent a considerable amount of time in the mountains. He was also a skilled tracker. It wasn't hard for him to follow the tracks Tsiyu Gansini and his warriors left as they traveled to Lookout Point and then turned north. William and the militia continued their pursuit into the night and then stopped just south of Crabtree Falls to eat, rest the horses, and get some sleep. They were up again before sunrise and, unbeknownst to them, at that moment, they were just a few miles from the spot where Tsiyu Gansini and his warriors were camped.

John Greer and William Davidson took the point, and the rest of the militia trailed about a hundred yards behind them. The sun had just come up when John saw smoke drifting up above the treetops directly ahead. William climbed down off his horse and motioned for the others to move up and join their position. William divided the men into three groups. He directed John Greer to lead a group that would move off to the west and his son George to lead a group that would move off to the east. William led a group that moved directly ahead towards the smoke. All three of the groups were instructed to keep moving forward until the natives were in sight and continue moving forward until William gave the order to open fire.

Tsiyu Gansini and his warriors were about to break camp and head towards Linville Gorge. Adahy walked a short distance from the camp, squatted against a tree, and was about to relieve himself when he saw men with guns approaching through the forest. He stood up and ran back towards the camp screaming as loud as he could to alert the others. Just as Adahy reached the edge of the camp, William gave the order to fire, and the militiamen sent a volley of musket shots into the camp. One struck Danuwoa high up on his right shoulder, shattering the bone and knocking him to the ground. One of the warriors took a shot directly to the chest and died instantly, and several others were wounded. Tsiyu Gansini yelled for the warriors to scatter. He knew they only had a matter of seconds before the militiamen reloaded their muskets and another barrage of lead balls would tear through the camp.

Tsiyu Gansini and the other warriors who were near their horses mounted up and raced off into the forest while others ran away on foot. A few who were too seriously wounded to escape remained behind and were shot dead minutes later. The militiamen who were deployed to the east and west of the camp opened fire on the warriors who fled in their directions, killing three and wounding several more. The wounded who couldn't keep running were executed. In total, of the thirty warriors that set out with Tsiyu Gansini, only twenty made it back home to their village. Tsiyu Gansini's son, Degataga, was one of the ten killed by Williams Davidson's militia. Uguku made it home uninjured. Adahy suffered a wound to his knee and for the rest of his life walked with a severe limp. Danuwoa lost a considerable amount of blood from the wound to his shoulder, and he barely survived the journey back to the village. It took the better part of a year for the wound to heal and when it did, the damage to the bone and muscle left his right arm weak and essentially useless. He and Adahy would never see battle again.

After William Davidson returned to Davidson's Fort, he didn't forget the rich soil and natural beauty of the Swannanoa Valley. It wasn't long before the Davidsons, the Alexanders, the Edmundsons, and the Smiths made their way up through the Swannanoa Gap and into the Swannanoa Valley where they cleared land and built farms. The western North Carolina mountains had once been the exclusive hunting grounds of the Cherokee, but the native people were outmatched by the heavily armed settlers who poured into the area in ever increasing numbers.

Major William Davidson and his wife Margaret and their family, John Alexander and his wife Rachel (the sister of Samuel and William Davidson), along with James Alexander and

Thomas Alexander (sons of John and Rachel) and their families, settled near Bee Tree Creek in what became known as the Swannanoa Settlement. William received a grant of six hundred acres of land on both sides of the Swannanoa River for his service in the Revolutionary War. William had played a prominent role in the Battle of Kings Mountain where he helped stop the advance of the British Forces led by Major Patrick "Bull Dog" Ferguson, who was killed on the battlefield and buried at Kings Mountain in an unmarked grave. A stone marker honoring Ferguson and the friendship between the United States and Great Britian was erected in 1930 in the Kings Mountain National Military Park. William died in 1814, and he's buried in the cemetery at the First Presbyterian Church of Swannanoa, which he and Margaret helped establish in 1794 near Bee Tree Creek. The church survived for two hundred and twenty years before it finally closed its doors in 2014.

A cousin of Samuel and William Davidson, who was also named William, settled just south of the Swannanoa River on land that later became part of George Vanderbilt's iconic Biltmore Estate that today is America's largest privately owned residence and Asheville's leading tourist attraction. Colonel William Davidson and his wife Elizabeth raised five children on that spot. William was elected to the North Carolina State House and then the State Senate, and in 1792 he introduced legislation that led to the creation of Buncombe County where he became the county's first judge.

Robert Craig immigrated to America with his parents from Ireland at the age of eight in 1721 and settled in Cub Run near the Shenandoah River in Augusta County, Virginia, not far from where the city of Harrisonburg and James Madison University are located today. Robert married Gritzel Crawford in 1739, and they built a farm and raised a family within miles of where Thomas Williams was born, and where Samuel and William Davidson lived before their family moved to North Carolina in 1748.

Robert and Gritzel Craig had eight children. The first child, John, was born in 1740 and died when he was five. Daughters Elenor and Jennett were born next, in 1741 and 1743, respectively. The fourth child was a boy born in 1746 that they named him John in honor of their firstborn son who died a few months earlier. Then came James a year later in 1747, followed by daughter Rebecca in 1754, son Robert in 1755, and daughter Anne in 1756. All of the Craig children were baptized by Reverend John Craig, the pastor at Tinkling Spring Presbyterian Church, founded in 1740 and the oldest Presbyterian church in the Shenandoah Valley.

Even though they were born and raised within a few miles of each other, it's doubtful that James Craig ever met Samuel or William Davidson or Thomas Williams when they all lived in Augusta County, Virginia. Samuel and William were born in 1740 and moved to North Carolina in 1748 when they were eight years of age and James was just a year old. Thomas Williams was born in 1758, when James was eleven years old. Given the difference in their ages, if they ever meet, they wouldn't have been close friends. They may have been acquainted later when they were both older. Thomas left for North Carolina in 1778 at the age of twenty. James would have been thirty-one at the time. He had married Hannah Davis, established a farm, and started a family. The U.S. Government didn't conduct the first census until 1790. At that time, there were fewer than eleven-thousand residents in Augusta County and the population would have been even smaller in 1778. Given the close geographic proximity of where they lived and the sparse population of the area at the time, it's entirely possible that James and Thomas were acquainted when they were adults and living in Virginia, but no one knows for sure. It's clear, however, that James had no connection with either Thomas or Samuel in North Carolina since both were killed in 1784, years before James and his family left Virginia for the North Carolina mountains. James and William, on the other hand, well, there's more to that story later.

James Craig, his wife Hannah, and their children made the trek to what is now Buncombe County in 1789, as did James's brother John, his wife Elizabeth, and their children. James initially acquired one hundred acres in Morristown, which later became Asheville, near the present site of the historic Grove Park Inn, and in the years that followed he continued acquiring large tracts of land. That included property along both sides of Bull Creek where he built a distillery and a grist mill. He used rocks collected from along the creek to build a dam that enabled him to harness the power of the rushing water to turn the stone wheel and grind corn. James built the mill just upstream from a little white oak tree that stood about seven feet tall and was about three inches in diameter. The young oak tree was the fruit of the acorn that was nurtured by the blood of Thomas Williams and the mother bear when they died beside the creek five years earlier.

James Craig was a prominent figure in the local area. He bought and sold hundreds of acres of land, and he bought and sold slaves. Bills of Sale recorded in the Buncombe County Register of Deeds Office show that on April 18, 1793, James bought "a negro man named Jacob abought twenty years of age for the sum of sixty pounds" from William Kennerly. On April 19, 1793, he bought "a certain negro woman named Fanny about twenty-four years of age" from Thomas Turk. On January 1, 1801, William Forester purchased "two negros to wit, Spencer and

Agee," from their owner, James Craig.

James and John Craig were among the founders of Buncombe County and John was elected the county's first treasurer. John died a few years later in 1801 and James served as coexecutor of his estate. Despite having purchased a residential lot in what would become the city of Asheville, James and his family built a home east of town near Bull Creek and started a farm that remained in the family for over two hundred and twenty-five years. James and Hannah raised their nine children – three boys and six girls – on the farm that became known as Craigsfield.

People considered Henry West a smart man, although those that knew him said he was eccentric and had a nasty disposition. He served in the Navy during the Revolutionary War under the command of one of America's earliest and most renowned Naval officers, Captain John Paul Jones. Henry suffered a shark bite – there are no details on how it happened – while in

Charleston Harbor, which left him with a deformed leg that caused him to walk with an awkward gait that favored his good leg.

In return for his military service, Henry received land grants in the mountains of western North Carolina, including one hundred acres near Bull Creek that he acquired in 1795. In October of 1803, he purchased an additional one hundred and fifty acres on Bull Creek from Major William Davidson – who had lived in Augusta County, Virginia, during the same period that Henry lived there – for one hundred pounds. Henry built a home on his Bull Creek property in 1804 and cleared land for a farm. Like James Craig, over the years, Henry West bought and sold large tracts of land in the area that lies between the Swannanoa and French Broad rivers.

While Henry was known to have a less than agreeable disposition with most folks, that was not the case with Martha Craig, James Craig's oldest daughter, who everyone called Mattie. Mattie was born in 1790, and she was fifteen when she first met Henry who was then in his forties. They met one afternoon in the summer of 1805.

Mattie walked with her mother Hannah from their house down to the mill where her father was working that afternoon. James promised Hannah when he left the house after breakfast that he would bring a sack of cornmeal home when he finished his work at the mill, but it was getting on into the afternoon and Hannah needed to start preparing dinner. James knew why they came to the mill as soon as they walked in the door. "Sorry, Hannah. I thought I'd be done sooner, but a problem with one of the pullies took me longer to fix than it should have. Here's the cornmeal you wanted," James said as he handed Hannah a small cloth sack. "Thank you. I don't mean to be impatient, but I need to get dinner started," Hannah said as she took the sack from James. "We'll get going and let you get back to your work. We'll see you up at the house in a bit," she said and then gave him a kiss on the cheek. James smiled, turned, opened the door, and Hannah and Mattie walked out with James following behind them.

As Hannah and Mattie were about to leave, their two dogs jumped up, looked towards the path down by the creek, and started barking. Just then, Henry West rode up on a horse with another horse on a lead trailing behind him with two sacks of corn draped over its back. Henry brought the corn to James, as he did from time to time, to grind into cornmeal and grits. "Afternoon, all," Henry said as he climbed down off his horse.

"Henry, you know my wife, Hannah. And this is my oldest daughter, Mattie."

"Good afternoon, Mistress Craig," Henry said as he removed his hat and nodded in Hannah's direction.

"Mattie, it's a pleasure to make your acquaintance," Henry said as he nodded towards her. Mattie smiled and blushed.

"It's good to see you Mister West. I hope you're doing well. Mattie and I are on our way home to get dinner started, so we'll leave it with you two," Hannah said and then she took Mattie's hand and headed towards the path that led back to the house.

"You ladies have a nice afternoon." Henry tipped his hat, turned, and started to unload the sacks of corn from the horse's back.

Henry didn't really think much about his first meeting with Mattie, or at least he didn't think much about it at the time. She was a child, and he was focused on his business with her father. Henry grabbed one sack of corn, James grabbed the other one, and they carried them both inside. James said he was about to shut the mill down for the day, but if Henry would come back the next afternoon, he'd have the corn ground and bagged up ready to go. Henry thanked him and said he would see him tomorrow afternoon.

The next morning, James walked with his son William and two slaves out to an area where they were working to clear trees and underbrush to expand the fields so they would have more acreage for planting in the spring. James was pleased with the progress they were making, and he commended them for their hard work. Then he rode down to Bull Creek and his mill. Dried corn remaining from last season and was waiting to be ground into cornmeal and grits, and it wouldn't be long before the next corn crop would be ready to harvest.

The female slave, Fanny, stayed at the house and watched over Jane and the baby, Elizabeth. Hannah, Mattie, and Sarah – the second oldest daughter who was four years younger than Mattie – spent the morning and part of the afternoon working in the garden pulling weeds and picking vegetables that were just beginning to ripen. When the work was done, Hannah looked at Mattie and Sarah, and said, "you girls are filthy. Why don't you run down to the creek and cool off a bit and wash up." "Yes, mother," they said in unison as they turned and headed towards the path leading down to Bull Creek

A quarter of a mile downstream from James's gristmill, the swift water fell several feet over a rock ledge and formed a pool about twenty feet wide and thirty-five feet long. At the center of the pool, the water reached a depth of about five feet, a little deeper than that after a good rain. The far side was dense with oaks, maples, pines, rhododendrons, and mountain laurels, but the near side was mostly clear with a small sandy patch between the big rocks on the bank of the creek and a worn path leading up the hill and back to the Craig's house. The Craigs called it "the swimming hole." Even in the heart of the summer heat, the creek's mountain water stayed cool, and a plunge in the swimming hole was refreshing after a long day working out in the hot sun. And during warm weather, the swimming hole also served as a place for members of the Craig family to bathe.

Mattie and Hannah took off their clothes, laid them across a rock next to the creek so they'd stay dry, and waded naked into the cool, clear Bull Creek water. It was a treat and one they savored. After splashing around to wash the dirt off their arms and legs from their work in the garden, both girls floated on their backs, arms out to their sides and their legs spread apart, basking in the sunlight, refreshed by the water's pleasant embrace, and relaxed by the sound of the water cascading over the rocks and into the pool where they floated.

Henry West saddled up his horse, put a halter and a lead on a second horse, and started out to James Craig's mill to pick up his sacks of cornmeal. He followed the path along the west side of Bull Creek. As he was plodding along, he heard noise off to his right. When he looked down towards the creek, he saw Mattie and Hannah, naked, floating on the water about a hundred feet below him at the swimming hole. It delivered quite a jolt. He hadn't set out expecting to see two young women naked, but well, there they were. He felt guilty for looking, but still he looked. Because of the sound of the water rushing over the rock ledge and crashing into the pool, Mattie and Hannah didn't hear the plop of the horses' hooves on the path above them or the sound of their occasional snorts. Mattie stood up in water that came about midway up her thighs and she turned towards the bank intending to walk out of the water to lay on a flat rock to let the sun dry her off before she put her clothes back on. It was only a few seconds, but the memory of her firm young breasts and smooth alabaster skin left an indelible mark on Henry's mind. The thoughts that raced through his head made him feel even more guilty, and after pausing briefly, he turned his head to look straight down at the worn dirt path ahead of him.

Mattie glanced up the hill and saw Henry just as he was about to turn his head. She froze momentarily and then fell backwards into deeper water so that only her head poked out above the surface. She watched Henry ride off down the trail and disappear into the forest. She was embarrassed at first that Henry West saw her naked, but her embarrassment was soon tempered by a notion she'd never entertained before … the notion that she had enticed a man. She smiled. She decided not to tell Sarah or anyone else that Henry West saw them naked. For the time being, it was her secret … and it was his.

Even though Henry was known for his disagreeable disposition, James Craig never had any quarrel with him and just considered Henry to be rather quiet and straight-forward when he spoke. But when Henry arrived to pick up his cornmeal that day, he seemed even more taciturn than usual. He didn't have much to say and he appeared to be in a rush. He and James carried the sacks of cornmeal out of the mill and loaded them on the horse, Henry paid James, and he left five minutes after he arrived having said no more than ten words the entire time. James didn't think much about it and just put it down to Henry West being Henry West.

Henry couldn't shake the thought of Mattie's naked body, even though he tried to convince himself that he was doing everything within his power to ignore those evil thoughts. He considered taking a longer, more looping route to return to his farm rather than the more direct route that would take him back past the swimming hole, but he decided – with little hesitation – that he should take the shorter and safer route home since it would get him there sooner. He told himself that the shorter route was less taxing on his horses, but it was really his own prurient interest that dictated his decision. Mattie and Sarah had already gotten dressed, and they were halfway home by the time Henry passed by the swimming hole. He hated admitting it to himself, but he was disappointed when he looked down towards the creek and saw that the swimming hole was empty.

Henry never made much of an effort to develop a love life. He was self-conscious about his disfigured leg and his awkward gait, which contributed to his laconic nature and his lack of self-confidence when it came to women and romance. It played a large part in his decision to venture up into the sparsely populated mountains rather than settling down in a city or town that would require him to have more interaction with people. He'd been a loner for a long time, and he recognized that he was indeed lonely.

The indelible memory of Mattie's naked body created quite the paradox. It was what Henry thought of on special occasions that brought him immense pleasure only to be followed by extreme self-loathing as he berated himself for harboring what his conscience told him were malign notions concerning young Mattie Craig. It was a recurrent cycle of pleasure and pain that Henry repeated more often than he would ever want anyone to know.

James Craig and his family attended the First Presbyterian Church of Swannanoa every Sunday. Beginning a few months after he moved into his cabin at Bull Creek, Henry West became a Sunday morning regular there as well. The Craig family always sat in the third row on the lefthand side of the church right behind William Davidson and his family. Henry West chose a seat on the righthand side of the church near the back the first time he attended, and that became his regular Sunday morning spot. While the congregation focused on the preacher as he delivered the sermon – not counting a number of parishioners, mostly the very young and the very old, who occasionally nodded off – Henry focused on Mattie Craig. The first time he saw her with her mother at the mill, he hadn't given her much thought because he viewed her as a child. The next day, however, after he saw her standing naked in the creek, he thought of her as something more than a child, a young woman on the cusp of adulthood. Henry knew that Mattie was all the things he was not – young, fit, and exuberant – and when he conjured up thoughts of the two of them together, he knew they would make an odd and unlikely combination. Still, it was a notion that became increasingly difficult for him to shake.

In the early summer of 1806, the First Presbyterian Church of Swannanoa held a homecoming; an annual celebration of the church's founding that involves the sharing of food and fellowship. The festivities were held just outside the church in the side yard right after the Sunday morning service ended. Long tables were set up and each family brought an assortment of dishes to share in a big communal meal. While the women were setting things up, the men stood around in small groups, smoking their pipes and talking as they waited for the signal that it was time to eat. Once everything was ready, the preacher gave a short talk thanking everyone for coming and for supporting the church, then he offered a prayer and exuberantly announced, "Now dinner is served!"

Folks queued up on both sides of the table and went down the line filling their plates from the assortments of delectable offerings. As Henry was making his way down the line and surveying the impressive spread, he reached for a piece of cornbread just as a hand from the other side of the table reached out to take the same piece, and their hands touched. Henry looked up and saw Mattie Craig smiling back at him.

"I'm so sorry, Mister West," she said. "You go right ahead."

Henry jerked his hand back and blushed. "Pardon me, Miss Mattie. I wasn't paying attention." Henry nodded towards Mattie, "I insist. Ladies first," he said as he motioned for Mattie to go ahead and serve herself.

Mattie took a piece of cornbread and put it on her plate. "I admire a gentleman with proper manners, Mister West," she said with a smile. "Would you care to join us?"

Henry hesitated a moment. "Thank you. It would be my pleasure."

Henry followed Mattie over to where James and Hannah Craig and their younger children were sitting in the shade beneath the trees. "I bumped into Mister West while we were in line, and I invited him to join us."

James motioned with his arm for Henry to join them. "By all means. Have a seat."

Hannah smiled. "Do join us, Mister West. Find yourself a spot to sit down and make yourself comfortable."

Henry nodded at James and Hannah. "Thank you. That's mighty kind of you." He took Mattie's plate with one hand and with the other he assisted her as she lowered herself to the ground. When she was settled, he returned her plate to her, and then he sat down on the ground next to her.

"I see you're trying my cornbread, Mister West," Hannah said.

"It looked too good to pass up," Henry responded as he picked it up and took a bite. "Umm! That is delicious."

Hannah smiled. "Well, thank you, Mister West. It's something that was handed down to me by my mother. The secret is to heat up the skillet before you pour in the batter, so it gets crisp on the outside and stays moist on the inside. And the cornmeal that James grinds, well it has just the right texture for making good cornbread."

Henry took another bite. "Whatever your secret is, it's outstanding. I hope you're planning on passing the recipe down rather than taking it to your grave. It would be a shame if future generations were deprived of something so fine."

Hannah faked an embarrassed look. "Now Mister West. You're just too kind."

After everyone ate and homecoming reached its end, the women began cleaning up the table and packing up the leftovers as the men milled around waiting to go home. Henry walked over to James and thanked him for allowing him to join them. "I don't get out and socialize very often and it was a real pleasure to get to spend some time with you and your family. I'm much obliged." James reached out and shook hands with Henry. "It was our pleasure too, Henry. We enjoyed your company."

Just before everyone departed, Mattie approached Henry to say goodbye.

"I hope you have a pleasant evening, Mister West."

Henry nodded. "I hope you do as well, Miss Mattie. I hope I get to see you again soon."

Mattie gave Henry a coy smile. "I believe you've seen more of me than just about anyone else ever has, Mister West."

Henry knew instantly what she meant. He blushed and averted his gaze, unsure how to respond. "I apologize for that. I didn't mean for it to happen; it was an accident. I'm so sorry and I'm so embarrassed," he stammered.

Mattie grabbed his hand and squeezed it. "No need for you to be sorry or embarrassed, Henry. I'm not," she said as she looked at him and smiled, and then released his hand, turned, and walked away. Henry stood there frozen and in silence.

James and Hannah climbed up on the wagon for the ride home from church and the Craig children piled into the back. "I've seen Henry West in passing here and there," Hannah said, "but I've never really had an occasion to talk with him much. I know some folks around here are put off by him, but he seems like a nice enough man to me." James nodded in agreement. "Henry's different, but I've never had any quarrel with him. He pretty much sticks to himself and tends to his farm. He stops by the mill on occasion, and I've always found him to be more likeable than a lot of others do." Hannah thought for a moment and added, "it's a shame that he's all alone. He must be lonely. It's too bad he hasn't found someone and fallen in love."

For the remainder of the year and on through the next, Henry and Mattie saw each other on Sundays at church where they would chat before and after the service. Often, Mattie would make a flirtatious remark or drop some subtle inuendo that would leave Henry red-faced and tongue-tied and send him home with his feelings in an uproar. By early 1808, Mattie was now eighteen years old, and she had grown into an attractive young woman. Several of the local young men her age took notice, and while she found their attention flattering and she enjoyed toying with them, she was infatuated with Henry West despite him being more than twice her age. And while Henry never said it directly to her, she knew that he was attracted to her too.

Mattie didn't know what to do about her feelings for Henry, which were as much in conflict as his feelings were for her. She was afraid to talk about it with her mother, fearing her mother would disapprove and would tell her father, and she worried how he would react. James Craig was a good father and a kind man in general, but he had made the decision to be one of the earliest settlers in an area where it was well known that others had died trying to put down roots there just as he was doing now. Survival in that environment meant a man had to be rugged and ready to use force when it was necessary to protect himself and his family. James was a slave owner. While he made sure they had adequate food, shelter, and clothing, and he wasn't abusive by nature, he believed a firm hand was required to keep slaves in line. Mattie remembered that not long after they moved to Bull Creek, when she was still just a little girl, a slave named Jacob cut down a big pine tree that fell the wrong way and landed on a wagon and split it in two. James ran over to Jacob and punched him in the face with his fist, knocking Jacob to the ground. "You damn fool," James yelled as he grabbed Jacob by the front of his shirt and lifted his head up off the dirt. "That wagon was worth a hell of a lot more than you!" James pulled his fist back and was about to deliver another blow when Hannah yelled, "James, stop it!" James froze and looked over at Hannah. "It was an accident," she said, "and beating Jacob isn't going to change a damn thing. Now you let him go." James paused for a moment, released his grip on Jacob's shirt, and let his head fall back on the ground. James walked away muttering to himself in anger. Mattie saw what happened and witnessing her father's temper firsthand scared her. She wrapped her arms around Hannah's waist and cried. She loved her father dearly, but she never forgot seeing his anger erupt that day.

Mattie had to talk to someone about her feelings for Henry West. She chose her sister, Sarah, who by then was fourteen years of age. One unusually warm Sunday afternoon in January of 1808, Mattie asked Sarah to walk home with her after church rather than riding in the wagon with the rest of the family. Sarah agreed and they set out on foot for home.

"If I tell you something, can you keep it a secret?" Mattie asked as they walked along.

"Sure. What is it?"

"I think I might have feelings – romantic feelings – for Henry West," Mattie said as she looked over at Sarah to gauge her reaction.

Sarah looked at Mattie with a surprised expression on her face. "Are you serious? Henry West? He's close to daddy's age, maybe just as old."

"I know that. But he's kind, and he's interesting, and I enjoy being around him, and I'm old enough to make my own decisions, and if his age doesn't bother me, it shouldn't be anyone else's business … should it?"

Sarah looked squarely at Mattie, "Mattie, I don't know. What about some of the other boys your age, like Will Cooper. I've seen how he looks at you. Wouldn't you be better off with somebody like that rather than an old man with a limp? My goodness, it wouldn't be long before you'd have to spend most of your time taking care of him. That wouldn't be much of a life for you, would it?"

Mattie looked down at the ground and walked on for a short time in silence.

"There's nothing wrong with Will Cooper or any of the other boys my age, but they're boys. Henry's a man. He's been places and he's done things. He's got his own farm, and I've heard daddy say that he owns a good bit of land. He'd be a good provider, and I know he'd treat me well. I don't know if he's interested in me in that way or not … we've never talked about it.

But I'm eighteen and I've got to decide at some point what I'm going to do with my life and who I'm going to spend it with. I just don't know what to do."

The two walked on in silence for a few minutes and then Sarah said, "Mister West is a nice man. He's always been pleasant enough when I've been around him, and he's handsome in a way, I suppose. I think it's something you've got to decide for yourself, Mattie, but I don't know what mama and daddy will say. I think they've always envisioned you marrying somebody your own age and giving them a bunch of grandbabies that they can make a fuss over."

"I know," Mattie said, "I know. I wish I knew what the right thing to do is. I've thought about it, and I've prayed about it, but I just don't know the answer."

As they were getting close to home, Mattie said, "There's something else I've never told you, and it's actually quite funny. If I tell you, you've got to promise me that you'll never tell another living soul."

"I promise," Sarah responded.

"A couple of years back, you and I went down to the swimming hole after we helped mama work in the garden. We took off our clothes and we waded in. Well, while we were splashing around, Henry rode by on his horse, and he saw us naked. I saw him looking at us and honestly, I think it embarrassed him more than it did me."

"Wait a minute!" Sarah said as she grabbed Mattie by the arm and stopped walking. "Henry West saw you and me naked, and you've never bothered to tell me?"

"You were just eleven and I thought you'd go run off and tell mama," Mattie replied. "And I was afraid she'd tell daddy, and he'd race over to Henry's house and do him harm. Besides, you were just floating in the water. I'm the one who stood up, so I was the one he got a proper look at … and to be honest, I think he liked what he saw," she said with a laugh.

"Mattie Craig, you should be ashamed of yourself. I'm pretty sure the preacher would tell you that you're going to hell for thinking naughty thoughts like that. Why, you're just an unrepentant flirt," Sarah said as she laughed, punched Mattie on the arm, and ran towards the house.

Mother nature dropped half a foot of snow on the Blue Ridge Mountains in mid-February. James had traveled down to Davidson's Fort for supplies and the snow delayed his trip home by a day. It was a heavy wet snow, and when temperatures plunged into the twenties that night in the Swannanoa Valley, it froze, and a hard crust formed on top. The next day, after the sun rose and the icy crust started to melt, the Craig children set out to do their chores. The two oldest boys were now in their twenties and had moved away leaving William as the lone son still living at home. William put on his boots, his hat, and his coat, and headed out to feed the livestock. Mattie and Sarah put on their hats and coats and went out to clear the ice and snow that had piled up on the front porch and the steps and the walkway. When William was about twenty-five feet away from the front porch, he bent down and scooped up two handfuls of the crusty snow and ice mix and molded it into a snowball. He turned and yelled, "hey Mattie!" as he flung the snowball in her direction. It would have struck her in the shoulder, but at the last second, Mattie ducked, and the snowball went past her and smacked Sarah right in the face. A trickle of blood flowed from Sarah's nostrils, and she started to cry.

William ran back towards the porch. "Oh God, Sarah, I'm sorry. I didn't mean to hit you. Are you alright?" Blood streamed down her face and Sarah shook as she cried. Mattie hugged her and said, "it'll be okay. It looks worse than it is. Let's get you inside and let mama have a look at you. William, you go on out to the barn, you've done enough." William patted Sarah on the shoulder, apologized again, and went off to feed the animals.

"What happened?" Hannah asked when the girls walked in. "William threw a snowball at me and missed, and it hit Sarah instead and gave her a bloody nose. I don't think it did any real damage." Hannah led Sarah over to the kitchen table and had her sit in a chair. Hannah told Mattie to get her a kitchen towel and when she did, Hannah pressed it against Sarah's nose.

Sarah screamed, and then she cried even harder.

"Oh, come on now, don't be a crybaby," Mattie said. "It's not broken. You're going to be fine." Sarah continued sobbing. "It hurts!" she protested.

"Don't be such a priss," Mattie said. "You're making more out of it than it deserves."

"Leave me alone!" Sarah yelled.

"Fine. You go ahead and be a crybaby," Mattie said as she turned and went back out to the porch to continue clearing the ice and snow.

Sarah was now as mad as she was hurt. She didn't appreciate Mattie calling her a "crybaby" and "a priss." In her mind, that was all the justification she needed to rescind some of the promises she had made.

"Mama, Mattie's in love with Henry West."

"What?" Hannah asked in surprise. "Mattie's in love with who?"

"With Henry West," Sarah answered. "She told me that when we walked home from church together a couple of weeks ago. And that's not all, mama. Henry West has seen Mattie with her clothes off."

Sarah's words struck Hannah like a bolt of lightning. Her little girl and a grown man who was old enough to be her father? And her little girl naked? Hannah didn't appreciate it at that

86

moment, but the anger that welled up in her was as intense as James's anger the day he hit Jacob for destroying the wagon. If Henry West was in the room, she would have grabbed a kitchen knife and plunged it into his stomach as hard as she could. Hannah liked to think of herself as a decent Christian lady with a kind heart, but she was as ferocious as a mother bear protecting her cubs when it came to her children. Whatever good thoughts she'd had for Henry West, well, those were gone, and they weren't coming back.

Hannah went to the door and ordered Mattie back inside. She directed Mattie to sit down at the kitchen table next to Sarah. Hannah repeated what Sarah had told her. Mattie looked over at Sarah in shock, but Sarah refused to make eye contact with her. Sarah had been slighted and now she had exacted her revenge. The dust up that day opened a wound between the two sisters, a wound that might have healed over time but for events that had yet to transpire.

Mattie tried to explain to her mother that yes, she had feelings for Henry West, and, yes, he had seen her naked, but it wasn't as bad as it sounded. They say that people can hear and still not listen; that is, you might understand that words are being spoken, but you are not comprehending the meaning the words convey. Hannah heard Mattie, but she didn't listen to her. She told Mattie that she was very disappointed in her, and she said they'd take it up with her father when he got home from Davidson's Fort. It was a long, quiet afternoon and evening in the Craig's house.

Few words were spoken again the next morning. William thought the frosty silence was because of the snowball incident with Sarah the day before, and he apologized to Sarah again, but his mother assured him that was not the case. James arrived in the early afternoon. In all honesty, he had enjoyed the beauty and the solitude of his ride back through the Swannanoa Gap under a blue sky and a blanket of snow. James loved his family, but with him and Hannah and the kids under one roof, a day of peace and quiet felt like a gift. The mountains were stunning all the time, but especially so after a snowfall. As James had joked to others before, "even a barnyard full of cow shit looks downright lovely when it's buried under a blanket of snow." The warm thoughts he carried home melted soon after he walked through the door.

James hugged Hannah, kissed her on the cheek, and apologized for his delayed return due to the snowstorm. It only took seconds for him to see the sullen faces and sense the chill that permeated the room. Hannah told William and Sarah to take the younger children into the side room by the fireplace and to play a game with them. She told James and Mattie to sit down at the kitchen table.

James asked Hannah what was wrong … and she told him. She told him that Mattie thought she was in love with Henry West and, if that wasn't bad enough, Henry West had seen Mattie naked. Mattie glanced at her father, and she could see the rage ablaze in his eyes.

"Daddy, it's not what you think. I can explain it."

"So, you're not in love with Henry West and he hasn't seen you naked? Is that what you want to explain to me?"

"No, daddy. I do have feelings for Henry, and yes, he saw me naked, but …"

"But nothing," James shot back as he stood up from the table. "Henry West is closer to my age than yours, and he's old enough to be your father. That son of a bitch ought to know better than to mess around with a little girl, and if he doesn't, I'll make sure he does."

Mattie stood up and tears rolled down her cheeks. "Please, daddy. Please don't do anything to Henry. It's not his fault. I can explain if you'd just let me. Please, sit down for a minute before you go and do something that you'll regret."

"No! Henry West is the one who's got some explaining to do." James grabbed his coat, his hat, and his gun, and he headed out the door as Mattie pleaded with him not to go.

Henry was out in his barn tending to his livestock when James Craig walked in with his gun at the ready. James had one hand on the flange with his finger resting on the trigger and the other hand gripped the stock.

"Afternoon, James. How are you?"

"Henry, this isn't a social call," James responded. "Me and you have some things we need to set straight, and you better have some damned good answers or we're going to have trouble between us."

Henry looked at James with a puzzled expression on his face. "What's wrong, James? I can see you're upset, but I don't rightly know why."

As they stood there in the barn, about six feet apart and James still gripping his gun, James told Henry what he'd heard from Hannah and Mattie.

"Would you care to explain, or should I just go ahead and whip your ass right here and now?"

Henry felt sick, like the blood had drained from his body and his knees were going to buckle beneath him. He collected himself and took a step towards James. "Stop!" James said as he took a step back and raised the barrel of his gun several inches. "You stay where you are. Now, what do you have to say about this?"

Henry put his palms up to show he meant no harm. "James, I think a lot of this is just a misunderstanding. Listen, I'll be totally honest with you; Mattie is a beautiful young woman, and I do enjoy her company … I'd be lying if I said otherwise. But I have never done anything untoward with her nor have I ever expressed any desire to do so. She's grown into a woman, and yes, I have had thoughts that it might be possible for me and her to maybe have a future together someday, but I've never said that to her, and I would never pursue such a thing without talking to you and Hannah first and getting your permission. As for seeing her naked, yes, that's true, but it was an accident. A few years back, I was riding over to your mill to pick up my cornmeal when I saw Mattie and her sister down in the creek at the swimming hole. I didn't sneak up on them or anything, they just happened to be there as I rode by … and I didn't stop and gawk or anything, I kept going. I felt bad about it, but there was nothing I could do, it was just an accident. So, that's the extent of it, James, I swear. I value your friendship, and Hannah's, and your family's, and I wouldn't do anything intentional to jeopardize that. You've always been decent to me, and I appreciate it. I swear to God above that's the truth and I'm truly sorry if there are any hard feelings between us."

James stood there for several seconds. He hadn't just heard what Henry said, he had listened to him, and he needed a moment to let it all sink in. James lowered his gun so that it was pointed at the ground, and he took his finger off the trigger. "I take you at your word, Henry. But you've clearly put thoughts in Mattie's head that me and Hannah don't approve of. For God's sake, you're old enough to be her father! Some folks might not have a problem with that, but I'm not one of them. So, I don't want you around me, Hannah, or any of my kids. I don't want you setting foot on my property, and you need to start taking your corn to somebody else to grind. I'm not going to tell you that you can't come to God's house on Sundays, but if you do, you stay away from us and especially stay away from Mattie. Are we clear on that?"

"Yes, James. We're clear. And I'm sorry, I truly am sorry."

"I don't wish you any ill will, Henry, but I'll do what I have to do to protect my family, and if I find you're messing around with Mattie, well, there's going to be trouble."

"I understand, James, and again, I'm sorry," Henry said as he extended his hand. James just stood there with both hands on his gun rather than shaking Henry's hand. "I don't want any more trouble," he said as he turned, walked out of the barn, and rode away.

When he got home, James told Hannah and Mattie that he and Henry talked, and he believed Henry and Mattie when they said nothing inappropriate had happened, but he said it wasn't right for a man Henry's age to have feelings for a girl Mattie's age, and he told Henry to stay away from the entire family and to stay off their property. James looked at Mattie. "Are we clear on that? I don't want any more trouble between us and Henry West, and you need to make sure that it won't be necessary for me to make another trip over there. You stay away from Henry West. I think he'll do right, and I expect you to do right, as well. And if you don't, what happens to Henry West will be on you." Mattie nodded in agreement, stood up, and ran outside to cry.

James didn't go into all of the details, but he told William that something had been going on between Mattie and Henry West that neither he nor Hannah approved of, and he said he told Henry to stay off their property and away from their family. "If you see Henry West around here or if you see him anywhere near your sister, you tell me, okay?" William nodded in agreement.

"Yes, sir. I will."

On Tuesday, March 15, 1808, the Swannanoa Valley was in the midst of Fool's Spring. It wouldn't be long before it was time to plant the seeds for this year's crops. Henry West had brooded over his dust up with James Craig for several weeks. He had come to accept that there would be no future for him and Mattie, but he hoped that at some point he could mend the rift with James. He didn't expect that they would ever be the best of friends, but he thought that they should at least be able to exchange pleasantries on Sunday mornings and conduct business like reasonable men. It was a nice day out, and Henry thought that he'd ride over to James's mill and try to set things right between them.

As Henry rode past the swimming hole, he looked down at the creek and for a moment the image of Mattie, wet and naked and vibrant, flashed in his mind. He pushed it aside and he berated himself for allowing it to surface again. When he was a short distance from the mill, he stopped next to a white oak tree that had now grown to a height of nearly forty feet and was over a foot in diameter. He climbed down off his horse and tied the reins around the tree. He saw James's horse tied up next to the mill. He was nervous and his mouth was dry, so he walked down to the creek and scooped up a handful of water to wet his lips. He walked back up to the path and stood there looking at the mill. As he did, Henry began to have second thoughts about going inside and confronting James. He worried about how James would react. Would there be trouble? With no one around to act as a witness or as a deterrent, would James do something bad to him? After a minute or two of reflection, Henry decided it would be better to try and talk with James one Sunday after church where the presence of other parishioners might have a calming influence and tamp down the chance of violence. He walked back to his horse, unwrapped the reins from around the oak tree, and rode back home.

James spent the morning making repairs inside the mill. Living in such a remote location made it difficult to obtain machinery and machine parts, so he had to do a considerable amount of improvising when he constructed the inner workings of his mill, and the whole apparatus was temperamental and prone to breaking down. It seemed he spent more time making repairs than he did running the mill. It could be aggravating, but James enjoyed tinkering and, while he wouldn't admit it to anyone, he derived a sense of satisfaction out of conquering the challenges he faced to keep his crude milling machinery in operation.

That morning, when Henry West was standing on the path contemplating whether to go inside to try and make peace with James, James was outside and down in the creek working on the paddlewheel he used to harness the power of the rushing water to turn the grindstone inside his mill. Henry hadn't seen James down by the paddlewheel, but James had seen Henry up on the path. James had looked up from his work just as Henry decided to turn around, mount up, and ride away. James was still angry at Henry because of the inappropriate relationship with Mattie, but James's anger wasn't as intense as it was before, and he didn't feel compelled to rush after Henry and confront him for coming onto his property. He thought it was sad that Henry had worked up the courage to ride down to the mill to see him and then lost his nerve and left without coming inside.

Shortly before noon, James heard his dogs barking from somewhere down the creek. He thought the dogs might have spotted deer and he hoped they hadn't spotted bears, which were becoming more active now that the weather was warming up. Mother bears were out and about with their young cubs, and they kept them under close watch and wouldn't hesitate to attack anything they perceived as a threat to their offspring's safety. In an encounter between a dog and a bear, the dog is guaranteed to lose every time. James grabbed his gun and headed outside to see what had aroused his dogs.

The sound of the barking was coming from downstream, and it was coming from the east side of the creek, so James crossed over on some rocks and proceeded along the top of the creekbank. He spotted his dogs about sixty feet away near a big stand of mountain laurels. He raised his musket and walked ahead slowly, worried there might be a bear lurking in the thicket.

He moved a few steps closer and then he saw something move amongst the laurels. Instantly, there was a flash and a loud boom, and James felt what seemed like a red-hot fireplace poker plunge into his belly. The impact knocked him backwards and he landed flat on his back on the ground. He put his hand over the spot where he felt the searing pain, and when he pulled his hand away and looked at it, it was covered in blood. James knew that he'd been shot.

A figure concealed in the thicket quietly disappeared. James's dogs walked over to him, licked his face, and whined. James knew his wound was bad, and his first thought was that he needed to get home before he bled out and died. He rolled over, got up on his knees, and used his musket as a prop to raise himself up to a hunched-over standing position. He slowly made his way down the bank to the edge of the creek, and he crossed over to the other side. He struggled up the western bank and made it as far as the white oak tree before he got lightheaded, slumped forward into the tree, and slid down to the ground. He managed to roll himself over so that he sat with his back against the tree, and he pressed his hand over the wound. He wasn't going to make it home and, unless someone found him soon, he was going to die right there beneath the tree. There wasn't much he could do, so he did the only thing he could; he placed the butt of his gun on the ground, placed his finger on the trigger, and fired a shot into the air hoping that someone would hear it and come down to the creek to investigate.

James told Hannah when he left that morning that he'd come home for lunch, but lunchtime had passed, and he wasn't there. It wasn't unusual for James to become engrossed in a project and lose track of time, so Hannah wasn't alarmed when he didn't show up. When her son William came home early in the afternoon, she asked him if he'd seen his father. "No, I haven't seen him since this morning. Why?" Hannah said he hadn't come home for lunch and opined that he'd probably just gotten busy and lost track of time. Williams said he heard a couple of gunshots an hour or so before that sounded like they came from down near the mill and suggested that perhaps his dad had spotted a deer or an elk or something, shot it, and was field dressing it before coming home. Williams asked Hannah if she wanted him to go and check on James. "Yes, please," she said. "If he's shot something, he could probably use your help with it."

Rather than saddling up a horse and riding down to the mill, William decided to walk. When he got there, he saw that his father's horse was still tied up next to the mill and he assumed his father was inside, but when he opened the door and went in, no one was there. William walked outside and yelled "dad! Are you out here?" He got no response. He recalled that the two gunshots he heard seemed to have come from somewhere between the mill and the swimming hole, so he followed the path downstream alongside the creek. He hadn't walked far when he saw his father sitting on the ground leaning up against an oak tree with his dogs standing beside him. "Dad! Are you okay," William yelled as he ran towards James. He saw that the lower portion of James's shirt, the top of his pants, and the ground around him were soaked in blood. "Oh God, dad! What happened? Who did this to you?" James had lost a lot of blood by that point, and he was drifting in and out of consciousness. He heard William's questions, but all he could do in response was mumble incoherently. "Who did this, dad? Did you see who it was?" James's mind was foggy. The only person he'd seen that day was Henry West, who he saw stop short of the mill and head away earlier that morning. "Henry," he muttered. It was the last coherent word James Craig ever spoke.

William removed his shirt and pressed it against the hole in his father's abdomen. He took James's hands and placed them on the bandage to hold it in place. "Hold onto that dad, you're bleeding really bad. Hang on, I'm going to get help. Don't you go and die on me now, you hear? I'll be back with help just as quick as I can. I love you, dad. Hang on!" William ran to the mill as fast as he could, jumped on James's horse, and raced back to the house.

As William approached the house, he saw the slave Jacob over by the barn. "Jacob, daddy's hurt and we need to fetch him home. Hitch up the wagon and make it fast." Jacob ran inside the barn and went to work. William jumped off the horse and ran into the house. "Mama, daddy's been shot. He's alive, but just barely. Jacob's getting the wagon ready so we can go get him. He's bleeding something awful, and he's barely conscious. Oh God, mama, it's bad. It's really bad."

"Okay, William," Hannah responded. She tried to keep her voice as calm as she could so that William wouldn't panic worse than he already was, but deep down inside she was a wreck, and it took all she could muster to hold herself together. "What do I need to bring?"

"He's bleeding … a lot … so bring some rags. We need to get him back here quick and see if we can patch him up before it's too late. Grab what you can and let's go."

Jacob had just finished hitching a horse to the wagon when William and Hannah ran out to the barn. "Jacob, James has been shot. We're going to get him and bring him up here to the house. I want you to take his horse and race over to the Alexander's place and tell Mister Alexander what's happened. And tell him we need his help just as quick as he can get here. Can you do that for me?"

"Yes, Miss Hannah. I'll get there in a flash," Jacob said as he turned, ran to the horse, climbed on, and rode away.

William and Hannah pulled themselves up onto the wagon seat. William grabbed the reins and used them to smack the horse on his haunches to get him to move. They headed down the hill and towards the mill as fast as they could go.

96

"Did your daddy say what happened," Hannah asked.

"No. He just mumbled. All he managed to say was when I asked him who shot him, and he said it was Henry West."

"Henry West shot him? Are you sure that's what he said?"

"Yes, ma'am. He said it was Henry West."

When they got close to the oak tree, Hannah jumped down off the wagon and ran over to James. "Oh, James! What happened?" He didn't respond. Hannah and William placed James flat on the ground, and Hannah pressed rags against his wound. They rolled him over a bit to see if there was an exit wound, but instead they saw a small, rounded bulge beneath his skin where a musket ball had lodged without exiting. "Hang on, darling. We're going to get you home. Hang on now. You're going to be okay." Hannah knew as she said those words that they weren't true.

William and Hannah loaded James into the back of the wagon. Hannah held bandages in place while William drove them up to the house, trying not to make the ride any rougher than it had to be on the rutted path. At the house, they carried him inside and laid him on the kitchen table. Hannah ripped open his shirt and examined the wound. It was still bleeding, but not as heavily as before. The flow of blood had slowed a bit, not because the wound was healing, but because James had already lost so much of it. Hannah washed the area around the wound and packed the hole with cloth. She could see that James's skin was turning ashen and he hadn't muttered a word since they got to him. Hannah wanted to hope for the best, but she knew in her heart that he didn't have long to go before he slipped away. She held his hand and told him over and over that she loved him. A few minutes later, James took a final, feeble gasp of air, and then his chest fell and remained still. James Craig died there on the kitchen table a little past three o'clock in the afternoon.

97

Thomas Alexander arrived a short time later. He walked into the house, removed his hat, looked over at the table, and asked Hannah if James had passed. She nodded, indicating that he had. Thomas hung his head and expressed his condolences. He said he'd sent Jacob on to alert others, and he said they should be arriving soon. He asked Hannah and William if they knew what happened, and William repeated the story of hearing gunshots, finding his father sitting against the tree, and his father saying that it was Henry West who shot him.

"Daddy and Henry West had a confrontation a couple of weeks back after daddy found out that Henry was messing around with Mattie. Daddy told him to stay off our property and away from our family or there was going to be trouble, and it looks like he was right." William paused for a moment and then headed for the door, "I'm going to kill that son of a bitch."

Thomas grabbed William by the arm. "Hang on there, son. Your mama is going to need you, and if you rush off and kill Henry West, you're not going to do anything but heap more trouble on her, and she don't deserve that. The others will be here soon, and we'll figure out how to handle this. You need to let the law take care of Henry West and you stay out of it. He'll get what's coming to him for what he did to your daddy, that I promise you. The best thing you can do is stay here and take care of your mother."

When Jacob returned, Hannah told him that James had died, and she asked him to take the wagon and go pickup Mattie and Sarah who were both visiting friends in Asheville. Jacob removed his hat and looked down at the ground. "I'm real sorry about Mister James, Miss Hannah. I'll go get the girls and I'll get them back here as quick as I can."

A half-dozen men gathered at James Craig's house that afternoon. William repeated what he told Thomas Alexander, and then Thomas suggested they all ride down to where William found James to see if there was evidence there that might be useful. At the site beneath the oak tree, William showed them where he found his father and they could all see where James's blood had saturated the ground. There were footprints around the tree that led up from the creek. It was apparent that some of the footprints were made by James. The other pair of footprints suggested they were made by someone who favored one leg, like Henry West. James's dying declaration to William that Henry West shot him and the footprints consistent with Henry West's awkward gait at the site where James Craig was found dying was enough to convince the men that Henry West was the culprit, and they set off on horseback to Henry's farm to apprehend him and deliver him to Sheriff James Hughey in Asheville to hold him until they could arrange for a trial.

No one ever ventured over to the other side of the Bull Creek to look for evidence. If they had, they might have seen blood on the ground where James Craig was shot and footprints around the mountain laurel thicket, footprints that were perfectly flat, like the smooth bottoms of a pair of moccasins. Had they followed the moccasin tracks a short distance deeper into the forest, they might have found hoof prints made by the horses the native hunting party rode as they made their way up the Broad River from the northern part of South Carolina and into eastern Buncombe County. The hunting party hadn't set out to kill James Craig, but when they saw that he had desecrated the land by damming up the creek and building a mill, and chopping down trees to clear fields and pastures, they made a plan to burn down the mill and bust up the dam at first light the next morning before they made their way back to their village in what later became Cherokee County, South Carolina. But their plan changed when James's dogs picked up their scent, started to bark, and led James, armed with his gun, in their direction. When James started to raise his gun when he spotted one of them hiding amongst the laurels, a member of the hunting party fired at him first in an act of self-defense.

It rained two days after James Craig died, and the rain washed away the bloodstain and the footprints that no one ever saw over on the east side of Bull Creek. And it caused the blood James Craig spilled under the oak tree to seep deep into the ground, just as the blood of Thomas Williams and the mother bear had done a quarter of a century before and gave birth to the oak tree where James was found.

William and Jacob used oak wood from trees they'd cut down at Craigsfield to build a coffin for James's body. His funeral service was held in the First Presbyterian Church of Swannanoa and afterwards his body was taken back to his farm and buried in a small clearing on a knoll about a hundred yards west of Bull Creek.

Henry West was taken into custody the afternoon James Craig died. While he proclaimed his innocence, on April eighth, a jury found him guilty based on James Craig's dying declaration that Henry West shot him, William's testimony about the bitterness between his father and Henry West over Henry's relationship with Mattie, and the unique footprints at the scene that were consistent with Henry's bad leg and his limp. On April twenty-eighth, Judge Archibald Locke sentenced Henry to death by hanging and he set Henry's execution date for the sixth of May at noon, just fifty-five days after James Craig's murder. Justice wasn't necessarily sure, but it was certainly swift.

One of the members of the jury that convicted Henry West was Thomas Patton. Not long after the trial ended, Thomas began to have doubts about the verdict and soon became convinced of Henry's innocence. Most notably, the musket ball that was removed from James Craig's body was larger in diameter than the barrel of Henry West's musket, making it impossible for the fatal shot to have been fired from Henry's weapon. Thomas Patton gave a sworn statement saying that had this evidence been presented at Henry's trial, he would have voted not guilty, and he believed others on the jury would have done the same. Henry's attorney, James Patton, with the help of his sister, Jane Erwin, prepared a petition to Governor Benjamin Williams for a pardon. Jane Erwin took a stagecoach to Raleigh to deliver the petition to the Governor's office and along the way she arranged for riders to be on standby to race the pardon back to Asheville, if the Governor signed it, to try and make sure it arrived before Henry West was executed. Governor Williams read the petition and the sworn statement from Thomas Patton, and he signed a pardon exonerating Henry West in the murder of James Craig. Jane Erwin delivered the signed document to the first of the riders, and the race was on to see if the pardon would get from Raleigh to Asheville before Henry West hung from the gallows.

Henry worried that as a convicted murderer, he wouldn't receive a proper burial. While he was in jail awaiting execution, he asked Sheriff Hughey if he could arrange for him to meet with Philip Creasman, the local undertaker, and Sheriff Hughey agreed to do so. Henry proposed a deal to Philip Creasman that in return for Creasman giving Henry a proper burial after his execution, he would give Creasman the deed to a large parcel of land he owned adjacent to the Craig property. Creasman agreed to the deal and Henry tendered the deed, which Creasman took straight to the Register of Deeds and had it recorded.

The sheriff assembled a team of men who agreed to construct the gallows for Henry's execution at the corner of Hillside and East Streets in downtown Asheville. The sheriff offered

William Craig the opportunity to participate in the execution of his father's murderer, but William declined. He did, however, ask if he could provide the wood they would use to construct the gallows. "Henry West shot my daddy under an oak tree on Craig land, and we buried daddy in a coffin we made from oak we cut there on the farm last fall. It seems fitting for Henry West to meet his maker hanging from Craigsfield oak." The sheriff agreed and the next day William and Jacob delivered a wagon load of thick, fresh cut oak planks to the site where the gallows would go up.

Henry West was scheduled to die at noon on Friday, the sixth of May. That day, as the execution time approached, Henry, accompanied by his attorney James Patton, climbed the steps up onto the gallows a few minutes before noon. Sheriff Hughey moved him into position, slipped the noose over his head, and secured it around his neck. Standing there waiting to die, Henry looked out at the crowd that had gathered to see him hang. He scanned their faces looking for Mattie Craig, but she was nowhere to be seen. Men and women came dressed in their Sunday finest, many with their young children in tow to witness the spectacle. On the opposite corner from the gallows, Henry saw Henry Creasman sitting atop his black funeral wagon waiting to haul his body away after he dropped through the floor and was pronounced dead. Sheriff Hughey was anxious to get the execution over with, and he was ready to press ahead, but James Patton argued that Henry had the legal right not to be executed until the prescribed time of noon and he added that the sheriff's watch was a few minutes fast and was depriving Henry of his right to live a few more minutes. Sheriff Hughey wasn't happy about it, but he acquiesced.

When noon finally arrived and James Patton couldn't stall the inevitable any longer, Sheriff Hughey asked Henry if he had any final words to say before he was executed. Henry looked out at the crowd, and in a clear and steady voice said, "I had no part in the murder of James Craig, either in thought, word, or action." Sheriff Hughey walked over to the lever that would release the trapdoor and drop Henry through the floor and to his death. "Henry West, you were found guilty by a jury of your peers and sentenced to die by hanging for the murder of James Craig. May God have mercy on your soul." Henry thought of Mattie Craig and held that thought firmly in his mind as he waited to meet his maker.

Sheriff Hughey yanked on the lever to release the trapdoor beneath Henry's feet, the crowd gasped … and nothing happened. Because of the heat and humidity, the oak wood William Craig provided to build the gallows had swollen, and now the trapdoor was stuck and refused to open and send Henry West plunging to his death. Sheriff Hughey yanked back and forth on the lever and shook it, still nothing happened. He walked over and stomped on the trapdoor with his boot several times. Still nothing. He moved Henry off the trapdoor, bent down, and started working to try and pry it loose. And as Sheriff Hughey was doing his best to free the trapdoor so he could proceed with the execution of Henry West, a rider raced into the intersection on horseback waving a document with his right hand, and yelling, "Stop! Governor Williams has issued a pardon to Mister Henry West." The rider rode to the base of the gallows, climbed down off his horse, walked up the steps, and handed the document to Sheriff Hughey. Everyone froze in place, and it was so quiet that Henry could hear a yellowjacket buzzing several feet away. Sheriff Hughey looked at the document for a moment and said, "it looks to be official. The governor has indeed pardoned Henry West."

James Patton walked over and lifted the noose over Henry's head as Sheriff Hughey unlocked the shackles and removed them from his wrists. "Good Lord, you're one lucky bastard, Henry West," James Patton said as he placed his hand on Henry's shoulder. "If that oak wood hadn't swelled up, you'd be a dead man, and that pardon wouldn't have been worth the paper it's written on." Henry rubbed his wrists, stretched his neck, smiled a bit, and said, "it's better to be a lucky bastard than a dead one." He shook James Patton's hand and thanked him, and then he turned to Sheriff Hughey and shook his hand. Henry climbed down from the gallows and limped off down Hillside Street.

Henry West returned to Bull Creek and his farm, and he went on buying and selling land around Buncombe County for many years thereafter. And Philip Creasman the undertaker, he refused to give Henry back the deed to the land he took from him in exchange for a proper burial. "When the time comes, Henry, I'll give you the burial that I promised you, but a deal's a deal, so I'll wait and bury you when you're ready for burying and not a day sooner."

Over the years, relations between Henry and the Craig family improved. In fact, in the 1830's, Henry sold a tract of land to William Craig and his brother James, and another tract to William Craig and his brother Thomas.

Mattie married Ashford Walker, and they moved away. She blamed Sarah for telling her secret about Henry West, which Mattie believed led to her father's death. The relationship between the two sisters was never the same as it was before the secret was revealed.

Hannah Craig remained at Craigsfield and continued to work the land with the help of her friends and neighbors. When she died, she was buried next to James in the family burial plot overlooking Bull Creek.

James and Hannah's daughter Jane married Eldridge Melton, and they lived on a farm at Bee Tree Creek where they raised three sons and two daughters. All three of Jane's sons and her husband were killed in the Civil War, so when Jane died, her daughter Harriet inherited the Bull Creek property and her daughter Mary Jane, who married John Wesley Coggins, inherited the Bee Tree property. Later, upon Harriet's death, Mary Jane's children inherited the Bull Creek property, which eventually became known as "The Old Coggins Place" and later as "Coggins Farm." That is, the property bore the Coggins name until it was sold to a real estate developer in June of 2015.

Part Three – The Swannanoa Gap Tunnel

Joseph Rice came to the Swannanoa Valley in 1782 to trade with the Native Americans who had established villages in the area and used the valley as hunting grounds. Even though Thomas Williams and Samuel Davidson were killed by Tsiyu Gansini's warriors two years later not far from where Joseph camped when he came to trade, he maintained good relations with the native people, and in the late seventeen eighties, they granted him a large tract of land where he built a cabin near a spring-fed lake, a lake that disappeared in 1811 when an earthquake rocked the valley. That's where he, his wife Margaret, and their three sons made a home.

Over time, Joseph accumulated a substantial amount of real estate, including property he acquired by grants from the Governor and property he purchased from Thomas Alexander and from a member of the Davidson family. The area around his home became known as Riceville, as it's still known today.

Joseph Rice notched a place in the region's history in another way as well. In 1799, while he was building a road to connect Bull Creek with Beaverdam Valley to the west, he heard a buffalo bellowing nearby. Joseph grabbed his gun, followed the sound until he located the buffalo, and shot it dead for its meat and its hide. That was the last wild buffalo ever seen in Buncombe County. The National Park Service erected a historical marker on the Blue Ridge Parkway at the Bull Creek Valley Overlook memorializing this milestone.

Colin McDonald and his wife Annie were proud of their little farm. They had worked hard for years and saved their money, and by 1842 they had scraped together enough to buy twenty-five acres of rich land along Shope Creek in Riceville from Robert Rice, one of Joseph Rice's three sons. Annie gave birth to their one and only child, a son named John Patrick McDonald, a few months after they settled along Shope Creek.

Colin worked from sunrise to sunset almost every day the weather permitted clearing out trees and brush in the early days, and then planting and tending to his crops, which he hauled into Asheville at harvest time and sold at the market. Colin was thrifty and never spent lavishly, hoping that in a few years he could save enough money to buy more land and increase the size of his farm.

Annie was pregnant when they moved to Shope Creek, and after she gave birth, she had John Patrick to take care of, so she couldn't help Colin with tasks that required heavy manual labor. Nonetheless, Annie stayed busy from sunrise to sunset as well, cooking, cleaning, nurturing John Patrick, tending to the chickens, and taking care of the area around the cabin. She shared Colin's dream of saving money, buying more land, and expanding the farm, and she envisioned John Patrick growing up and inheriting a prosperous operation that would one day make him a prominent figure in the Swannanoa Valley. Sure, it required them to make some sacrifices now, but like a mother bear and her cub, Annie was willing to do whatever she had to do to provide for her offspring.

Colin managed to eke out a small profit in 1843, and by putting most of it back into the farm, he earned a larger profit in 1844. Putting the money back into the farm meant there wasn't much leftover to save, but a good profit in 1845 would enable him to maximize what he could produce on the acreage he had and start to save in earnest to purchase more land. If they stuck to the plan and the good Lord continued providing the fine weather they'd had the first two seasons, Colin and Annie believed they would be able to double the size of the farm by 1850.

The spring of 1845 started out the way most springs begin in the Blue Ridge Mountains. The first of the six spring pseudo seasons, Fool's Spring, was relatively mild and brief. Second Winter wasn't bad at all; it turned chilly for a few days, but it never dropped below freezing and no snow fell. The Spring of Deception was hotter than normal with temperatures reaching the mid-eighties and no appreciable rain. Third Winter, if you could call it that, saw high temperatures in the sixties and lows in the mid to upper forties, and because of the warm air and the lack of moisture, there was no frost. Yellow dust fell and covered most everything, and wreaked havoc on allergy sufferers, during The Pollening. You could wipe off a chair on the front porch, walk away for an hour or so, and when you came back you had to dust the pollen off again before you sat down to avoid getting a stain on the seat of your pants or the back of your dress. The one comforting thought for those suffering with runny noses, sneezing, and sinus headaches was knowing that The Mudding would come soon and wash away the pollen and usher in the arrival of Actual Spring. But in the spring of 1845, the suffering that began during The Pollening didn't end. It was just a prelude to what was to come.

Colin's primary cash crop was corn, but this year, he was going to add small patches of wheat and cabbage to diversify his crops and to test which was easiest to grow and proved to be the most profitable. In preparation for planting season in April, he ordered and paid for the seeds in early March, and he picked them up a few weeks later. He planned to plow his fields as soon as The Mudding ended and the soil dried out a bit, so he could get the seeds in the ground by mid-April and let the April showers work their magic.

But The Mudding never ended ... because The Mudding never began.

March eighth was a Saturday. Colin and Annie heard rain pattering on the roof of their cabin, which made it a good morning for them to stay in bed for as long as they could until John Patrick awoke and demanded their attention. Sleeping in was a treat they rarely got to enjoy.

"I love the sound of the rain," Annie said as she gently rubbed Colin's cheek. "It's so soothing. I could just lay here all day and do nothing; well, at least until John Patrick wakes up."

"I know," Colin said as he rolled onto his side to face Annie. He reached up with his hand, pushed her hair away from her face, leaned forward, and kissed her. "Let's just lay here and enjoy it while we can." Annie smiled and squeezed his hand.

By mid-morning, the sound of the rain hitting the roof stopped, and a short time later the sun came out. Neither Colin nor Annie nor John Patrick would ever hear the sound of rain falling on their roof again.

On April 4, 1845, the Mecklenburg Jeffersonian newspaper reported that there had been no measurable rain in over a month. "The consequence is a cloud of dust almost dense enough to suffocate," it said. According to the Charlotte Journal, no rain fell again until September 5, 1845, too late for crops that should have been in the ground and growing months earlier. Normally, by that time of the year, farmers had already started harvesting their corn crops. This year, they hadn't even planted their fields. It was the worst drought to hit the region in many years and it resulted in food shortages throughout the Carolinas. Those who suffered the most were those who lived in the Blue Ridge Mountains.

Colin and Annie made do with cornmeal, tomatoes, and beans that Annie canned the prior fall, and eggs and chickens, and they did their best to make what they had last for as long as possible. While he was unable to plant his fields, Colin did plant a small garden near the cabin with corn, cabbage, tomatoes, and beans, and he watered the garden with buckets of water he carried up from Shope Creek. By late June, the creek was nearly dry. Colin had killed and cleaned the last chicken several days before and Annie had used up most of the provisions she had canned and stored in the fall. She was doing her best to stretch what remained, but there was only so much she could do. She and Colin saved the best for John Patrick, but now the best was gone and all three of them were beginning to feel the debilitating effects of malnourishment. Colin and Annie prayed, and they kept a close eye on the sky hoping that their prayers would be answered, and rain clouds would come rolling over the mountains and rejuvenate the valley.

Robert Rice stopped by one afternoon in late June and told Colin that six wagons loaded with food had arrived at the newly erected Berea Baptist Church where Pastor Thomas Stradley would oversee its distribution. He told Colin to hurry up and head over to the church, a crowd was already assembling. Colin took what little money was left, saddled up his horse, and rode to the church. Hunger was rampant throughout the Swannanoa Valley, and Riceville was no exception. By the time Colin got to the church, the churchyard was crowded with wagons, horses, and people. The crowd wasn't in a panic, but it teetered on the edge of it as dozens of hungry souls waited anxiously for whatever food they could get.

Food grown in the northeast and deep south arrived by ship at the ports in Wilmington and Charleston. From there, it moved inland on trains to the cities, and then by wagons out into the countryside. There were no rail lines that came anywhere near the Blue Ridge Mountains. The rail lines ended in Salisbury, over a hundred miles east of Asheville. From there, it was five days by wagon up through the Swannanoa Gap and over into the Swannanoa Valley. The valley wasn't necessarily the end of the line for commerce at that time, but some said you could see the end from there.

The men who made the journey up the mountain with wagons loaded with food wanted to help those in need, but they also wanted to get paid for their effort. At first, they planned to auction off their cargo to the highest bidders, but Reverend Stradley persuaded them that the Christian thing to do was to charge a set price that would still earn them a nice profit but was fairer than letting the richest buy disproportionate shares and leave poorer residents to go hungry. Once he finished negotiating with the merchants, he turned his attention to the crowd gathered in the churchyard.

Reverend Stradley climbed up into the back of one of the wagons to address the crowd. He raised his hands to get them to quieten down so he could speak, and after a few seconds, a hush fell over the assemblage.

"Ladies and gentlemen, we're all suffering. That includes me and my family. We're fortunate that these men made the arduous journey to get here and to bring us food. God bless them," he said as he nodded towards the merchants who were standing next to their wagons. "Folks, we're all in this together. While I wish there was enough here to where we could all take as much as we want, that's not the case. We're going to have to ration what's here to feed as many people as we can, and we're going to have to pray that more food will arrive soon.

And we've got to keep praying for rain. So that means that for every man, woman, and child in your household, you can buy one bag of cornmeal, one bag of wheat flour, one bag of rice, and one sack of beans. If you have slaves, you can buy one half that amount for each one of them too. Not everyone can afford to buy their full share. If you can, remember what it says in the good book about helping those in need and spare whatever you can to help your neighbors.

Now, lineup here and let's get started. Be patient, don't be greedy, and keep praying for the good Lord to bring us some rain and some relief."

There was some jostling amongst the crowd, but things settled down once the process got underway, and the line moved slowly, but in an orderly fashion. When it was his turn, Colin bought all that he could, and after he paid, there wasn't much left to slip back into his money pouch. He loaded the sacks on the back of his horse and led it back to the cabin. He thought to himself as he walked along that he needed to sell one of his two horses or a piece of his farm equipment to make sure he had money to buy more food when the next shipment arrived, but he wasn't sure there would be any buyers since he and his neighbors were all in the same dire boat. There wasn't much demand for farm equipment when no one could farm.

"Thank God," Annie shouted as Colin walked in with the first two sacks. Colin brought in the remaining sacks, and he told Annie what happened in the churchyard. "This will get us through for a couple of weeks perhaps," he said, "but we need to make it last for as long as we can. I don't know when more food will arrive or how we'll pay for it when it does." Neither

Annie nor Colin had eaten until they were full in weeks, and it was tempting to prepare a big meal just this once and gorge until they couldn't eat any more, but Annie let that notion fade away and began preparing a modest meal that would sustain them and make the meager provisions they had last longer.

Colin and Annie did all that they could to make the most of their rations. As the creek began to dry up and they began to grow weaker, they couldn't keep their garden going, except for several hardy cornstalks that by August had produced ears of corn that they picked out of necessity before they were fully mature. Colin managed to shoot a rabbit or a squirrel from time to time, and the meat was a welcome addition when they sat down at the table to eat.

111

Colin took his gun and ventured off in search of game one morning in the middle part of August. When he reached the point where Shope Creek and Wolf Branch merge, he saw someone lying face down on the bank near the water, and he rushed over to see if he could help. He turned the person over and saw that it was a man who appeared to be in his thirties. The man was extremely pale and gaunt. He was unconscious and breathing weakly. From the stench, Colin could tell that the man had soiled his pants and vomited on himself. He was drenched in sweat, but he shivered like he was freezing cold. Colin propped up the man's head and shook him by his shoulders. "Mister. Mister. Can you hear me?" No response. Colin removed a tin cup from his pack, took it over to the creek, and scooped up some water. He lifted the man's head, held the cup to his lips, and poured some water into his mouth. The man coughed and when he stopped, he mumbled incoherently. Colin tried again to give him more water. The man seemed to swallow it, and then he coughed and mumbled. Colin gently lowered the man's head back down to the ground. "Mister, if you can hear me, you hang on. I'm going home and get my horse and wagon and get you to town and find you some help. I'll get back here as fast as I can. You hang on now. I'll be back soon."

When Colin arrived at the cabin, he told Annie about the man he found lying by the creek. "He's in bad shape and I don't know if he'll still be alive when I get back there, but if he is, I'm going to take him into town and try to get him some help." Annie offered to take John Patrick and go back to the creek with Colin, but Colin told her to stay at home with their child and he would take care of the stranger. He went out and hitched a horse to his wagon. He tossed a shovel into the back of the wagon before he left, and he prayed that he wouldn't need to use it.

Nearly two hours passed between the time Colin left the man beside the creek and the time he returned with the wagon. Before he even climbed down, he could tell that the man was dead. He placed his hand on the man's chest to determine if he was breathing or had a heartbeat, and he detected neither one. He took the shovel from his wagon and started to dig a grave a few feet above the edge of the creekbank. When he was done, he pulled the man's body over to the hole, lowered it inside, and positioned the man's arms so they were folded across his chest. Colin leaned on his shovel and looked down at the man's body lying in the crude grave. "Mister, I don't know who you are, where you came from, or what brought you here, but I'm sorry about what happened to you. No one deserves to die all alone like this. I pray the good Lord will have mercy on your soul." Colin covered the man's body with dirt, returned to his wagon, and went home.

A few days later, Colin woke up feeling achy and his head hurt. By the afternoon, he felt a tickle in the back of his throat, and he started to cough. The next morning, he woke up soaked in sweat and shivering. Annie had made a stew from rice, beans, and rabbit meat, and she tried to get Colin to eat some, but he said his stomach hurt and he wasn't hungry. She tried again that evening, and this time she insisted he eat something to keep up his strength. Colin relented and ate a few bites, and then he leaned over and vomited on the cabin floor.

Colin developed a rash on his chest and stomach, and the fever and the shivering got worse. Just a couple of days after Colin fell ill, Annie woke up with a headache and joint pain, and John Patrick had a fever and cried in discomfort. Over the course of the next several days, each one of them had periods where it seemed like the fever was going to break and their condition was improving, but within hours things would take a turn for the worse and the fever would rage once again. Colin and John Patrick were nauseous and constipated, while Annie was nauseous and had diarrhea. The smell of sickness lingered in the hot, stale, dry air inside the little cabin.

The afternoon of September 5, 1845, was warm and windy. By evening, clouds had formed over the mountains off to the west, and by dark, rain started to fall, slowly at first, and then in a downpour mountain folks call "a gully washer" or "a frog strangler." It was the first rain in the Swannanoa Valley in six months, and the sound of it hitting the roof echoed throughout Colin and Annie's cabin all night long and through most of the next day. At long last, the draught of 1845 had come to an end.

September 8, 1845, was a Monday. The sky was clear and the temperature in the morning was in the fifties. Robert Rice rode down Shope Creek on his horse headed into Asheville to visit the blacksmith. He smiled when he saw that for the first time in months, the creek was once again flowing, not as strong as it often did after a good rain, but better than it been recently when it was nearly dry. Along the way, he noticed that a lot of the vegetation that had turned brown during the drought had sprung back to life after getting a nice drink of water from the good soaking rain. Off from the road in the distance, Robert saw Colin and Annie's cabin. As he got closer, he noticed there was no smoke coming from the chimney, which seemed odd since there was still a chill in the air and normally Annie would be making coffee or cooking something over a fire at that time of the day. He hadn't planned to stop in to see Colin and Annie, but he thought he should check in on them and make sure they were okay.

The awful stench drove Robert backwards when he opened the door of the cabin. It was the putridly sweet smell of sickness and of death. Robert removed the bandana from around his neck, rolled it up, and put it over his nose and mouth before he tried to venture inside. John Patrick was in his crib, Annie was in bed, and Colin was lying face down on the floor next to the kitchen table. All three of them were dead. From the ghastly look of things, Robert figured they died sometime before the rain fell.

Between the drought that caused a total crop failure and a typhoid fever epidemic, the summer of 1845 was catastrophic for many in the Blue Ridge Mountains. It highlighted the fact that the mountains were isolated and not easily accessible. That stymied efforts to deliver enough food to the area to sustain mountain folks when they were unable to grow crops and sustain themselves. It led to calls for the government to do something to improve transportation into and out of the mountains. Rail service was the answer, but it would be a long time coming and it would come at a very steep price for some.

In 1855, the North Carolina Legislature chartered the Western North Carolina Railroad Company to extend passenger and freight rail service from Salisbury to Asheville. The rail line was to be constructed in sections beginning in Salisbury and proceeding west, and each section had to be financed and paid for through stock subscriptions. The legislature included this provision to prevent the state from incurring a huge debt at the outset of the project and allowing it to spread the debt out over time as each section of the line was completed. A twelve-person board of directors was selected to oversee the project, with eight directors appointed by the governor and four by the individuals and the counties who held stock in the railroad.

In 1854, James Turner conducted a survey for extending the rail line westward, and after the board of directors was appointed, they named him to be the chief engineer for the project. Turner proposed a route from Salisbury to Morganton, a distance of about seventy-six miles, with an estimated cost of nearly two-million dollars. Work on the rail line began in 1857, and by August 1858, twenty miles of new track between Salisbury and Statesville was in place and pressed into service.

The second phase was to extend the rail line from Statesville to Old Fort and then from Old Fort to what would be the western opening of the yet-to-be-built Swannanoa Tunnel. The rail company chose to publicly finance this phase of the project at the start rather than seeking financial assistance from the state. Turner estimated that this forty-three-and-a-half-mile section would cost about two-and-a-half million dollars, and contracts were awarded to build it in 1859. The contracts specified that no payments would be made until the section to Morganton was completed at which time the state would step in and help fund the segment that extended past Morganton to Old Fort. Work on the section to Morganton was supposed to be completed by the end of 1860, but it took longer than expected and contractors were not getting paid for their work. To remedy the problem, the legislature made the entire line from Salisbury to the western entrance of the Swannanoa Tunnel one single section, which triggered the state's obligation to begin making payments for work performed west of Morganton.

Due to a downturn in financial conditions, Governor John Ellis ordered the suspension of all payments on the rail project. Work came to a halt on April 29, 1861, and contractors were not paid again until the legislature authorized the treasurer to pay out two-hundred-thousand dollars in December 1861. The legislature also specified that the second section of the line would end at Asheville and a third section would extend the rail line from Asheville to Waynesville. Work proceeded at a slow pace, and by the time the Civil War intervened, the line was still a few miles short of reaching Morganton.

The war exacerbated the shortage of men available to work on the rail line, so the rail company rented slaves from slave owners to do the work. Slave owners were paid from seventy-five to two-hundred-and-fifty dollars a year per slave, depending on their skill level. But slave labor was no cure for the labor shortage. Slaves had to be trained for the duties they were to perform, which took time and money, and slave owners needed most of their slaves to work their farms, which limited the number of slaves they could make available to the railroad.

In June 1863, Colonel George Kirk led a Union attack on Camp Vance, a Confederate training camp located near Morganton. Kirk had hoped to commandeer a train and use it to move his troops quickly down to Salisbury to free Union prisoners being held there, but he was unsuccessful. He did, however, manage to burn down a depot, destroy some rail cars, and damage an engine before he was forced to flee west back over into Tennessee.

General George Stoneman was more successful in disrupting rail service. During what became known as "Stoneman's Raid" in 1865, he captured Salisbury and then moved west destroying rail lines and rail assets along the way as he passed through Statesville, Morganton, and Asheville on his way to Tennessee. Hundreds of slaves accompanied Stoneman and his troops as they left the area, further reducing the labor pool. When the Civil War finally ended, most of the rail line was destroyed, funds were depleted, and the labor force was decimated.

Restoration of the nearly destroyed rail line began during Reconstruction, and by the summer of 1867, contracts were awarded to build the line from Morganton to Old Fort, and in 1868, contracts were awarded to build the line to the western end of the Swannanoa Tunnel and from the tunnel on to Asheville. At the State Constitutional Convention of 1868, a two-and-a-half million-dollar bond issue was approved with most of the funds to be used to build the line from Old Fort, through the mountains, and into Asheville. That was in addition to the four-million dollars the state had already spent on the project to extend it as far as Old Fort.

Reconstruction was a period ripe for opportunists to exploit the government for personal gain. In late 1868, North Carolina native George Swepson convinced the legislature to divide the Western North Carolina Railroad Company into two divisions, an eastern division and a western division, and to increase the capital stock of the company to twelve-million dollars. With the help of a New Yorker, General Milton Littlefield, Swepson secured control of the western division, and Swepson served as the division's president from October 1868 to October 1869.

Swepson and Littlefield, through fraudulent stock subscriptions, convinced North Carolina's Reconstruction Governor William Holden that they satisfied the conditions required for the state to issue them nearly six-million-four-hundred-thousand dollars in state bonds in payment for the state's two-thirds interest in the railroad company. Those bonds were sold in New York City for about half their face value, and Swenson pocketed nearly one-million-three-hundred-thousand dollars for himself.

In 1870, the legislature appointed a commission chaired by Asheville attorney Nicholas Woodfin to investigate Swepson's misappropriation of funds and to recover whatever remained and could be recouped. For the next decade, Swepson's sketchy investments were the subject of numerous lawsuits. In an effort to complete the line to Asheville, the rail company issued mortgage bonds in 1870, but it was unable to keep up with the interest payments. As a result, the company went into receivership in 1872.

On June 22, 1875, Augustus Merrimon, acting as agent for the state, purchased the rail company for eight-hundred-and-twenty-five-thousand dollars and a new board was appointed to oversee it. They arranged for the men and materials necessary to extend the line up the mountain, and they hired mathematician and Confederate veteran James Wilson to lead the effort. But it wasn't long before the board was caught up in a political squabble in the state legislature, which led to the removal of all the board members and the appointment of a new board in 1877. James Wilson was named president of the board, as well as superintendent and chief engineer for the project. A contract was awarded to James Wilson and Company to complete the Swannanoa Tunnel, paying Wilson's company two dollars per yard to remove the tons of rock that had to be excavated to carve the tunnel through the mountain.

Wilson was presented with a host of difficult challenges. The passage from Old Fort up the slope of the Blue Ridge Mountains to the Swannanoa Valley was an eleven-hundred-foot change in elevation over less than three and a half miles of distance as the crow flies, seven feet of elevation change per one-hundred feet of linear distance. That exceeded the limits for trains at the time of not more than twenty-six inches of elevation gain per one-hundred feet of linear distance. To handle the steep grade, Wilson designed sweeping turns and switchbacks to traverse the mountains, which required nearly eight and a half miles of rail to cover less than three and a half miles of linear distance. In some places it was necessary to go through the mountains rather than over them, so seven tunnels had to be cut through mostly solid rock. The longest of those was the eighteen-hundred-and thirty-two-foot Swannanoa Tunnel. Finally, Wilson needed a large labor force to perform the hard and dangerous work. The state obliged and provided convicts from the state's penitentiaries.

Cornelia Wilson almost died giving birth to her son, Tobias. Cornelia was twenty years old and a third-generation slave on a cotton and tobacco plantation on the Cape Fear River north of Wilmington. She went into labor in the early morning hours on a sweltering August day, and it was past dark before Tobias finally made his entrance into this world. Cornelia was a cook who prepared breakfast and dinner for the field hands who toiled in the heat from sunrise to sunset, six days a week. It was hot in the kitchen and the work was hard, but Cornelia knew it wasn't nearly as hard as working out in the fields, so she felt that she was more fortunate than many of the others. She expected she'd be out for a day after giving birth, but she hadn't foreseen how difficult a labor it was going to be. The two other women who worked in the kitchen with her covered for her for almost a week before Cornelia finally gained enough strength to return to her cooking duties.

Tobias was born on Monday, August 5, 1861, just a few months after the Civil War began. His father was a field hand who escaped the plantation in December 1862 when Major General John Foster and his Union forces marched through the area and destroyed the Goldsborough Bridge, disrupting rail traffic on the strategically important Wilmington and Weldon Railroad that was used to transport Confederate troops and supplies.

Cornelia and Tobias moved to Goldsboro when the war ended. Cornelia felt that she was fortunate once again when a merchant named Hiram Cohen hired her to cook and clean for him and his family. The job didn't pay much, but it came with food and shelter, and it allowed Cornelia to keep an eye on her young son. It wasn't until later in his life that Tobias realized just how good his childhood was. He was too young to remember much about his time on the plantation. Instead, most of his early childhood memories were of his time with his mother at the Cohen's place in Goldsboro.

There were other boys and girls like Tobias, the children of former slaves who were recently freed, and he recalled fondly the hours he'd spent playing with them. Like the other mothers, Cornelia reminded Tobias regularly to avoid white folks and to stay out of trouble, and for the most part he complied. There was an occasional encounter that led to a white man or woman yelling "you colored kids get away from here," but Tobias didn't think much about it because that was the world he had been born into and it was all that he'd ever known. It never occurred to him to question whether it was right or wrong, it was simply how it was.

One evening when Tobias was thirteen, he walked to the backdoor of the main house that led into the kitchen where his mother was preparing the evening meal for the Cohen family. As he peered through the glass, he saw his mother standing over the stove stirring a pot with her back towards him. Before he could turn the knob and open the door, Mister Cohen walked up behind Cornelia, placed his hand on her butt, and squeezed it. Cornelia spun around and pushed him away. Tobias couldn't make out what they were saying, but it was clear there was a heated exchange. Mister Cohen raised his hand to slap Cornelia in the face, but she blocked it with her left arm and raised the big wooden spoon she had in her right hand to defend herself. Mister Cohen pushed her in the chest with both hands and knocked her backwards and onto the floor, and then he walked away. Cornelia stood up, straightened her clothes, walked back over to the stove, and continued stirring the pot.

Tobias turned and went back to the little one-room cottage on the back edge of the yard where he and Cornelia lived. Cornelia came home about an hour later carrying a basket with leftovers that they would have for dinner. Normally, there was a lively conversation around the dinner table with Tobias sharing stories about what he had done that day. That night, however, it was quiet. Cornelia knew that something was wrong, and she tried to get Tobias to tell her what

121

it was, but he responded, "it ain't nothing, mama." After several more minutes of silence, Cornelia decided to try again.

"Baby, you say it's nothing, but I know better than that. You and me, we don't keep secrets. So, tell me, why are you so quiet? What happened today?"

Tobias looked down at his plate for a few seconds, and then he looked at his mother. "Mama, I walked over to the kitchen a little bit ago to see you, and when I got to the door, I saw Mister Cohen grab your behind, and I saw you two arguing, and I saw him push you to the floor. Mama, that ain't right. You can't let him get away with doing that to you."

Now it was Cornelia's turn to be quiet. She looked down at her plate and pushed her food around with her fork as she pondered how to respond. After she collected her thoughts, she looked at Tobias and said, "Baby, it ain't right, but there ain't nothing I can do about it. Mister Cohen is usually pretty good to me, but sometimes when he's had too much to drink, well it's like he becomes a different man. When he's like that, I just do my best to stay away from him, but sometimes I can't, and when I can't, I do the best I can to keep things from getting out of hand. But it would be my word against his, and they'd believe him, and I'd get fired, and I need this job or me and you will be living out on the street. Baby, that's just how it is. It ain't right, but we can't do nothing about it to try and make it right. I'll be okay, and don't you worry about it. I can handle it."

Tobias continued looking straight at his mother. "Mama, maybe there's nothing you can do about it, but if I see him do anything like that again, I'll kill him. I ain't afraid of that man. I'll kill him if he tries to hurt you again."

Cornelia stood up, walked around the table to Tobias, and put her hands on his shoulder.

"Baby, listen to me. You stay away from Mister Cohen. I can take care of myself and I'm not going to let you throw your life away on account of me. I know in your head you think you can win that battle, and maybe you're right, but I'm telling you, you'll end up losing the war. That's just how it is, even if it's wrong, it's how it is. So, you need to let it go. Can you do that for me?"

Tobias huffed and then nodded his head. They never spoke of it again.

Tobias got a job working on a farm just outside of town. It was hard work, but the extra money allowed him and his mother to afford a few luxuries they had to forgo on just her pay. They settled into a comfortable rhythm, and their lives seemed to be going well ... and then Cornelia fell ill.

Cornelia cut her arm when she stumbled and fell against a sharp piece of metal in the chicken coop. She washed the cut with water, put some grease on it, wrapped it in a cloth bandage, and continued working. Within a few days, the cut began to ooze a yellowish discharge, and her arm began to swell and burn. Not long after, she developed a fever. Tobias could see that his mother was sick, so he stayed home from work to tend to her. As a result, he got fired from his job at the farm.

Cornelia became delirious and disoriented. Her speech was rambling and slurred. Tobias went to the Cohens and begged them to get medical help for his mother, and they agreed to do so. When the doctor arrived and examined Cornelia, he said she had sepsis and that it had progressed beyond the point where it could be treated. The doctor said it was just a matter of time until her organs started to shut down and eventually, she would die. All he could do was to provide some medication to help alleviate her pain, but death was inevitable. Cornelia slipped into a coma the morning of September 10, 1877, and she died that night at the age of thirty-six. Tobias was sixteen when his mother passed away and left him behind and all alone.

Mister Cohen waited a few days after Cornelia's death before he went to see Tobias to deliver an unpleasant message. "Son, I'm sorry about your mother," he said. "She was a good woman, and I know you miss her greatly. My family misses her too. I hate to do this, but I'm going to need for you to move out of here by the end of the week. Since your mother passed, I had to find somebody else to take her place working in the house. I hired a lady this morning and she's going to start next week. She's going to move in here over the weekend."

Tobias was stunned. "Sir, mama and me lived here pretty much my whole life. I ain't got nowhere else to go. I wasn't expecting to stay here forever, but can't you give me a little more time? I lost my job when mama got sick. I've got to find work before I can get a place to live."

"I'm sorry, son. None of this is your fault, I know that, but none of it is my fault either and I've got to take care of my family." Mister Cohen reached into his pocket, pulled out some money, and handed it to Tobias. "Take this. It's not a lot, but hopefully it'll help tide you over until you can find work. I wish you well, son. I mean that. I really do."

Tobias walked out to the farm where he used to work and explained why he had stopped showing up. His old boss said he understood, and he was sorry about Tobias's mother, but they already hired a replacement for him, and it was coming up on the end of the farming season, so they wouldn't need as many farm hands until next spring when it was time for planting again. He told Tobias to come back then and if there was an opening, he'd hire him back.

The money Mister Cohen gave Tobias was enough for him to find a place to stay in the home of a widow who rented out rooms by the week. He tried to find work at some other farms, but they were all in the process of winding down for the season too and didn't need to hire more help. The druggist in Goldsboro gave him some part-time work making deliveries to customers who couldn't travel to the drug store to pick up their medications and performing janitorial duties in the store. It was only a few days a week, and it didn't pay enough to cover his room and board, and after several months, he had to move out of his room at the boarding house because he couldn't pay the rent.

There was an old one-room shack in the woods on the banks of the Neuse River that Tobias remembered seeing a couple of years earlier when he and some other kids ventured out that way. It had been abandoned for as long as anyone could remember, and it looked like it would collapse if a middling storm blew through. Tobias packed his belongs into two burlap sacks and headed to the cabin. It was February and it was cold. When he got to the cabin, it was in as bad a shape as he remembered it. He sat his things down on the floor and went to work boarding up the windows to block the cold wind. When he finished, he went outside, gathered up fallen tree limbs, and broke them into pieces that would fit inside the fireplace. As he lit the fire, he prayed it wouldn't end up burning the place down with him in it. He had kept a hunk of bread from the last meal he had before leaving the widow's boarding house, and he sat down by the fire, ate it, and thought that if he could just survive until spring, he could get a job working on a farm and then everything would be alright. He would in fact have a job by the time spring came, but despite his earnest wishes, everything would be far from right.

Zeb Vance was born in May 1830 in a log cabin on Reems Creek several miles east of Weaverville and just up the road a piece from Asheville. His father was the son of a member of the North Carolina House of Commons who had been a colonel in the Continental Army and served under General George Washington at Valley Forge. His mother's father was a state senator. His uncle, Robert Vance, was a close friend of frontiersman Davey Crockett and they served together in Congress. Robert Vance died when he was on the losing end of a duel with his political opponent, Samuel Price Carson, in Saluda Gap three years before Zeb was born. Davey Crockett attended the duel, and he transported Robert's body back to Reems Creek for burial.

Despite both of his parents coming from influential families, Zeb's mother and father were not wealthy by any means. When Zeb was three, his family moved from Reems Creek to Lapland, now known as Marshall, on the French Broad River, where his father sold supplies to the drovers who moved livestock down the river to the market in Asheville. When Zeb was thirteen, he left to attended Washington College in Limestone, Tennessee, but he returned home before the end of the school year after his father was killed in an accident. His mother was forced to sell much of the family's property to pay her husband's debts, and she moved the family to Asheville. Zeb studied law there under John Woodfin, and when he was twenty-one, he wrote to former governor and the then head of the University of North Carolina at Chapel Hill, David Swain, and asked for a loan to enable him to study law at the university. Swain, who was from Buncombe County and had been an elementary school classmate of Zeb's mother, arranged for a three-hundred-dollar loan.

Zeb Vance was admitted to the North Carolina Bar in 1852 and elected to the state senate in 1854. While serving in the senate, he was an advocate for extending rail service into the mountains of western North Carolina and he hoped one day to see rail service go all the way to Knoxville, Tennessee. He was elected to Congress in 1858 where he was pro-slavery – his family at one time owned as many as eighteen slaves – but anti-secession. When North Carolina was set to vote on whether to secede from the Union, Vance traveled around the state urging

North Carolinians not to follow the path South Carolina chose when it seceded. His views on secession changed, however, after Union forces fired on Fort Sumpter in Charleston Harbor.

Zeb resigned from Congress and returned to Buncombe County where he organized the Rough and Ready Guard, which became part of the North Carolina Infantry. He was promoted to colonel and was placed in command of the 26th North Carolina Infantry Regiment in August 1861. In the Battle of New Bern in 1862, his troops were outnumbered, but held off Union forces for five hours and they were the last Confederate troops to retreat from the battlefield. In July 1862, he and his troops were involved in the Seven Days Battles – a series of seven battles fought over the course of seven days outside of Richmond, Virginia – where he earned high praise for his courage and exceptional leadership.

North Carolina needed a governor, and many believed it should be Zeb Vance. Zeb agreed to run, but he refused to leave his troops. Without giving a single speech, knocking on a single door, or even crafting a platform to run on, Zeb Vance was elected governor with seventy-three percent of the votes, which to this day remains the largest margin of victory in a governor's race in the history of North Carolina. When he learned that he had been elected governor, he resigned his commission and traveled to Raleigh where he was sworn into office on September 8, 1862, at the age of thirty-two.

As governor, Zeb Vance was a staunch supporter of the Confederacy. He used blockade runners to transport cotton grown in North Carolina overseas and he used the proceeds to support North Carolina's citizens and keep its textile mills running. North Carolina was the only Confederate state that managed to arm, clothe, and feed its troops throughout the war. He was a firm believer in individual rights. When Confederate President Jefferson Davis ordered states to imprison any of their citizens believed to be disloyal to the Confederacy and to do so without trials, Zeb Vance refused and threatened to call North Carolina's troops home to defend the rights of its citizens if it became necessary. Jefferson Davis backed down and North Carolina was the only southern state where the courts remained open, and the right of habeas corpus was honored throughout the war. Zeb also opposed the conscription practice that allowed rich plantation owners to pay others to go off and fight in their places. He lamented what he called "a rich man's war and a poor man's fight."

Zeb was hugely popular with North Carolinians because of his efforts to reduce the effects of the war on the state and his efforts to preserve the rule of law. As a result, he was reelected governor in 1864. When Confederate forces began to surrender to their Union counterparts in 1865, Zeb issued a proclamation to both citizens and soldiers telling them to "retire quietly in their homes and exert themselves in preserving order," and then he surrendered to General John Schofield in Greensboro on May 2, 1865. General Schofield accepted his surrender and told him to go home to his wife and children in Statesboro as there was no order for his arrest. Less than two weeks later, he was arrested by General Hugh Judson Kilpatrick and transported to Raleigh where he was imprisoned for a short time before he was transferred to the Old Capitol Prison in Washington. He arrived there on May 20, 1865. While he was confined in Washington, Zeb shared a cell with John Letcher who had been the governor of Virginia during the war. He was paroled by President Andrew Johnson on July 6, 1865, and pardoned on March 11, 1867, having never been charged with the commission of any crime.

Zeb ran for the U.S. Senate in 1872, but he was defeated by Augustus Merrimon. He ran for a third term as governor in 1876 and won, but he only completed two years of his four-year term. He stepped down in 1879 when he was elected to replace Merrimon in the U.S. Senate and he held that senate seat from then until April 14, 1894, when he died at his home in Washington.

President Grover Cleveland and Vice President Adlai Stevenson attended a service held for Zeb in the U.S. Senate where his chair and desk were draped in black velvet and adorned with pine branches symbolizing North Carolina. His body, escorted by seven congressmen, was transported by train to Raleigh where another service was held, and then he was carried home to Asheville. Thousands of people lined the train tracks throughout North Carolina to pay their final respects to a man they loved dearly.

The funeral service in Asheville was held at the First Presbyterian Church and then Zeb's casket was transported to Riverside Cemetery for burial, escorted by more than seven hundred carriages and many of the surviving members of his former Rough and Ready Guard. An estimated ten thousand people turned out for Zeb's funeral service and burial: a number equal to the entire population of Asheville at the time.

Zeb Vance had been a supporter of extending rail service to Western North Carolina since his days in the state senate in the early 1850s. For more than two decades, the state spent millions of dollars – some of it later embezzled – funding multiple efforts to build a rail line to Asheville and beyond. When the effort started up again after the Civil War, there was little appetite or ability to commit large sums to the endeavor. James Wilson needed laborers, and lots of them, to perform the hard work required to run train tracks up the mountain from Old Fort, through the Swannanoa Gap, and into the Swannanoa Valley. Since the state would not provide enough money to hire contractors to perform the work, the state offered up an alternative; a cheap labor force pulled from the state's prisons.

The state agreed to build three stockades to house up to seven hundred prisoners who would be committed to James Wilson and the rail project. There was one problem: there were not enough inmates in the state prisons to fill all the stockades and provide the labor force

Wilson needed. The solution was to create a bigger pool of convicts. Governor Zeb Vance sent word to sheriffs and prosecutors throughout the state to bring more offenders before the courts in order to grow the state's prison population … and they obliged.

Scores of mostly African-American men were arrested, tried, and convicted for petty offenses like vagrancy and shoplifting. From 1875 until the railroad's completion in 1892, three-thousand-six-hundred-and-forty-four inmates worked on the rail project and four-hundred-and-sixty-one of them died from injuries or illnesses. Most of the inmates were from the eastern part of the state where the ground is flat, and the winters are mild. They weren't prepared for the harsh conditions they'd face up in the Blue Ridge Mountains.

They say that slavery officially ended on December 18, 1865, with the ratification of the Thirteenth Amendment to the Constitution. Others say that slavery never really end, it just transformed.

It was the middle of March and Tobias thought that at last there was light at the end of the tunnel. Local farmers would soon start preparing for the spring planting, and Tobias would go see his old boss in a few days to inquire if there was a job for him at the farm where he had worked before his mother died.

Sheriff Ollin Coor, the sheriff of Wayne County, and a deputy showed up at Tobias's cabin early one morning while he was still asleep. They roused him awake, ordered him to get dressed, placed him in shackles, loaded him into the back of a wagon with two other young African-American men, and carted him off to the county jail. That afternoon, Tobias appeared before Judge R. M. Saunders. He was convicted of vagrancy and sentenced to twelve months in the state penitentiary. The next morning, Tobias was taken from the Wayne County jail and escorted over to the train station. A short time later, the train pulled in, and he was placed into a railcar loaded with other African-American inmates and a few guards. The train wasn't headed to the state penitentiary in Raleigh, it was headed to the Blue Ridge Mountains.

It was a cold, dreary, overcast afternoon when the train stopped in Old Fort. The inmates were ordered out of the railcars and directed to lineup next to the tracks and remain quiet. Tobias followed along in the queue and took his place in line under the watchful eye of an armed guard, a young white man about his own age. As he stood there awaiting instructions, Tobias looked off to the west and saw something he'd heard about before, but he'd never seen ... the Blue Ridge Mountains.

"Damn, that's something, ain't it," the inmate next to him muttered.

"It sure is," Tobias responded seconds before the guard struck the back of his leg with a wooden baton.

"You boys keep your damned mouths shut," he said, his face so close to Tobias's ear that Tobias could feel the heat of his breath. "If I want something out of you, I'll knock it out of you. You hear me? Now shut your damned mouths and do as your told."

Two days before, Tobias thought spring was coming and he was on the cusp of things taking a turn for the better. He couldn't have imagined that a short time later he'd be standing in shackles in the cold and looking up at the Swannanoa Gap just as Joseph Rice, Thomas Williams, and Samuel Davidson had done many years before him, although they did it by choice while he did it by compulsion.

Tobias and the other inmates stood silently in a long line beside the tracks. The train moved about a hundred yards to the west to a turntable where it rotated slowly in preparation for its trip back to the east. A group of men came out of a small wooden building situated a short distance from the railroad tracks and they walked towards the line of inmates. The group stopped, and a middle-aged white man in a leather duster coat and a wide-brimmed hat stepped forward.

"I'm Henry Miller. I'm the supervisor of convicts for the Western North Carolina Railroad. You are going to be with us for as long as the State of North Carolina sees fit, and you are going to be working on the construction of the rail line from here on up to Asheville. In a few minutes, you are going to get into one of these wagons," he said as he gestured towards a group of horse-drawn wagons waiting nearby, "and you'll be taken to one of the stockades where you'll reside for the duration of your time with us up here in the mountains. You're going to work from sunup to sundown every day except for Sunday, and on Saturday work will end at four in the afternoon, at which time you'll bathe and put on a fresh uniform. You will follow the directions of the guards, the engineers, and the walking boss for the gang you're assigned to. If you break the rules, you'll be punished. If you try to escape, you'll be shot. If you do as you're told and you do your time, you'll be free to go back home. We've got a lot of work to do, so rather than standing here wasting more of it, let's get moving."

Miller turned and walked away with his little entourage in tow.

"Alright now, you boys from here on down, come with me. We're going to take those wagons over there up to the Swannanoa Tunnel camp. Mind your business and don't give me any shit, and we'll be alright."

The guard was short and pudgy with a scraggily beard and a plurality of his teeth, and he appeared to be in his late thirties. He and the younger guard who had struck Tobias with his baton escorted the prisoners over to two wagons where inmates in striped prison uniforms were

132

at the reins and waiting. Tobias and the others piled into the back of the wagons, the two guards climbed up on their horses, and they headed west towards the mountains.

Tobias was assigned to the camp dedicated to excavating the Swannanoa Tunnel, the longest of the seven tunnels required for trains to make their way from the base of the mountain west of Old Fort to the top of the Swannanoa Gap east of Black Mountain at Ridgecrest. To build the one thousand-eight-hundred-and-thirty-two-foot tunnel, Wilson had crews start on both sides of the mountain and he hoped that with a little luck the two halves would eventually connect up in the middle. The work had to be performed by hand, and it was grueling and dangerous.

James Camber was an engineer and explosives expert. He developed a blasting technique using a dough-like compound made from nitroglycerine mixed with sawdust and cornmeal to make it less volatile. It became known as Nitro Mash. The Nitro Mash paste was packed into holes carved about two feet deep into the rock using a pike and a sledgehammer. Once the fuse was lit and the Nitro Mash exploded, the rock fragments were carried out by hand, and the process was repeated over and over as the inmates burrowed further and further, inch by inch, into the mountain. Camber also perfected a method for wrapping Nitro Mash paste in an oil paper covering to create an explosive akin to the sticks of dynamite that Swedish chemist Alfred Nobel – benefactor of the Nobel Prize – developed in 1867. Blasting is inherently dangerous work, and blasting conducted by unskilled prison inmates inside a rock cavern using a nitroglycerin-based explosive was especially dangerous.

The wagons pulled into the Swannanoa Tunnel camp late in the afternoon. The inmates were instructed to climb down and form a line, and then they were herded into the yard in the middle of the camp. Standing there and waiting, Tobias surveyed the place that would be his home for the foreseeable future.

There were four, one-story, rectangular buildings – one on each side of the camp and the other two spaced about twenty-five feet apart and set parallel to one another on the third of the camp's four sides. These were the bunkhouses for the inmates. Behind the bunkhouses were two narrow rectangular buildings, each one an eight-seater outhouse, and a square building in between that served as a bathhouse. Across from the bunkhouses were two slightly smaller rectangular buildings. One was the kitchen, and the other was the laundry, which also served as the quarters for the few female inmates in the camp. Next to the kitchen was a long building with walls at each corner and large open spaces in between with oil clothes rolled up overhead. That was the open-air chow hall, which doubled as a meeting spot when it was needed. In the center of the grounds was a square building that served as the office and armory for the guards and the company officials. Short structures, about four feet tall and with thick walls about six feet in length, sat on both sides of the office. These were known as "the hole," and they were used to confine inmates who were being punished for breaking the rules or sometimes it seemed just to serve as an example to keep the others in line. Two rectangular buildings sat about fifty feet behind the chow hall. Those buildings housed the guards and company employees when they needed quarters at the site. Finally, a short distance away and set close to the mountain, there was a tall square building where tools, equipment, and other supplies were stored. The buildings were constructed out of rough-hewn lumber milled from trees harvested nearby and stones, which were plentiful even before they started blasting the mountain.

Three men came out of the office and walked over towards the inmates.

"I'm Major Curtis Warren," said a man with a substantial gray beard and long hair and clad in an oilskin coat that came down almost to the top of his bowed knees. "I'm in charge of this camp. This here is Mister John Hamilton, an engineer for James Wilson and Company. He's overseeing this end of the tunnel work. This is Sergeant Charles Owens. Sergeant Owens is the head guard for this camp. Next to him is Clayman Hill. Like you, Clayman's an inmate, and he's the chief inmate. If there's something you think I need to know or if there's something you think you need, you go to Clayman Hill with it. And if any of us tells you to do something, the only thing we want to hear back from you is yes sir. Are we clear on that?"

"Yes Sir," several of the inmates responded.

"What did you say," Major Warren asked with a look of anger on his face.

"Yes Sir," the inmates responded in unison and with more gusto.

"That's better. The crews that are working in the tunnel now will be coming out shortly. Tomorrow, you'll all start working alongside them. Right now, you'll be assigned a bunk in one of the bunkhouses and you'll be issued a uniform that you'll change into. Your personal clothing will be bagged up and returned to you when it's your time to go home."

"The rules around here are straightforward and simple; do your job and don't cause any trouble. You'll notice that there's no fence. Don't take that as an invitation to escape. If you run, you will be shot. If you get away, we won't stop until we find you and you'll be whipped real good before you're hung. I'm not going to lie to you and tell you that your life here will be easy, it won't, but exactly how hard it will be is mostly up to you. It'll be chow time here in a bit, so between now and then, guards will show you where to go. Get changed, get settled in, and get yourself a good night's sleep. You're going to work tomorrow, and you need to be ready for it. Are there any questions?"

"Yes bossman," said an inmate a few spots down from Tobias who stepped forward from the line. "I get the sweats and the shakes when I'm all cooped up in a tight space, so I ain't able

135

to work in your cave. I'll lose my damned mind and go crazy. You're going to have to find me something else to do around here where I ain't cooped up, bossman."

A guard standing behind the inmate smacked him hard in the back of the legs with a wooden baton causing the inmate to drop to his knees. He raised the baton again and struck the inmate in the back of the head sending him face-first into the dirt, moaning and bleeding.

Major Wilson looked at the inmate, paused for a second, and slowly shook his head. "If there aren't any more questions, you're dismissed," he said and then turned and walked away.

"You four come with me." A guard motioned for Tobias and three other inmates to follow him. "You're in barracks four. We're going to the laundry first to get your uniforms and then we'll go to the barracks for you to change clothes."

Tobias and the others got in line behind some of the other inmates who were already in the queue at the laundry. When he had made his way to the door, a petite African-American woman about his age and dressed in prison stripes looked him over, walked inside the laundry, and returned with a pair of pants, a shirt, and a denim jacket that were neatly folded and a wide brimmed felt hat. "Here. This ought to fit you. If it doesn't bring it back and exchange it." Tobias took the bundle, nodded, and walked away.

Barracks four was on the western end of the camp between the laundry and the supply building. There were doorways in the center of the building on both sides, one facing east towards the center of the compound and the other facing west towards the entrance to the tunnel. Once inside, Tobias saw that there were eight wooden bunks on the left – four on the righthand wall and four on the lefthand wall – and eight more on the right side of the building, each with three racks, for a total of forty-eight beds. Stone fireplaces were located at each end. There were rolled up pine straw-stuffed mattress pads and coarse blankets on seven or eight of the beds. A

136

thin, elderly inmate with tufts of white hair on his head and chin and protruding from his ears was using a makeshift straw broom to sweep the floor. He paused for a moment and looked at

Tobias, and then he went back to sweeping. "You boys can see the bunks that aren't taken. Choose one of them and that's your bunk. Once you've done so, change into your uniform and put your civilian clothes in here," the guard said as he passed out small burlap bags. "When you're done, come outside and I'll collect up your bags."

Tobias chose a bottom bunk about halfway down the back wall on the righthand side of the building. He unrolled his mattress pad. It had a bristly burlap cover and was loosely filled with pine straw. He sat down on it and thought to himself that it wasn't any worse than where he'd been sleeping on the cold floor of the old cabin outside of Goldsboro. He took off his clothes and pulled on the prison uniform. The shirt was a little baggy, but it would do. The pants fit loosely around his waist, but he was able to sinch it up with a piece of cord that he'd been provided. He put on the jacket and the hat, placed his regular clothes in the burlap bag, walked outside, and waited with the others.

"Alright now, listen up. I'm Corporal Collins. I'm the walking boss for this barracks. Private Haggard and Private Allen work with me. They're out now with the other inmates from barracks four, but you'll meet them later. The three of us are responsible for keeping an eye on you when you're working. Mind your business, keep your mouth shut, and do your job, and we won't have any problems. You saw Charlie when you were inside. Charlie's too old for heavy work, so he's responsible for the upkeep of the barracks. If somethings broke or you need something, you go to Charlie, and he'll take care of it, and if he doesn't, you go and talk to Clayman Hill."

"Barracks four has two main jobs: digging the tunnel and cutting timber. Most of you will be working in the tunnel, but some of you will be on the timber detail. For those working in the tunnel, there are several different jobs you might do. We have teams of two who use a pike and a sledgehammer to make the holes for the Nitro Mash we use to blast the rock. Some pour the

Nitro Mash and load the fuses, but that takes some training, so you won't have to worry about that at first. Most of you will be working on extracting the rock. After the blast area has cleared, the rock fragments are loaded into buckets, carried out, dumped into wagons, and hauled away. The timber detail is mostly responsible for cutting the ties that will be used when we start laying rail and for what we need now to brace inside the tunnel. It also involves cutting the wood we burn here in the camp. In the morning, each of you will be paired up with another inmate who's been here a while who'll show you the ropes. Does anybody have any questions?" The guard paused for a few seconds and added, "and don't be afraid to ask a question, I promise I'm not going to club you or anything."

One of the inmates raised his hand. "Bossman, what do we do about food?"

"Right. That's a good question. Breakfast is just after sunup and dinner is just before dusk. When you hear the dinner bell ring, you line up at the door at the kitchen and wait for one of the girls to hand you a plate and you take it over to the chow hall to eat. Lunch will be brought out to the worksite. Anything else?"

No one responded.

"Alright then. You boys are dismissed. You're free to go back inside the barracks or you can mill about out here in the yard until dinner time. But let me remind you of what Major Warren said. If you try to make a run for it, you'll be shot, so I don't recommend you try."

That was the third time that day Tobias was reminded that he'd be shot if he tried to escape. He figured his best bet was to make do as best he could and hope to leave the mountains upright and as a free man come next March.

Most of the sixteen new inmates, including Tobias, chose to stay in the yard. Even though they'd spent a considerable amount of time together on the train and in the wagons on their way to the Swannanoa Tunnel camp, they hadn't had a chance to get to know one another, so they took turns introducing themselves. Eventually, it was Tobias's turn.

"I'm Tobias Wilson. Me and my mama lived down in Goldsboro, or at least we did until mama died a few months back. We lived in a little place where mama worked, and I got kicked out of it after she passed. I'd been working as a farm hand, but I lost my job when I had to stay home and take care of mama after she took sick. I'd been doing whatever I could to make do, and I'd planned to go back to working on a farm here soon when it turns spring. But the sheriff come and snatched me up, charged me with vagrancy, and the judge gave me twelve months, so here I am. I just want to keep my head down, do my time, get the hell out of here, and head up north where I hear folk like us fare a lot better than we do down here in this sorry-assed state."

The others all had similar stories: arrested, charged and convicted of some petty crime, and shipped off to the North Carolina mountains to build Governor Vance's railroad. With just a couple of exceptions, the men were all young and had little if any family to speak of. They all had the same goal: To survive and leave the mountains in one piece. They got the message from seeing the inmate who asked a question and was clubbed: It doesn't pay to be a smart ass.

Soon, the inmates and guards returned to the camp from the tunnel worksite. With the arrival of Tobias and the fifteen other new inmates, there were now one hundred and ten inmates at the Swannanoa Tunnel stockade.

A short time later, the dinner bell rang, and the inmates began to line up. When Tobias made his way to the front of the line, the young female inmate who had handed him his uniform earlier handed him his plate. He looked up at her and smiled. "Thank you, ma'am. And that uniform you gave me earlier fits me just fine." She looked at him, forced a little smile, and said, "Glad to hear it."

Tobias carried his plate to the chow hall and took a seat on a long bench next to one of the new inmates who was assigned to barracks four. Dinner consisted of beans, cabbage, and cornbread. It wasn't much, but Tobias thought to himself that it was the best meal he'd eaten in the weeks since he had to leave the boarding house. The State of North Carolina allocated six cents per day per inmate for rations, so meals were strictly no frills. Beans and cornbread were staples, often augmented with cabbage, potatoes, or corn. Every week or so there might be a little bit of pork or chicken. On special occasions, if a guard managed to shoot a deer, some venison might make its way onto the menu.

The bed wasn't exactly what Tobias would call comfortable, but it had been a long day, and the room was nice and toasty, so he fell asleep in a matter of seconds despite the irritating sound of snoring echoing throughout the barracks. It only seemed like he'd been asleep for a few minutes when he heard Corporal Coggin's voice yelling, "come on boys, it's time to get up and get started." Tobias noticed that the darkness was beginning to give way to the light, and he realized that while it seemed like he hadn't slept long, he'd managed to sleep for several hours. He sat up on the side of his bunk, rubbed his eyes and yawned, put on his boots, stood up, and stretched. All things considered, he felt pretty good.

Breakfast was beans and biscuits. As he was finishing up, a guard announced that they'd be leaving for the tunnel in twenty minutes, so tend to whatever needed tending to and prepare to head out. Tobias walked down to one of the latrines. Four of the eight seats were already taken, and Tobias chose an empty slot down at the end. There was no talking in the latrine, but that's not to say it was quiet; you might say the sound was reminiscent of a thunderstorm rolling through the valley, just not quite as romantic. When he was done, there was no paper or towels to wipe his ass, just a wad of corn husks.

Tobias went back to the barracks, grabbed his coat and hat, and made his way to the yard to wait for the group to depart. As he stood there, he looked over towards the kitchen. The young female inmate he spoke to earlier was standing at the doorway. While she was slight in stature, she had perfectly sculpted features and supple skin the color of chestnuts. Her hair was wrapped up in a kerchief, and her eyes were strong and focused. To Tobias, she was a contradiction. On one hand, she reminded him of his dear mother. On the other hand, she was sultry and exquisite. She happened to glance up at the same time and she saw Tobias looking at her. She smiled at him for a second, then turned and walked back inside. Tobias sensed that it felt like his heart might have skipped a beat.

Tobias was assigned to one of the teams that carved holes in the rock where the Nitro Mash mixture was inserted. An inmate who appeared to be about thirty with arms like piledrivers was given the task of training Tobias.

"What's your name," he asked.

"Tobias. What's yours?"

"I'm Henry. So, Tobias, this job ain't complicated. One of us holds the pike. The other one pounds it with the sledgehammer. And we keep pounding away until we've made a hole about two feet deep. And then we move a few feet down the line and we do it again."

141

Henry grabbed the sledgehammer and pointed at the pike. "Take that, and let's go."

Tobias picked up the iron pike – it was heavier than he had expected – and followed Henry into the tunnel.

They walked several hundred feet inside. Tobias could smell the kerosene from the lanterns hung along the walls to illuminate the area, which otherwise would have been pitch dark at that depth. Other inmates were using sledgehammers and picks to bust big rocks into smaller ones, and the smaller rocks were shoveled into buckets that inmates carried them two at a time back to the entrance where they emptied them into wagons to be hauled away.

When they got to the face of the tunnel, another team was punching holes on the lefthand side, so Henry said they'd work on the righthand side. He instructed Tobias on where to place the pike and how to hold it, and then he raised the sledgehammer over his head and brought it down hard. Tobias wasn't expecting the strong vibration the blow generated, and he let go of the pike and it fell to the ground with a clatter. Henry shook his head. "Come on now. Hold that thing tight. It ain't going to bite you, boy." Henry swung the sledgehammer eight to ten times per minute and in less than fifteen minutes they'd made a hole of sufficient depth and were ready to start on the next one. "Okay. Now it's your turn to swing the hammer," Henry said as he handed the sledgehammer to Tobias, picked up the pike, and moved into position. "But you better make damn sure you hit the pike and not me, or you'll be begging Major Warren to put you in the hole so I can't get to you and rip your damn head off."

By late morning, the loose rock remaining from the day before had been removed and the holes were punched for another round of blasting. Tobias stood outside in the sunlight with the others and before long he heard the shout, "fire in the hole!" as the fuse was lit. A minute later, he heard the rumble from within the tunnel and he felt the ground shake beneath his feet.

Seconds later, a cloud of dust and smoke came billowing out of the tunnel opening. Everyone stood around waiting for the dust to clear until one of the guards yelled, "it's cleared up enough, you boys get back in there," and everyone returned to work.

The guards called for a lunch break shortly after noon. Tobias walked outside and got in line with the others for his meal. When he reached the front of the line, the young woman he had admired before was handing out metal cannisters containing beans and a biscuit.

"Nice to see you again, Miss ..." Tobias said inquisitively, hoping it might allow him to discover her name.

"Addie. Addie Green," she said. "And you?"

"Tobias Wilson. I'd say it's a pleasure to see you again, Miss Green, but given the circumstances, pleasure probably isn't the right word for me to use."

She smiled. "I agree, Mister Wilson."

Tobias spent the rest of the day shoveling rocks into buckets to be carried out of the tunnel and hauled away. By the time the guards told everyone to pack up and head back to the camp at the end of the day, he was exhausted.

At dinner, Tobias couldn't talk with Addie, but they did see each other from a distance and exchanged glances and smiles. After dinner, Charlie, the old man who tended to barracks number four, and two other inmates brought out a banjo, a fiddle, and a harmonica, and most of the camp gathered around a fire in the middle of the yard to listen to the trio play and sing. When it was time for bed, Tobias's head barely hit the pillow before he was sound asleep.

The next day, it was more of the same. Tobias spent the morning shoveling loose rock to clear the tunnel, and then he and Henry returned to punching holes for another round of blasting.

Everyone cleared out of the tunnel in mid-afternoon, the fuse was lit, and an explosion shook the ground. Then, once the air cleared, it was back inside to excavate the loose rock.

Tobias and Henry worked near the face of the tunnel. It was Tobias's second day, and he could see that they had progressed just a couple of feet since he first started. Henry stepped to the left side of the tunnel where several boulders were jammed in place holding back the loose rocks trapped behind them. He grabbed a long metal pry bar, placed it between the two largest pieces in the center of stack, and pulled back to try and break them loose. When the pieces suddenly shifted, Henry fell to the ground just as the entire pile tumbled forward with a loud rumble and generated a cloud of dust. Tobias rushed over to try and pull Henry to safety. Just as he grabbed one of Henry's arms and was about to pull him to safety, a boulder crashed down on Henry's chest with a sickening thud, and then it rolled forward and knocked Tobias backwards and pinned him against the wall. Several inmates raced over to Tobias, pushed the boulder away from him, and freed him.

Tobias stood up. His right arm ached. He could see that the boulder had torn his skin, and he was bleeding a bit, but nothing seemed to be broken. He looked over at Henry. A couple of inmates were kneeling over him, and it was apparent that Henry was dead, his chest crushed by the weight of the falling boulder. A guard arrived and instructed the inmates to carry Henry outside. He looked at Tobias, saw the blood running down his arm, and told him to head back to the camp and have one of the female inmates bandage him up until he could see the doctor who traveled daily between the camps and would arrive later in the day.

Addie took a wet rag and wiped the blood off Tobias's arm. The wound didn't appear to be too deep. Once she had cleaned it, she wrapped a clean strip of cloth around it and tied the ends in a knot to hold it in place.

"You're lucky you weren't hurt worse. In the time I've been here, I've seen men lose limbs and break bones. And the guards don't care. They get more upset when a piece of equipment breaks than when a man gets hurt."

"I was lucky," Tobias said. "Henry wasn't. The same rock that hit me killed him. It just squashed him like a bug. One second, he was there, and the next second he was gone."

"Well, he wasn't the first one to die in the tunnel and I guarantee you he won't be the last," Addie said as she rolled Tobias's sleeve back down. "You be careful. A lot of men have died and a lot more will trying to dig through this mountain. Don't you go and be one of them."

Addie made a sling from a long piece of cloth, draped it over Tobias's shoulder, and helped him position his arm in it. "The doctor will be around shortly and can take a closer look. You take it easy until then."

Tobias walked back up to the tunnel. A short distance from the entrance, off to the side of the path leading back to the camp, Clayman Hill and a couple of inmates had dug a hole in the ground and were about to place Henry's body in it. Tobias walked over and watched them lower Henry into the crude grave. He removed his hat and stood there as they began shoveling dirt on top of Henry's body. There was no service, no prayer, no mourners, and no marker. In the grand scheme of things, Henry's death hadn't been anything more than a momentary inconvenience. As soon as the last shovel of dirt was tamped down, Clayman Hill looked at the group assembled by Henry's grave and said, "okay now, there's nothing more we can do. Let's get back to work." Tobias put his hat back on and walked away, wondering if Henry had a family or anyone who cared about him who might be heartbroken to know that he lost his life in the Swannanoa Tunnel.

The months ticked by, and Tobias kept toiling away. He had heeded the advice he got the day he arrived on the train: he kept his head down, his mouth shut, and he did as he was told. Nearly a year passed. In some respects, it seemed like it had only been a few weeks. In others, it seemed like he had been there for all of eternity. In any event, Tobias would be free to leave soon, free to head up north where he could start a new life, he hoped, far from the injustice and inhumanity he'd experienced in the divided North Carolina. Once again, he sensed there was light at the end of the tunnel. All he had to do was stay safe and out of trouble for just a few more days, and then it was on to begin a new life.

March 11, 1879, was a Tuesday. Tobias had six days to go until he was released. Some of the other inmates had started to call him "short timer." That morning, Old Charlie said, "hey, short timer, this here be your last Tuesday in this hell hole. If you want, I can talk to the major and see if he'd be willing to extend your stay." Tobias laughed. "No thanks, Charlie, I'm happy to give up my bed to the next young fellow who gets the privilege of working on Mister Vance's railroad."

That morning, Tobias and another inmate punched the last hole for what would prove to be the final blast in the Swannanoa Tunnel. When the dust cleared and the inmates went back inside the tunnel, they found that they had carved clear through and, low and behold, the two halves of the tunnel married up perfectly. It had been a gamble for sure, but crews working from both ends somehow managed to meet up right dab in the middle. At long last, the inmates had carved out one-thousand-eight-hundred-and-thirty-two feet of stone and created a passage right through the mountain. James Wilson, Major Warren, and the engineer James Cambar all came to see this historic achievement. Wilson rushed back to his office and fired off a telegram to

Senator Vance: "Daylight entered Buncombe County this morning through the Swannanoa Tunnel." When it reached the senator's office in Washington, Senator Vance read it, leaned back in his big chair, and smiled. It had been a long time coming, but soon trains would be rolling up the mountainside and into Asheville.

Tobias looked forward to leaving, but he was glad he was there to see the two ends of the tunnel connect. He had worked hard the past year. He had seen men get hurt and he had seen men die to make it happen. On paper, it may look like the twenty-three miles of railroad between Old Fort and Asheville didn't cost all that much, but Tobias and the other inmates who were forced to build it knew the true cost; an astronomical cost paid with their blood, sweat, and tears, and with the lives of many more like them left behind in unmarked graves to rest for eternity all along the railway's path.

There was still a lot of work to do, including work on six other tunnels. The first train wouldn't pass through the Swannanoa Tunnel until October 3, 1880, more than a year and a half later and some thirty-five years after the drought of 1845 called attention to the urgent need to extend rail service to the mountains.

A short time after the two halves of the tunnel were joined together, the celebratory mood ended, and the arduous work resumed. Tobias joined the bucket line carrying buckets of loose rocks outside to the wagons to be hauled away. He had just made his fifth trip out, dumped his buckets, and had turned to walk back to the tunnel when he paused for a moment to wipe the sweat and dust off his face. A second later, he heard a loud rumble and felt the ground tremble beneath his feet, and then a cloud of dust came billowing out of the tunnel's entrance.

147

"Cave in! Cave in!" screamed a guard as he ran towards the tunnel. Tobias and the others went back inside as soon as the rumbling stopped and the dust cleared, and they began pulling away the rocks that had come crashing down when the roof of the tunnel collapsed at the point where the two halves of the tunnel met. They worked all afternoon, through the night, and until the next morning to free those who were trapped in the debris and to recover the bodies of those who had been crushed to death. Twenty-one men died, including one guard, the highest single day death toll in the history of the Western North Carolina Railroad, eclipsing the nineteen deaths that occurred in December 1882 when a boat carrying nineteen inmates who were shackled together capsized as they tried to cross the Tuckasegee River west of Asheville. Fourteen inmates sustained injuries, six of them serious enough that they had to be evacuated for treatment and never returned to the Swannanoa Tunnel stockade. Inmates dug a large hole not far from where they buried Henry the year before, and the twenty dead inmates were buried together in a mass grave. The body of the dead guard was placed in a rough-hewn coffin and sent home to his family for a proper Christian burial.

The mood in the camp was depressed the remainder of the week. Even Tobias, who was set to be released on Monday, found little comfort in the fact that his freedom was just around the corner. Saturday night was normally the most boisterous night of the week in the camp. The workday ended early on Saturdays and inmates got a bath and fresh uniforms. After dinner, the musical instruments came out and it was an evening of singing and joking and telling lies. Not this Saturday night. The fiddle player died in the cave-in and the banjo player suffered a broken arm. Old Charlie played his harmonica, but it was mournful rather than raucous. Tobias went to bed that night thinking that when he woke up on Sunday, he was just three meals away from leaving the Blue Ridge Mountains and never coming back.

"Well, it's your last day here and it's a Sunday, so you can just lay around and think about what you're going to do tomorrow and the day after that once you're a free man," Addie said as she handed Tobias his breakfast.

Tobias gave her a faint smile. "Won't be much I miss about this place … except for your cooking and your smiling face. I will most truly miss that."

He took his plate to the chow hall, and he chose a spot where he could be alone. As he sat there and ate, a couple of inmates paused briefly as they walked past to slap him on the back and comment on his "short timer" status. After breakfast, he went back to his bunk. He tried to take a nap, but he kept thinking about what he was going to do after he was released. He didn't really have a plan, other than to get out of North Carolina and to head up north. He also thought about Addie. Her kindness was about the only bright spot there was in his memories of his year at the Swannanoa Tunnel stockade. She was due to be released soon too, and Tobias wondered if she might allow him to stay in touch with her after they were both freed. Breakfast was over and he knew that she would be in the kitchen preparing for lunch, and he decided it would be one of his last opportunities to talk with her before he got his freedom.

Tobias walked around to the backside of the kitchen building intending to knock on the door. He saw Addie standing out back at a waist-high wooden table peeling potatoes. As Tobias started to walk towards her, a guard came around the other side of the building, walked up behind Addie, and slid his hand up the back of her skirt. Addie spun around instantly and plunged the knife she was using to peel potatoes deep into his stomach. She pulled the knife out and then plunged it into his chest, and the guard fell to his knees and then slumped over face first onto the ground. Addie stood over him for a moment, and then she began to tremble and cry.

149

Tobias ran to Addie and grabbed her by the shoulders with both of his hands. "Are you okay?"

"I don't know. He was drunk and he'd tried messing with me before breakfast, but one of the other guards pulled him away. And then now, he came back and started up again, and I just snapped. What am I going to do? They're going to hang me for this."

Tobias thought for a second. His mind instantly raced back to the time when Mister Cohen accosted his mother, and he was too young and too small to do anything about it. Well, that was then. He was a fully grown man now. He couldn't do anything to help his mother back then, but this time he was determined to see the wrong set right. He wasn't going to stand by and see another decent black woman suffer for a deviant white man's drunken transgressions.

"You're not going to do anything. Wash that blood off your hands and go back inside the kitchen and act like nothing happened. I'm going to take care of this." Tobias reached down and picked up the knife off the ground. "You take care of yourself, Miss Addie. You finish up your time and then get on out of here and enjoy your freedom. Don't you ever tell a living soul what happened here today. I've got this." And then Tobias turned, walked around the corner of the kitchen building, paused for a moment as he looked back one last time at Addie, and then he ran across the yard with the bloody knife in his hand. "I killed that asshole," he yelled as he ran towards the entrance to the tunnel. For a moment, the inmates and the guards were stunned and didn't know what to think or what to do.

It was just a couple of minutes before a guard discovered the lifeless body of Private Biggers face down behind the kitchen in a pool of blood. Major Warren ordered Private Haggard and Private Allen to go after Tobias. "I don't care if you bring the son of a bitch back dead or alive, just bring him back to teach the others a lesson." Haggard and Allen drew shotguns from the armory, saddled up two horses, and set out after Tobias.

Tobias ran through the tunnel and emerged through the western entrance. He kept going west following the path of the Swannanoa River. He ran for as long as he could run and when he couldn't run any more, he walked. He finally stopped to rest when he reached the spot where Bull Creek merges into the river. As he sat there, it occurred to him that he had no idea what he was going to do or where he was going to go. For that matter, he had no idea where he was. He had planned to escape and to draw attention away from Addie, but he had no plan whatsoever beyond that. He knew that he wouldn't be safe until he was far away from the Blue Ridge Mountains. As he pondered what to do next, he heard horses off in the distance behind him. He decided it was time to change course, so he left the river and headed north along the eastern bank of Bull Creek.

Private Haggard and Private Allen saw footprints in the sand by the river that turned north and seemed to follow along beside the creek. "You cross over the creek and come up on that side and I'll keep going up this side, and let's see if we can't hem him in down in the creek bed up ahead." They continued riding north knowing they weren't far behind their quarry.

Tobias knew that he couldn't outrun the guards who were on horseback. He decided his best chance to escape was to hide in hopes that they wouldn't see him, and they'd pass him by. There was a thick grove of rhododendrons up ahead on the eastern bank of the creek. He got down on his hands and knees and scurried inside. A large section of an otherwise healthy oak tree had broken off and fallen amongst the rhododendrons, a common occurrence that arborists can't explain called sudden limb failure or summer branch drop. Tobias slid behind it, stretched out flat on his back, and covered himself as best he could with twigs and leaves. He tried to control his breathing and to lay as still and as quiet as he could. Soon, he heard horses approaching over the steady rumble of the creek as it flowed nearby.

"Dole, you see anything over there?"

"No. How about you?"

"There were some tracks back there a little piece. It looks like he's still headed up this side of the creek. We've got to be close, so keep your eyes peeled."

A few seconds later, Private Allen saw a boot and the black and white stripes of prison uniform pants poking out from behind an oak log amidst the Rhododendrons. Tobias didn't know it, but his foot and the bottom part of his leg extended past the end of the tree branch, and it gave away his hiding spot.

"Hold on, Dole. Well, well, looky here at what I found," Allen said as he climbed down off his horse. "You might as well come on out of there boy and let's get this over with. We're supposed to whip you before we kill you, but if you make it easy on us, we'll spare you the whipping part and make it fast."

Tobias jumped to his feet, ran out of the brush and across the creek towards a big oak tree. As he got to the tree, Private Haggard stepped out from behind it and punched him in the face, knocking Tobias to the ground. "I got him, Robbie," Private Haggard yelled out and then he kicked Tobias twice in the ribs. Private Allen wrapped the reins of his horse around a Rhododendron and then he walked across the creek towards Tobias and stood over him. "You killed Biggers, you worthless piece of shit," he said as he stomped his boot hard into Tobias's stomach. "Major Warren said we could bring you back dead or alive, but it'll be easier to tote your ass back dead. Dole, go get your rope. We got ourselves a good hanging tree right here. We'll string him up and then we'll haul his dead ass back for the others to see."

152

Private Haggard turned to walk back to his horse and retrieve the rope that was draped over the butt of the shotgun that protruded above his saddle. He'd only taken two steps when suddenly a six-hundred-pound black bear came out of the woods, stood up on its hind legs, bared its teeth, and snarled in the most menacing fashion. "Shit! Robbie, it's a bear!" Both horses sensed the danger, pulled themselves free, and galloped away carrying the shotguns with them. Private Allen looked up, saw the bear, and yelled "run!" As Private Haggard and Private Allen ran towards the creek, the bear dropped down on all fours and chased after them. It passed within a foot of Tobias without giving him so much as a glance. Haggard and Allen scurried up the creekbank on the other side and ran back down towards the Swannanoa River with the bear in hot pursuit. A few seconds later, Tobias heard screams. He didn't stick around to find out what had caused it. He rose gingerly to his feet and leaned against the oak tree for a moment as blood from his nose and lip dripped onto the ground. When he regained his composure, he turned north and headed up Bull Creek.

Tobias Wilson was charged with the murder of Private Leon Biggers, but he was never apprehended and never convicted. Private Biggers's family got his body back for burial and collected the thirteen dollars in cash he was owed for a month's work as a prison guard, but they never got the justice they thought they deserved.

Addie Green completed her sentence a few weeks after Tobias left, and she went back home. She got married and had a family. She always wondered what happened to Tobias and she never forgot what he'd done for her. She never told a living soul that she was the one who killed

Private Biggers or that Tobias Wilson took the blame for it in order to spare her life. She'd remain grateful to him for as long as she lived.

Private Haggard sustained serious injuries when the bear raked its claws across his back and sunk its teeth into the flesh of his thigh and tore it away. If Private Allen hadn't stopped, grabbed a limb, and used it to poke the bear and turn it away, Haggard would have died. He was thankful to be alive, but he could no longer work as a prison guard and returned home where he started a small farm and eventually got married. For years thereafter, his children and then their children asked to see his scars and for him to tell them the story about the time he wrestled with a black bear alongside Bull Creek.

Zeb Vance finally got his railroad. He rode it in 1894 when a train carried his body back to Asheville for burial. As he'd predicted, the railroad brought growth and prosperity to Asheville and to the Swannanoa Valley.

Tobias Wilson made his way up north … all the way to Canada. After meandering about for a time, he settled in Ontario where he was able to put the expertise he developed working on the Swannanoa Tunnel to use. Nickle and cooper deposits were discovered in Ontario in 1883. Tobias got a job with a mining company drilling holes and setting explosives to extricate the ore. Hardly a day went by that he didn't think about Addie, and he often wondered how her life had turned out. He never knew that the oak tree from which he was almost hung was the product of the acorn that was watered by the blood of Thomas Williams and the mother bear almost a century before he was knocked flat on the ground next to it, or that the bear that came along and saved him from hanging was a descendant of the yearling that, like Tobias, had headed north up Bull Creek and never looked back.

Part Four – Oakwood Farm

When Kelli Halstrom left the embassy at ten o'clock for a morning meeting in Uhuru Park, the temperature was still in the low sixties, so she grabbed her jacket off a hook on the back of the door as she left her office. People tend to think that Africa is brutally hot, but that's not the case in Nairobi, the capital of Kenya, where at an elevation of nearly six thousand feet, high temperatures in August typically hover in the seventies. The population of Nairobi was just over two million in 1998, less than half the size it is today. Kelli reached her destination early, which gave her time to pop into a coffee shop for a cup of Kenyan coffee. When her coffee was ready, she took it, walked over to the park, and sat down on a bench to wait.

Brian Kirby arrived in Nairobi the day before. According to the travel itinerary attached to his visa, he was there for three days to look at potential sites for an American corporation that was interested in setting up an office in Kenya, so meeting with an economic development officer from the U.S. Embassy wasn't anything that would arouse suspicion. Brian was in his late fifties, and he was just beginning to get a touch of gray around the edges of his brown hair. He was dressed in slacks, a sport coat, and a shirt with an open collar. There was nothing remarkable about his appearance that would set him apart from the scores of other westerners who came and went regularly in and out of Nairobi.

"Good morning, Kelli," he said as he approached the park bench where she was sitting.

"Good morning to you, Brian," she said as she stood up and gave him a hug. "I haven't heard from you in a long time, and I was beginning to think Langley had forgotten about us."

Brian – who Kelli knew as Max Schauer back when he was a field agent and operating under deep cover – smiled. "Never in a million years. We just wanted to make sure that you and Andy had a nice long break after your last job. That was a big one and it generated a lot of

155

chatter among our friends. We don't want anyone getting suspicious of two of our best, so we thought we'd let things settle down a bit before we called on you again."

"Alright," she replied. "I think Andy enjoys the diplomatic stuff he's doing, and it keeps him busy, but to be honest, I'm starting to get bored. I'm ready for a new challenge and I'm sure he will be too whenever you decide to tap us again."

"Well then, you're in luck. Here's a thumb drive with information on your next target. There's no intel suggesting that he's planning anything in the immediate future, so it's not urgent. We have intercepts indicating a couple of places where he's likely to be over the next few months, so you guys decide where you think it's best to make the approach, preferably some place where disposal won't be a problem, and you can get in and out without exposing yourselves to too much risk."

Kelli took the thumb drive and slipped it into her jacket pocket. "Okay. We'll check it out and come up with a plan, and then we'll forward it up to you to review, and we'll wait until you give us a green light before we proceed. But let me ask you something, Brian. Why did you travel all the way out here to give me this? You could have had it delivered to us without having to travel all the way from Langley to Nairobi."

"I know," he said and then he paused for several seconds. "The boss wanted me to lay eyes on you and make sure you're okay before saddling you with another job. You know Director Neal feels like he has a personal stake in you and Andy. You really put yourself out there on the last job, and we were worried that you might need some more time to recover before we throw you back in the game. Listen, you and Andy have done great work, you always have, and you need to know that you can tap out at any time with no regrets. You've put your necks on the line plenty of times and there's no shame in saying enough is enough and letting someone else step up and take their turn. You don't owe us anything, so when you decide the time is right, all you have to do is say so and you can walk away knowing you've done more for your country than anyone will ever know. Director Neal wanted to make sure that you understood that you've done your duty and that it's entirely up to you and Andy to decide when it's time to say no mas."

"I appreciate that, and I know that Andy will too. I'm forty-four and Andy's forty-five, so we've still got some good years ahead of us, but you're right that a time will come when it's best for us to step aside, but that time isn't right now. Tell Director Neal thank you for us and let him know that we're still good to go for a while longer."

As Kelli was about to say goodbye to Brian, an explosion boomed a short distance away and the ground trembled. "What in the hell was that?" she said as she glanced at her watch and saw that it was half past ten.

"I don't know, but from the sound of it, it's not likely to be anything good. You'd better get back to the embassy and I'm going back to my hotel. I've got meetings this afternoon to look at properties to maintain my cover, which should be exciting. I'm flying home tomorrow night, and I'll be back in my office on Monday. Let me know if you need anything."

Brian stood up and gave Kelli a hug. "It's great to see you, Kelli. Give my best to Andy." They both turned and went their separate ways.

Andrew Halstrom, who everyone called Andy, fell in love with Kelli McArthur in 1980 when they were students at the Defense Language Institute in Monterey, California. They were both captains in the U.S. Army, and they were classmates in a year-long Arabic language course. Andy had worked on the Middle East desk at the Defense Intelligence Agency on the banks of the Potomac River in Washington when he was selected to attend the language school. Kelli was an intelligence officer at U.S. Central Command located on MacDill Air Force Base in Tampa, Florida, when she was chosen to go to the language school as well. They had met briefly once before at a social gathering during a conference they'd attended, but they really didn't get to know each other well until they arrived in Monterey.

On the first day of class, when Andy saw Kelli walk into the room, he remembered that they had met at a conference the year before. He remembered her distinctly because she was stunningly beautiful. There weren't many female officers in the Army in 1980, and a rare few were as drop-dead gorgeous as Kelli McArthur. She had short brown hair that came down to the top of her collar. Andy recalled staring at her that first day in class and thinking to himself that the statement, "this woman has the perfect nose," was a thought that had never occurred to him before until that morning, and it was true. Plus, Kelli had full lips and the most radiant smile he'd ever seen. Even in unflattering Army fatigues, it was clear that she was in excellent physical condition and had a knockout figure. Captain Kelli McArthur was one of the most exquisite women Andy Halstrom had ever seen, and he was dwelling on that thought when he realized the instructor was calling his name. "Captain Halstrom. Captain Halstrom, are you having some sort of medical issue? You look like you're in a trance. How about you rejoin us here in the real world and stand up and introduce yourself to the class." Andy's face turned beet red with embarrassment, which was made even worse when he noticed that Kelli was laughing at him.

At the end of the first week, Andy worked up the courage to approach Kelli and ask her if she would be interested in going out to dinner with him. When she said yes, he had to make a conscious effort to contain his excitement and avoid appearing overly eager.

Kelli had taken notice of Andy as well and she thought he was quite handsome. Andy was over six feet tall and in excellent physical condition. He had been a running back on his college football team, although he never was a starter except on special teams. After he joined the Army, he continued his daily workouts. He was an avid runner and cyclist, and he competed in triathlons as often as he could. He had dark brown hair that was cut short, which gave away the fact that he was in the military, even when he was out of uniform. When he first joined the Army, Andy had a mustache. Every morning at the start of Officer Training School, his drill instructor told him his mustache was not in compliance with Army regulations and needed to be trimmed it in closer so that the outer edges didn't extend beyond the corners of his mouth. Every morning, Andy brought the sides of his mustache in a little bit further, but it was never enough to pass muster, and by the end of the week he looked in the mirror and realized that his mustache was beginning to make him look like Adolph Hitler. He breathed out a heavy sigh of dejected resignation knowing that his stache had to go. He shaved it off and he never grew it back.

Their first date was on a Saturday night. Andy picked Kelli up at her apartment and they went out for pizza and beer. Andy was surprised by how easy it was to talk with Kelli. It was like they'd known each other for years and they were entirely comfortable in each other's presence. They talked about their Army careers and their future ambitions. They found that they had a lot in common: Both of them had lost their parents, had no siblings, and neither one had any real close family to speak of. They were both into athletics and the outdoors, and they both considered themselves to be loners who tended to look after themselves rather than relying on others. When they finished eating, they decided to go to a nearby bar.

Thanks to the John Travolta and Debra Winger movie, Urban Cowboy, which had come out a few months before Andy and Kelli got to Monterey, country music and line dancing had become hugely popular. Andy wasn't keen on dancing, but he obliged, and he managed not to embarrass himself or Kelli, well at least not too much. Truth be told, he found that he really enjoyed dancing when the band played a slow song, and he got to hold Kelli's body close to his. He could feel her warm breath on his neck and the sweet botanical fragrance of the Herbal Essence shampoo she'd used to wash her hair. It made him think that the Army selecting him to attend the language school might have been the best thing the Army had ever done for him, and he was grateful.

Kelli goaded Andy to ride the mechanical bull that occupied a corner of the barroom, and after she "double-dog dared" him, he had no choice but to mount up. When his turn came, he climbed on, gripped the saddle horn with his right hand and lashed it tight with a leather strap, dug in his heels, and gave a nod to the guy who worked the controls. Two seconds later, he picked himself up off the rubber mat that softened the blow when he flew off the bull and landed flat on his back. Kelli laughed and gave him a hug when he walked over to her, his head hung down in shame. Now it was her turn. She climbed on, let out a deep breath, and yelled "go!" The guy operating the controls was easier on her than he'd been on Andy, and after she'd been on the bull for seven or eight seconds, Kelli let go of the saddle horn, leaned back, and replicated the sensual bull ride Debra Winger did in Urban Cowboy to try and make John Travolta jealous. The crowd, particularly the guys, clapped and hooted in delight. After a few seconds, Kelli spun around, hopped off, and totally nailed the dismount. As the crowd clapped and cheered, she ran over to Andy, threw her arms around his neck, and kissed him. Andy thought that at that moment, he was the luckiest man on planet earth.

They had dinner together two nights later and again a couple of nights after that. It wasn't long until they were spending nearly all their free time together, and by Thanksgiving they were sleeping together most nights. Andy knew that at some point they'd finish school, and then the Army would give them assignments, and they would go their separate ways. He dreaded the thought of it. This was the happiest he had ever been, and he had to find a way to make sure it would never end.

One Saturday evening in early December, Andy and Kelli went out to a club where Roger McGuinn and Chris Hillman were playing. When the band took a break between sets, Andy and Kelli went to the bar to order a round of beers. As they waited for the bartender to return, a couple about their age stood next to them and waited as well.

"I hadn't heard Roger and Chris play since Gene Clark left the group. I think they sound just as good, maybe better, without him."

Andy looked over at the guy standing next to him and nodded. "I never got to see them in-person back when it was McGuinn, Clark, and Hillman, so I don't know," Andy said. "They sound pretty good to me now as a duo."

"I agree." The man stuck out his hand. "I'm Alex and this is my girlfriend, Kris. Pleased to meet you."

Andy shook his hand, nodded at Kris, and said, "I'm Andy and this is Kelli."

After the four of them got their beers, they stood and talked for a few minutes. Alex and Kristen said they were originally from Canada, but they had lived and worked in California for several years. Alex said he worked for a company that managed commercial properties and Kris said she was a technician in a medical practice. They asked Andy and Kelli what they did, and Andy said they were both in the Army and they were in Monterey attending language school. As the band came out for the second set, the two couples got ready to return to their seats.

"It was a real pleasure to meet you. I hope we see you again sometime," Alex said as he shook Andy's hand.

"Likewise," Andy replied.

Andy had dated other women in college and after he joined the Army, but none of them ever made him feel the way he felt when he was around Kelli McArthur. The more time they spent together, the more he knew that she was the one he wanted to spend the rest of his life with. They occasionally joked that at times they acted like they were an old married couple, but they never had a serious discussion about becoming a real married couple. Army life isn't easy, even less so for married couples when both are serving on active duty, but other couples managed to do it and make it work, and Andy believed that he and Kelli could make it work too. Now he just had to summon up the courage to ask her to marry him, and he knew he had to do it sooner rather than later since they'd complete their course in a few months and leave for follow-on assignments. Time was of the essence and the clock was starting to tick fast.

In the early part of 1981, several weeks after they had passed the halfway point of their year-long course, Andy was summoned to the Commandant's office. After a short wait, the administrative assistant said the Commandant was ready to see him. Andy walked into the Commandant's office, stood at attention, saluted, and said, "Sir, Captain Halstrom reporting as ordered." Colonel John Tomosky looked up from a stack of correspondence he was signing, returned the salute, and told Andy to stand at ease.

"Captain Halstrom, I've received information that you've had contact with foreign nationals, and you failed to report it. As you know, students at the school are prime targets for our foreign adversaries, and we remind students constantly to stay alert for potential approaches that might be a first step in an adversary's effort to cultivate a student as an intelligence asset and of the obligation to report any contacts with foreign nationals. You're going to need to answer some questions before I decide whether you should continue in your course or be disenrolled from the school. You're going to go with these folks," Colonel Tomosky said as he gestured towards two people standing in the doorway behind Andy, "and I encourage you to cooperate with them so we can get this resolved quickly. Do you understand?"

"Yes, Sir," Andy replied.

"Very well then. You're dismissed," Colonel Tomosky said, then saluted, and returned to signing correspondence.

"Yes, Sir." Andy saluted, did an about-face, and walked out of the Commandant's office followed by the two people who were waiting to question him.

The two people, a man and a woman dressed in civilian attire who appeared to be in their late twenties, looked solemn. The woman – who was African-American, had creamy caramel skin, and close-cut black hair that suggested she was in the military – told Andy to follow her, and she led him out of the Commandant's suite and down the hall to a small room where there was a narrow table with a single metal chair sitting on one side and two metal chairs with arms sitting on the opposite side. Andy was instructed to take a seat in the single chair and then the woman and the man took seats across the table from him.

"I'm Special Agent Valerie Bronson, and this is Special Agent Dennis Allen." The agents pulled out small leather wallets from their inside jacket pockets and showed Andy their badges and credentials. "We're from the Army Criminal Investigation Division, and as Colonel Tomosky told you, we're investigating whether you failed to report contacts with foreign nationals. Before we ask you any questions, I'm required to advise you of your rights under Article Thirty-One of the Uniform Code of Military Justice. I advise you that under the

163

provisions of Article Thirty-One, you have the right to remain silent, that is, you have the right to say nothing at all. Any statement you make, whether it's oral or written, may be used as evidence against you in a trial by court-martial or in other judicial or administrative proceedings. You have the right to consult a lawyer and to have a lawyer present during this interview. You have the right to military legal counsel free of charge. In addition to military counsel, you are entitled to civilian counsel of your own choosing, but that would be at your own expense. You can request a lawyer at any time during this interview. If you decide to answer questions, you can stop the questioning at any time. Do you understand your rights?"

"Yes, I do."

"Do you want a lawyer?"

Andy paused. His mind raced as he thought to himself, "what in the hell have I done?" He rubbed his sweaty palms on his thighs and looked down at the table. When he looked up, he said, "No, I don't want a lawyer."

"Good. And are you willing to answer some questions for us?"

"Yes, I am."

Agent Allen – who had pale white skin, an abundance of freckles, and short red hair – took a piece of paper out of a folder, laid a pen on it, and slid it across the table to Andy. "This form documents that you were advised of your rights, and you chose to waive them. Initial here and here and then sign and date it at the bottom."

Andy skimmed the document quickly, added his initials and signature, and slid it back across the table to Agent Allen, who picked it up and returned it to the folder. Andy thought to himself that Agent Allen's hand and the white sheet of paper were an exact color match, and then he thought "why in the hell am I thinking about trivial shit like that at a time like this."

"We received information that in the past couple of months you and Captain McArthur were observed with individuals we believe are agents of a foreign intelligence service. Our colleagues are questioning Captain McArthur right now in another room and she's told them that you met a couple named Alexander and Kristen at a bar, that you saw them a few times after that and had drinks with them, and that you went out to dinner with them last week. Is that true?" Agent Bronson leaned back in her chair and waited for Andy's response.

Andy thought to himself for several seconds. "Yes. We met Alex and Kris sometime before Christmas. After that, we bumped into them a few times when we were out in public, and we chatted and had drinks, and not long ago they asked us to go out to dinner, which we did four or five nights ago. They've never said or done anything that seemed out of the ordinary. They seem like nice, ordinary people. I have no reason to believe that they're a couple of spies or anything of that nature."

Agent Allen asked, "did you know they're foreigners and, if so, why didn't you report the contact as you're required to do?"

"No. They said they were originally from Canada, but they immigrated to the States several years ago. I never had any reason to suspect they were anything other than residents or citizens – whatever the proper term is – of this country. I never had any reason to think that there was anything I needed to report."

"They were identified by a reliable source as Russian intelligence agents who were sent here to develop and recruit assets the Russian government could exploit in the future, and that students at the language institute are of particular interest to them. Can't you see how you and Captain McArthur would be attractive targets for them?" Agent Allen asked.

"I never really thought about it," Andy responded. "I understand that students here could be considered valuable intelligence assets, but I just never had any reason to suspect Alex and Kris were trying to recruit us for anything other than as friends."

For nearly an hour, Agents Bronson and Allen pressed Andy on the details of each meeting he and Kelli had with Alex and Kris. Andy provided as much detail as he could, and he continued to deny that anything suspicious had ever occurred. Agent Bronson asked Andy if he needed to take a break, and he said no. She said she needed to take a break, and she instructed Andy not to leave the room until they returned. Agents Bronson and Allen stood up, walked out, and closed the door behind them.

As Andy sat there and waited, he thought to himself that his career in the Army might be over, and he worried that he could end up doing time in the stockade at Fort Leavenworth before the Army let him go. He worried about Kelli and how she was holding up. He knew she was tough, and he hoped she was doing okay.

Five minutes later, Agents Bronson and Allen returned. They took their seats, and they both looked squarely at Andy.

"Captain Halstrom," Agent Allen said, "you need to cut out the bullshit and start telling us the truth. Captain McArthur confessed. She admitted that she suspected Alex and Kristen were foreign intelligence officers all along, and that recently they started blackmailing her to cooperate with them by threatening the lives of her family members. At their behest, she said she's been working on you to try and find information they could use to coerce you into cooperating with them too. You've been dating a spy, Captain Halstrom. Your girlfriend is a traitor to you and to this country."

Andy had suspected that something wasn't right about Agents Bronson and Allen, and now he was convinced his suspicion was accurate. They said Alex and Kris were blackmailing Kelli by threatening her family, but he knew that Kelli, like him, didn't have any close family. That's why they stayed in Monterrey over the Christmas holiday while most of their classmates took leave to go home to visit their families. But why would Agents Bronson and Allen lie to him? What were they up to? Andy didn't know, but he decided he would play along with them a little bit longer and try to figure it out.

"That's not true. Captain McArthur is as dedicated to this country as anyone I've ever known. She'd never betray America, and she'd never betray me. So, if we're talking about cutting through the bullshit, why don't you start by telling me what you're up to? Why are you lying to me about Captain McArthur? Why are you trying to turn me against her?" Andy folded his arms across his chest, leaned back in his chair, and looked directly at Agents Bronson and Allen as he awaited an answer. When neither one responded, Andy leaned forward and slammed his hand on the table. "What the fuck are you up to? Why are you lying to me? What's up with this line of bullshit?"

Agent Allen pounded his fist on the desk. "Listen to me, Captain. You and your girlfriend are in some deep shit, and unless you drop this high and mighty act and start cooperating with us, it's going to get a lot worse. Now tell us the truth about Alex and Kris. This is your last chance, and I suggest you take it."

"Go fuck yourself. If you've got the evidence to arrest me, then arrest me, otherwise I'm walking out of here and you can both go to hell. I don't know what kind of game this is, but I'm through playing it." Andy stood up and took a step towards the door.

"Time out, time out!" Agent Bronson said as she stood up and put her palms out towards Andy to try and stop him and calm him down. "Please, please, just have a seat for a minute."

Andy stopped and looked at her. "Please, Captain Halstrom. Have a seat. We want to get this resolved as much as you do. Please, sit down and just give us a minute. Let's see if we can't get this all straightened out."

Andy walked back to his chair and sat down. "Okay. I'll give you a few minutes, but then I'm done."

"Thanks. Now, just hang tight for a little bit longer and we'll see if we can't wrap this up. Can you do that, please?" Agent Bronson asked.

"Yes. Like I said, I'll give you a few more minutes, but then I'm out of here," Andy responded.

"Good. We're going to step outside. It won't take long. I'm sure we can finish this up quickly, just give us a minute." Agents Bronson and Allen walked out of the room and closed the door behind them.

Andy sat there in silence for not more than ten minutes, which to him seemed like an eternity. Then the door opened, and Colonel Tomosky walked in. "Captain Halstrom, if you'd come with me, please. I know you're wondering what this is all about and you deserve some answers." They walked down the hall and back to Colonel Tomosky's office. When they entered, Colonel Tomosky closed the door. Seated at a small conference table off to the side of the room were Kelli and an African-American man in a suit who looked to be in his forties. He stood up and extended his hand to Andy.

"Captain Halstrom, it's a pleasure to finally meet you," he said as they shook hands. "Have a seat and I'll cut to the chase and explain to the two of you what just happened and why

I'm here." Andy pulled out a chair and sat down next to Kelli. Colonel Tomosky took a seat at the head of the table facing the gentleman in the suit.

"What Mister Neal is about to tell you is classified. You are not to discuss it with anyone else and if you do you will be held accountable. Are we clear on that? Colonel Tomosky asked.

"Yes, Sir," Andy and Kelli replied in unison.

"Alright then. My name is Carson Neal. I'm the Deputy Director of Operations at the Central Intelligence Agency. We're constantly searching for new talent, and the language institute is one of the places we look at regularly for potential candidates. The two of you were recommended as good prospects. I reviewed your records, and I concurred, so we've been vetting you. The people you know as Alex and Kris – that's not their real names, by the way – work for me as do the folks you met today who posed as CID agents. They all say you have the traits we're looking for in our field agents and they recommended to me that I extend offers to you to join us at the CIA. That might not be something you've ever thought about before, and I don't expect you to decide right this minute, but I'll need for you to make a decision fairly soon. Does this sound like something you'd be willing to consider?"

Andy and Kelli looked at each other. "Wow! That's a lot to take in," Kelli said as she looked over at Andy again. "I guess our plan to meet up with Alex and Kris next weekend is off the table now."

Mister Neal chuckled. "Yes. I'm afraid it is. You'll need to make some other plans."

"Are we allowed to talk about this amongst ourselves or would that violate Colonel Tomosky's order?" Andy asked.

"You two can talk with each other but use good judgment and only do so here when you're in a secure environment. Don't talk with anyone else, and if you decide to turn us down, you're never to talk about this again, not even with future spouses or with other military members, not even if they have security clearances. I'll give you until the end of next week to make up your minds, but if you haven't decided to join us by then the offer expires. Does that sound fair?"

"It does," Kelli responded. "It's flattering to get the offer, and I promise you I'll give it serious consideration."

"Can I ask you a few questions?" Andy said as he leaned forward and placed his hands palms down on the table.

"Sure, Captain Halstrom. Ask away," Mister Neal said as he leaned back in his chair.

"Okay. First, what about our commitments to the Army and what about this course? If we say yes, will we have to drop out of the course?"

"No. Your language skills are a valuable asset, and we want you to complete your training. As for the Army, we'll make the necessary arrangements and facilitate your transition out. In all likelihood, you'll finish the course, each of you will go on to your next assignments, and then we'll figure out a way for you to leave the Army without arousing suspicion and then we'll onboard you with us, but we can sort all of that out later. Did you have another question?"

"Yes, Sir. Are you recruiting us individually or as a couple? Captain McArthur and I are in a relationship, and I won't speak for her, but from my perspective, it's a relationship I'm hoping continues for a long time. I don't know how that would work if one of us says yes to you and the other one says no."

"I'm aware of your relationship. We'd love to have you both, but we'll take either one of you if that's the decision you come to. I know it's a challenge for the Army to try and accommodate the needs of couples, and it's a challenge for the Agency too, but we deal with it.

There are quite a few couples in the Agency, and I think most of them would tell you that we do our best to accommodate their unique situations. So let me ask you something. Are you two planning on getting married?"

Andy and Kelli responded at the same time, but not with the same answer. "No," she said just as Andy said, "I hope so."

"What?" Kelli said in exacerbation as she looked over at Andy. "When were you planning on telling me?"

"I ... I ..." Andy stammered.

Mister Neal chuckled. "Well, it appears you two have a lot to discuss and you don't need me or the Colonel around for that. It's been a pleasure to meet you. I can see why the team you knew as Alex and Kristin was so impressed and gave you such glowing recommendations. Think about it and when you come to a decision, let Colonel Tomosky know and he'll get in touch with me. I'm hoping you're going to say yes, but there'll be no hard feelings if you turn me down. This is an opportunity for you to do something vitally important for this country, so give it some serious thought."

"Alright, then. You two are dismissed," Colonel Tomosky said. Andy and Kelli stood up, saluted, and walked out of the office.

They walked down the hallway outside Colonel Tomosky's office, and then Kelli pushed Andy into an empty classroom, pinned him against a wall, and stuck her finger in his face. "What the hell was that back there? What's this shit about us being a couple for a long time? And marriage? Why would you say that when you haven't bothered to talk with me about it?"

Andy reached up and took her hand, moved it away from his face, and then he took her other hand. "Here's the deal. I love you. I love you more than anyone or anything I've ever

171

known. I can't imagine my life without you. When I think about us leaving here and going our separate ways, my heart feels like it's going to explode, and I feel like I'll just fall apart. I've been thinking about asking you to marry me, but I just haven't worked up the courage to do it. I thought there was still time for me to ask you before we graduated, and I never expected what happened today was going to happen. All of this just sort of came out of the blue."

"So, wait a minute. Are you asking me to marry you?" Kelli inquired as she looked directly at Andy.

"If I did, what would you say?" Andy asked.

Kelli paused for a second. "I'd say yes," she said and then she leaned forward and kissed him. She pulled back a bit and smiled. "Well, that's one decision out of the way, but we still have the other one to make."

Andy smiled back at her. "The other one doesn't matter nearly as much as this one. As long as we're together, I don't care if it's in the Army or at the C.I.A. I love you Kelly McArthur, and I promise you that I always will."

"I love you too," she responded. "But I'm going to miss Alex and Kris. We're going to have to try and make some new friends."

The next day, Andy and Kelli went to see Colonel Tomosky and told him they were accepting Mister Neal's offer to join the C.I.A. They also told him that they were getting married.

Andy and Kelli got married in the chapel at the Presidio of Monterey. It was a military wedding complete with an Honor Guard composed of some of their classmates. In keeping with military tradition, the couple walked out of the ceremony beneath the raised swords of the Honor Guard and the last member of the Guard detail, in accordance with custom and protocol, popped

Kelli on the butt with his sword as she went by. They enjoyed a weekend-long honeymoon in Huntington Beach and then returned to school for their final weeks of classes.

After they graduated, the Army assigned them both to the Washington, D.C., area. Kelli was assigned to U.S. Army Intelligence and Security Command, known as INSCOM, where she worked for Major General Albert "Bert" Stubblebine, and Andy was assigned to the Defense Intelligence Agency where he worked for Lieutenant General James Williams who was nicknamed "The Giant Grummer" because of his serious demeanor. Since they were assigned to the National Capitol Region and worked in intelligence organizations, their frequent trips to C.I.A. headquarters in McLean, Virginia, was nothing out of the ordinary.

Generals Stubblebine and Williams knew that Andy and Kelli were leaving the Army and joining the C.I.A. and they helped craft the cover story for their exit from the military. According to their official military records, Andy developed a heart condition that made him medically ineligible for continued military service, so he was administratively separated from the Army for medical reasons. Kelli applied for an administrative discharge on humanitarian grounds due to her husband's medical condition and the Secretary of the Army approved her request. Andy Halstrom's and Kelli Halstrom's military service officially ended on March 31, 1982. Their careers in the diplomatic corps at the State Department began a month later.

It was December of 1991, and Christmas was approaching. Bob Gates became the Director of the C.I.A. the month before after he was nominated by President George H.W. Bush and confirmed by the Senate by a vote of sixty-four to thirty-one. Gates had been nominated for the same post in 1987 by President Ronald Reagan, but he withdrew his name from consideration after it became clear that his involvement in the Iran-Contra scandal was likely to derail his confirmation. That wasn't a problem for him four years later. Carson Neal, who brought Andy and Kelli into the C.I.A., was now the Agency's Director of Operations, third in command behind Gates and Deputy Director Robert Kerr.

Andy was waiting in line to pay for two cups of coffee in the C.I.A. gift shop on the ground floor of the headquarters building on the Langley campus. Kelli walked over to him and took one of the cups. She glanced up and smiled when she saw a sign that advised, "If you are clandestine, no checks or credit cards, cash only." She nudged Andy and gestured towards the sign. "Do you have cash?" He smiled. "I do ... for me. How about you?" Kelli elbowed him gently in the ribs. After Andy paid for the coffee – with cash – he and Kelli took the elevator up to the top floor and walked down to the office suite for the Director of Operations. They had just sat down in the reception area when Director Neal walked in. "Good to see you," he said as he shook Andy's hand and then gave Kelli a hug. "Come on in my office."

Kelli surveyed the Director's office. "Wow! This is quite a step up from your old office." Carson Neal smiled. "Well, I'm not complaining. It took me a lot of years to get here, so I sort of feel like I earned it." The Director had a big desk and a palatial looking chair. Behind it was a credenza with two computers and two monitors, and two telephones: One system for unclassified information and the other for classified information. There was a conference table that could seat a dozen next to a bay of windows that overlooked the Langley campus. On the other side of the room was a couch, two chairs, and a coffee table. Carson Neal directed Andy and Kelli to the two chairs, and he sat down on the couch.

"Thank you for coming in this morning. It really is good to see you. How long are you going to be in Washington?"

Andy sat his coffee down on the coffee table and leaned back in his chair. "We flew in Monday night. We had meetings in Foggy Bottom on Tuesday and Wednesday, and we'll fly back to Amman tomorrow."

"Well, listen, one of the reasons I wanted to see you is to commend you on the job you did in Tripoli last summer. It took us a long time to locate and neutralize Hassan, and you two pulled it off brilliantly. I spoke with Ambassador Crocker a couple of weeks ago and he said no one over there has any inkling what happened to Hassan and most people think he got crosswise with Zumar and he's in hiding somewhere in Iran. It's a very small circle of people who know what really happened. The Secretary and the Chairman were the only people in the Pentagon who were in the loop on it, but I know everyone would be appreciative for what you did as would the families of all those Marines, Sailors, and Soldiers who died in eighty-three."

"Thank you," Kelli said. "Honestly, we thought it was going to be more difficult than it turned out to be. Hassan Abadi had a reputation for being smart and cautious, but it turned out he was neither. We made sure he knew that this was payback for Beirut, and we made sure people will go on wondering about what happened to him for a long time."

"You guys have earned quite a reputation among the handful of people who are in the loop on wet ops. There's never been a trace of evidence or a hint of U.S. involvement in any of the jobs you've done over the years. Often there's some little piece of evidence or some little screwup along the way that we have to try and clean up after the fact, but that's never been the case with you. The nation will never know the risks you've taken or how much you've done to keep the country safe, but if it did, I hope you know that everyone would be extremely grateful." Andy and Kelli thanked Director Neal, and then the rest of the conversation turned to more trivial matters.

After ten minutes or so, Director Neal glanced at his watch. "Listen, I've got to head to another meeting. It's been wonderful to see you and I hope you have a safe trip back to Jordan. And thanks again for the great work you're doing." Director Neal stood up and extended his hand to Andy and Kelli. As he walked them to the door he added, "And FYI. Things are starting to get interesting in parts of Africa and we're beginning to focus more attention on it. When it's time to move you again, that might be an area where we could use your talents."

Andy smiled. "Well, you know where to find us."

Officially, since April 1982, Andy and Kelli worked for the State Department, but that was to provide cover for their primary jobs as covert operators for the C.I.A. They underwent an extensive psychological evaluation to assess their suitability for the stresses they would face in the field, including the realistic possibility of being detected, captured, tortured, and killed. Once they were determined to be good candidates for the program, they received specialized training on the techniques they would use to conduct the missions they were assigned. They wouldn't be running a network of foreign spies or collecting intelligence information. Their job would be to "neutralize" certain individuals who posed serious threats to America's national security. The term "neutralize" was just a more sanitary way of saying that their job was to assassinate high value targets. They weren't called upon often, but when the Agency determined that their skill set was the best match, they were tapped to devise and execute a plan to make people disappear without leaving a trace. The Tripoli mission in the summer of 1991 was the tenth mission they'd completed. Two others were aborted before they could carry them out. In one instance, the target was neutralized a short time later in a Predator drone strike on the target's car as he drove along a remote mountain road in the Agency's first use of this new remote-operated weapons system. The other target was still active and remained on the Agency's high value targeting list.

Andy and Kelli spent the vast majority of their time on their diplomatic duties. Andy worked on environmental and climate matters and Kelli worked on economic development, and over time they'd developed genuine expertise in their respective fields. Their diplomatic duties allowed them to travel within their regions without arousing suspicion since the issues in their portfolios were regional in nature rather than country specific. Their ability to travel freely, their expertise in their fields, their language skills, and their personable demeanors made them a perfect pair for the lethal tasks the C.I.A. assigned them. Not many people knew what Andy and Kelli did for the C.I.A., but those who were in the loop respected them greatly for their unique ability to make targets vanish without a trace.

Killing people and disposing of their bodies is stressful, and Andy and Kelli were not immune to the stress. They were, however, adept at compartmentalizing and walling off the emotional impact of taking another person's life. In nearly every case, one or both of them had to make a personal connection with the target so that at the right time the target could be lured into a scenario where he – and it was always a he – could be disappeared discretely.

Any personal feelings they might develop for a target they tried to ignore and instead they focused on the grave harm the target had done and the future threat he posed. It made things more palatable to believe that their work was a net positive in the grand scheme of things. Once a job was done, they never discussed it again unless some aspect of it became relevant in the planning for another mission. At first, it took time for the psychological impact to dissipate after the job was done, but with each assignment, the recovery process got shorter and easier. Andy recalled that after their last job in Tripoli where they "neutralized" Hassan, dismembered his body, carried it out in cases, and then handed the cases off to a Special Forces team who jettisoned them from a helicopter far out at sea, he had turned to Kelli and asked, "well, what do

177

you think?" and she looked at her watch and answered, "I think if we hurry up, we can make it out of here in time for dinner."

Traffic from the morning rush had died down in Nairobi when the beige Toyota Dyna truck loaded with a ton of cargo left from a villa just a few miles from the U.S. Embassy. It was August 7, 1998, and it was the eight-year anniversary of American troops arriving in Saudi Arabia for what would become Operation Desert Storm, the U.S.-led multinational effort that expelled Saddam Hussein and the Iraqi Army from Kuwait.

Ambassador Prudence Bushnell had warned the leadership at the State Department that additional resources were needed to beef up security at the embassy, but for two years she was told to stop nagging and let it go. Ambassador Bushnell had hoped to get a new, more secure building, that would better protect embassy personnel, but instead the State Department decided some renovations to the existing building would suffice.

At the time the truck was enroute to the embassy, Ambassador Bushnell was next door in the Cooperative Bank Building in a meeting with Kenyan Minister of Commerce Joseph Kamotho to discuss an upcoming trade delegation visit. Andy and a few other members of her staff accompanied the Ambassador to the meeting, but Andy left early to go back to his office for a conference call scheduled for half past ten.

Azzam's palms were sweaty as he drove through the streets of Nairobi towards the U.S. Embassy. Both he and his passenger, Mohamed Rashed Daoud Al-Owhali, rode in silence. In his head, Azzam kept repeating over and over, "Allahu Akbar," God is the greatest. Throughout his training, he had been confident and steady, but now that the time had arrived to carry out the mission, he did his best to hide the fact from his companion that he was trembling.

The gate at the rear entrance leading to the embassy's underground garage was about a hundred-and-fifty feet from the building and adjacent to the Co-op Bank. The two gate guards were both Kenyans and they were unarmed. One of the guards got up from his chair and raised the gate to allow a mail truck to drive out of the compound. He lowered the gate back down and then stood in the doorway of the guard station and lit a cigarette. Moments later, as he ground the remnants of cigarette under his boot, he saw a beige truck coming towards the gate at a rapid pace. The truck's driver suddenly slammed on the brakes to avoid hitting a car that was exiting the Co-op Bank's underground parking garage. Azzam blew his horn and shook his fist at the car's driver. The other driver waved back as if to say I'm sorry, and then he backed the car up to let the truck pass.

The guard who was standing in the doorway saw what happened and yelled to the other guard, "hey, come here." The truck pulled up to the gate seconds later and the passenger jumped out. "Raise the gate! Raise the gate!" When the guards just stood there, he yelled "do it, do it now!" The plan had been for Mohamed to shoot the guards and then raise the gate himself so that Azzam could drive into the underground garage, but in his haste, Mohamed jumped out of the truck and left his pistol sitting on the seat. From the driver's seat, Azzam tossed a concussion grenade towards the guards, and they ran off towards the embassy. One of the guards tried to use his radio to alert those inside the building, but the lone radio frequency was in use, and he couldn't get through. Mohamed ran away too. He knew what was coming and he wanted to get as far away from the truck as possible before it exploded. The sound of the concussion grenade detonating caught the attention of some who were working inside the embassy, including Andy who walked over to his window and looked out towards the guard station. Azzam hesitated for a second, then he reached under the dashboard of the truck, said Allahu Akbar once last time, and pressed his finger on the detonator button.

Three buildings closest to the site of the detonation suffered the brunt of the blast. The Ufundi Cooperative Building – a four-story office building sandwiched between the U.S. Embassy and the Cooperative Bank – was leveled and reduced to a smoldering pile of rubble. The windows were blown out of the embassy building and out of the side of the Co-op Bank building facing the detonation site, and both buildings sustained major structural damage.

The windows of the office in the Co-op Bank where Ambassador Bushnell was meeting with Minister of Commerce Komotho were blown out and the Ambassador was knocked to the floor. She suffered a serious wound to her head and a concussion caused by flying debris. U.S. Commercial Officer Riz Khaliq, who was in the meeting and was injured himself, rushed over to Ambassador Bushnell and administered first aid. When she regained consciousness and it appeared she was mobile, Khaliq, Foreign Service Officer Steve Nolan, and Foreign Service National George Mimba assisted her down multiple flights of stairs. The building trembled as they made their escape, and Ambassador Bushnell thought it might collapse and kill them before they could get out. She was relieved when they finally made their way out into the open. They hurried across the parking lot and over to the embassy. Blood from Ambassador Bushnell's head wounds flowed down onto the green suit she wore to the meeting and today that bloodstained suit is on display in the National Museum of American Diplomacy in Washington.

Even though he had run as fast as he could, Mohamed was still close enough to the detonation that it threw him down face first onto the pavement. Shards of metal and concrete had torn into the back of his head, his shoulders and torso, and his legs. He stayed down on the

180

ground for several minutes, his ears ringing from the deafening sound of the explosion. Mohamed was stunned and not sure what he should do. When his head cleared and he was finally able to stand, he hobbled back to the hotel where he was staying. When he had left hours earlier, he never thought he'd be back to see the hotel room again. The farewell note he had written to his family was still there on the bed where he'd left it. He looked in the mirror at his injuries and he knew they were more serious than he could tend to on his own, so he went downstairs and asked a hotel clerk for directions to a hospital.

The doctors who treated Mohamed were suspicious of him. His story seemed implausible, and his injuries were all on his back side, which suggested he knew there was going to be an explosion and he was moving away from it when it detonated. The medical staff notified the police who apprehended Mohamed at the hospital. A copy of the plan for the attack was found in his pocket. The plan had called for the truck to drive into the parking garage located beneath the embassy and then detonate, but when the guards refused to raise the gate and Mohamed forgot his pistol and ran off, the plan changed. Had the truck made it into the underground garage and exploded, the devastation would have been much greater.

Once he was in police custody, Mohamed confessed to his role in the bombing. The Kenyan government later turned him over to the United States and he was transported to New York for prosecution in federal court. He was convicted of murder in June 2001 for the deaths of two-hundred-and-thirteen people. Ambassador Bushnell testified at Mohamed's trial, and she described the bloody aftermath of the terrorist bombing. The jury could not come to a unanimous agreement on the death penalty, so Mohamed was sentenced to life in prison without the possibility of parole. He has been in confinement at the federal prison in Florence, Colorado, known as the "Supermax," for more than two decades.

Kelli started to run as soon as she realized that the smoke plume was coming from the direction of the embassy. When she got there, she couldn't believe what she saw. The Ufundi building was totally destroyed and there was no glass in the windows of the embassy or the Coop Bank building. She looked up towards Andy's office on the fifth floor of the embassy. Nearly the entire side of the building had been blackened by the explosion. Her heart sank. She and Andy had planned to meet for lunch at noon. He told her earlier that he had a conference call that he expected to end before lunch, but if he hadn't come to her office by noon, she should come to his office. She hoped that something had come up and he hadn't been in his office when the bomb exploded, but she knew that wasn't likely. Kelli wasn't religious, but at that moment she prayed to God that Andy was still alive.

Kevin Strand was twenty-six. He earned a master's degree in environmental policy from the University of Pennsylvania and joined the State Department a short time later. He had only been at the embassy in Nairobi for two months where he worked for Andy Halstrom. Kevin's desk was about twenty-five feet from the door to Andy's office. Since he was so junior, Kevin didn't rate a window and he was assigned to one of several desks in a large open area in the interior part of the fifth floor. He had thought that not having a window so he could see outside was a curse, but it proved to be a blessing that day in August when the truck exploded.

Kevin's ears were ringing from the sound of the blast, but otherwise he wasn't hurt. One of the other junior staff members, Cara Yelton, who had a desk near Kevin's, asked if he was okay, and he said that other than the ringing in his ears he was fine. The secretary who sat just outside Andy's door had been knocked to the ground. After a few seconds, she sat up on the floor with her back against her desk. Blood ran down her face and her arms from shrapnel wounds. Kevin and Cara walked over and helped her up to her feet. "We need to get out of the building," Kevin said. "Cara, you help Maria get out and I'll check on Andy."

Because of the smoke and dust billowing in the air, Kevin could barely see as he made his way into Andy's office. He stepped over chunks of concrete and walked over broken glass as he made his way towards Andy's desk near the window. He found Andy lying on his back behind the desk. He wasn't moving. Kevin knelt beside Andy and put two fingers on his neck.

He was relieved to feel a pulse. Andy's face was bloodied, and Kevin could see gashes in his side and arm where his shirt had been ripped away. Kevin retrieved a pillow that used to be on the couch, and he placed it under Andy's head. Andy was unconscious, but he appeared to be stable. Kevin knew he couldn't move Andy alone, so he went to find some help.

Kevin and two Kenyans who worked at the embassy picked Andy up and carried him down the stairs to the front entrance of the building where the injured were assembling. Motorists who had been driving by stopped and were helping to transport the wounded to local hospitals. Kevin waved at a man who was seated in his car, and the man got out and opened one of the rear doors. They loaded Andy into the back seat of the car and Kevin climbed in next to him. As he rode along, Kevin thought about the dead and mangled bodies he had seen and the sound of the screaming and crying from those who were injured. He put his hands over his face, and he cried.

Kelli was in a panic. She tried to enter the building to look for Andy, but she was turned away by security personnel because it was too dangerous for her to go in. She made her way around to the front of the building where scores of injured people were spread out on the ground as those who were able did their best to provide care. She saw Cara, who was still with Andy's injured secretary Maria, and she asked if Cara knew what happened to Andy.

"Kevin and some other guys carried him out a few minutes ago and put him in a car to take him to a hospital. Kevin went with him. I'm sorry, I don't know where they went."

"Could you tell how bad he was hurt?" Kelli asked.

"No. It looked like he was unconscious, and he was bleeding quite a bit, but obviously he's alive or they wouldn't have rushed him out of here the way they did."

The driver stopped outside the emergency entrance at the M.P. Shah Hospital. The scene was beginning to get chaotic, but it was fortunate for Andy that he was among the first to arrive there. The chaos was going to get a lot worse soon as medical facilities throughout Nairobi were overwhelmed by the scores of injured victims brought in from the embassy and the area around the blast site. Kevin flagged down what appeared to be a doctor and led him over to the car. The doctor yelled for a medical attendant to get a stretcher, and then they gently took Andy out of the car, placed him on the stretcher, and wheeled him inside. There was nothing more Kevin could do there, so he asked the driver if he could take him back to the embassy.

When they arrived, Kevin spotted Kelli in the crowd near the steps to the front entrance and headed in her direction. She was relieved to see him and gave him a hug.

"How's Andy? Where is he?"

"We took him to the M.P. Khan Hospital and they're treating him. I don't really know the extent of his injuries. He was unconscious, but he seemed to be stable, and he had a steady pulse. He got hit with a lot of glass fragments and he was cut up pretty bad. I don't know if there's any internal damage. I wish I could tell you more, but that's all I know."

Kelli squeezed Kevin's hand. "Thank you. Thank you for taking care of him. I really appreciate it. I'm going to head over to the hospital. Do you want to go?"

"No. I'll stay and see if there's anything I can do here to help. This is bad, really bad. It's going to take a long time for us to recover from this."

By the time Kelli reached the hospital, there was a crowd outside, and the emergency room was packed. It took her several minutes to find someone who looked like she worked there who wasn't tending to the injured.

"Excuse me," Kelli said. "My husband is Andrew Halstrom and they brought him here from the ambassy. Who do I need to see to find out how he is?"

"I can go and check for you," the young woman said. "What was his name again?"

The young woman went through a door and back into the emergency department. It seemed like an eternity to Kelli, but less than ten minutes later she came back out.

"Your husband's injuries are serious, but his vital signs are stable. He's currently in surgery with Doctor Opuko. They've been in surgery for about half an hour, so it's going to be a while before we know more about his prognosis. If you want to wait, I'll check on him periodically and I'll let you know as soon as more information is available."

Kelli gave the young woman a hug. "Thank you so much. I appreciate it. Please let me know as soon as you hear anything."

The young woman came out every hour or so and updated Kelli on the status of the surgery. Finally, near midnight, Doctor Kimani Opuko came out with the young woman, who directed him over to Kelli.

"I'm Doctor Opuko," he said as he extended his hand. "I operated on your husband. The good news is that he's stable and I'm optimistic that he'll survive. He's not out of the woods yet, but I expect in the next twelve to twenty-four hours we'll see signs of progress. The bad news is that he suffered some serious injuries, and he lost a significant amount of blood. I take it from the

185

way the wounds were dispersed on his body that he was turned slightly when the impact of the blast hit him because the wounds are predominantly on his left side. I removed a lot of glass fragments from his face, and there's likely going to be some permanent scarring. There was a fairly large glass shard imbedded in the outer side of his left eye. I didn't see any damage to the lens and the vitreous body wasn't penetrated, but it did protrude into the nerves and may have caused some damage that could impact his vision in that eye. We won't know until he's conscious. His left arm sustained a lot of damage. It appears that his arm was down at the time of the blast, and it took the brunt of the impact. That likely prevented any of the projectiles from penetrating into his chest and abdomen where they could have damaged his lungs, heart, and other organs. I repaired his arm as best I could, but he's going to need additional surgeries on it.

We won't know until we can do a more thorough assessment exactly how much long-term damage was done. He struck his head on something, most likely when the blast knocked him backwards. There're no skull fractures, but he did suffer a concussion. Again, until he regains consciousness we won't know if there's any neurological damage. He's going to remain in intensive care, and he'll be out of it for several more hours and he'll be heavily sedated after that. I know that's a lot to take in. The good news is that he's alive. The bad news is that he's got a long road ahead of him. Are there any questions I can try to answer for you?

Kelli breathed out a heavy sigh. "No, I don't think so. Thank you for filling me in on all the details and thank you for taking care of Andy. I'm grateful and I know he will be too. Can I see him?"

"Not right now. As I said, he's still unconscious and he'll remain that way for several more hours. It's also very hectic back there given the number of injured who've come in here. I'd suggest that you go home and get some rest and come back in the morning. There's really nothing you can do here right now. Well then, if you'll excuse me, I need to help take care of some of the other victims."

Kelli took Doctor Opuko's advice. She thought about returning to the embassy to see if she could help there, but she knew it was chaotic, and she thought that she'd just be in the way. Instead, she drove to the housing compound where she and Andy had a townhouse. Even though it was well past midnight when she approached the gate, she could see that there was a lot of activity going on inside. There were normally two guards stationed at the gate, but now she spotted six or more and there were several police vehicles parked nearby. She passed through the gate, parked her car outside the townhouse, and went inside. She walked to the kitchen and poured herself a glass of wine, then she went into the office and sat down at her desk. She logged into the classified computer network and sent a short message to Langley to let Director Neal know that she was okay, and Andy was seriously injured but expected to live. After she hit send and logged out of the classified network, she went upstairs and stretched out on the bed. She had been awake for nearly twenty hours, and it had been about as stressful a day as she had ever experienced. She fell asleep in less than a minute.

Kelli returned to the M.P. Shah Hospital the next morning. It was still as crowded and as hectic as it was when she left several hours earlier. After more than an hour of waiting, a young woman came out and escorted her back to see Andy. He was still in intensive care and remained heavily sedated. As Kelli approached the side of Andy's bed, she could see that the left side of his face was a mess. There appeared to be dozens of cuts that had been sutured shut and a white gauze bandage covered his left eye. A strap held a facemask in place over his mouth and a tube pumped oxygen into his lungs every few seconds. His left arm was heavily bandaged and was suspended by two straps that held it in place at a slight angle to his body. Kelli walked around to

187

the other side of the bed. There were intravenous lines attached to his right arm, but otherwise Andy's right side looked completely normal.

Kelli took Andy's right hand and squeezed it softly. She felt a lump forming in her throat and she concentrated on suppressing it and holding herself together. She leaned over next to Andy. She didn't know if the explosion had damaged his hearing, but she decided to talk to him.

"Hey babe. I don't know if you can hear me, but I'm right here by your side. You scared the shit out of me. For a while, I didn't know whether you were still here or whether you had left me. You've been the center of my world the past eighteen years, and I didn't know how I'd survive if I lost you. I was so relieved when the doctor told me you're going to be okay. You probably don't feel like it right now, but you're going to get through this … we're going to get through this. You just rest and focus on getting better. I'm right here … I'll always be right here. I'll take care of you, I promise. It's going to be okay."

Kelli bent down and kissed Andy on the cheek. The young woman who escorted Kelli back to see Andy brought her a chair, and Kelli sat down and held his hand.

The next day, an Air Force C-9 medevac aircraft arrived at the Nairobi Airport. Doctor Opuko said that Andy was stable enough to travel and put him on the schedule for transport to the airport for the flight out. Kelli sat with Andy in the back of the ambulance and held his hand for the duration of the short drive. Andy and two dozen other patients were carried aboard on litters that were specifically designed to clip in securely onboard the aircraft. Several hours later, the C-9 landed at Ramstein Air Base near Frankfurt, Germany. Andy and three others were loaded into an ambulance for transport to the military medical facility in Landstuhl. Kelli and the others who had accompanied the injured from Nairobi were loaded onto a bus that followed behind the procession of ambulances.

Andy stayed at Landstuhl for a week. He had two more surgeries on his arm and shoulder, and an ophthalmologist checked the injury to his eye daily. From there he was transferred to the Walter Reed Army Medical Center on a sprawling campus in northeast Washington, D.C. Over the course of six weeks, he underwent additional surgeries and began a grueling physical therapy regimen. The glass shard that imbedded in Andy's left eye severed some of the optic nerves causing optic atrophy. He was fitted with glasses to correct for the blurriness in his left eye, but there was no treatment for the halo effect he experienced, which was worse at night. The neurological assessment found no evidence of significant impairment. While Andy had frequent and intense headaches, they were expected to dissipate over time and hopefully disappear entirely at some point. Finally, nearly two months after the bombing, he was ready to be released from the hospital and go home.

Kelli found an apartment in downtown Washington on M Street near Dupont Circle. She had been reassigned to the State Department and given an office in the headquarters building on C Street. Her superiors were aware of the significant injuries Andy suffered, and they afforded Kelli wide latitude to be with him and assist in his recovery.

Director Neal invited Kelli to C.I.A. headquarters to have lunch with him in the executive dining room. When they finished eating, they went to his office to talk about Andy and their future with the C.I.A.

"I'm glad to hear that Andy is making progress. I know he'll be happy to get out of the hospital and go home with you. I want you both to know that there's a place for you here for as long as you want it, but you're under no obligation. When you decide it's time to cut ties with the Agency, just say so. You don't owe us anything. And you'll still have your diplomatic duties and that can be your sole focus for a change. Let me know when the two of you figure out what's best for you."

Kelli smiled. "I really do appreciate that. We've never regretted for a minute accepting your offer to leave the Army and join the Agency. We know that we've been able to do more here to serve the country than we ever could have done in the Army. For now, if it's okay with you, let's give it some time. Let's see how Andy progresses and what the lasting impact will be from his injuries. I suspect that if he's physically able he'll want to return to duty. He'll probably be anxious to do what he can to hold those who were behind the bombing accountable and prevent anything like that from ever happening again."

"That's fine with me. You two take as much time as you need. Just keep me posted."

A young noncommissioned officer helped Andy into a wheelchair. He rolled him to the elevator, and they rode down to the ground floor. He wheeled Andy out through the front entrance to the car that Kelli had pulled up to the curb to take him home. Andy's left arm was still in a sling, and he wasn't allowed to do anything strenuous with it, so the attendant helped him up out of the wheelchair and into the car. "Good luck, sir," the young man said after he had Andy seated in the car. "Thank you, sergeant. I appreciate you and everyone here taking such good care of me, but I'm not going to lie and say I'll miss seeing you."

The young man smiled. "I totally understand that. Take care of yourself and get better."

Andy surveyed the apartment. "I like it. It's nice. And it sure beats the hell out of that hospital room."

"Well, I'm glad you do because I signed a six-month lease, so like it or not, we're stuck with it for a couple of more months at least."

Like Kelli, Andy had been reassigned to the State Department. The plan was to keep them in D.C. for as long as it took for Andy to heal and then, if they were ready, they could go back out into the field. Andy had physical therapy appointments every other day for the first few weeks and then twice a week after that. He went into his office at the State Department headquarters daily and soon fell into a comfortable routine. His superiors made sure to assign him enough work to keep him busy but not so much that he would be overwhelmed.

Andy and Kelli had the Friday after Thanksgiving off from work. Keeping with tradition, they ate to excess on Thanksgiving and then fell into a turkey-induced tryptophan coma before it was even dark outside. They were up early the next morning and decided to walk to a neighborhood bakery for pastries and coffee and to read the Washington Post. Andy had been able to take his left arm out of the sling for short periods of time for about two weeks. The arm was weak, and he had a limited range of motion, but he could use it. It occurred to him as he sat there drinking coffee and reading the paper that people tend to take little things for granted. He hadn't realized how much he enjoyed going through a newspaper page by page from front to back until he injured his arm and couldn't hold a newspaper up to read it. Instead, he had to lay it down on a flat surface and use his good arm to turn the pages, which just wasn't the same. It was good to be able to read a newspaper properly again.

"You know, Christmas is just a month away," Andy said.

Kelli looked up from her newspaper. "I know, and I haven't done any shopping yet."

Andy paused for a second. "You know, I was thinking ..."

"Oh God," Kelli interjected, trying to sound like she was shocked. "Nothing good ever comes from you thinking."

"Smart ass," he responded. "No, seriously. I was thinking that we ought to go somewhere for a couple of days over Christmas. From that day in Nairobi until now, our lives have been pretty intense. It would be nice to get away somewhere where we can just kick back and relax."

Kelli nodded. "I'm up for that. Do you have any place in mind?"

"No, not really. I'd just like to go somewhere nice where it's quiet and Christmassy. Not a beach or anywhere that's hot. It would be nice to go somewhere where it feels like Christmas, a Norman Rockwell kind of setting."

"I have an idea," Kelli said as she folded her paper and placed it on the table. "I saw an article in Southern Living not long ago about a town in the mountains of North Carolina named Asheville. There's a place there called Biltmore with hundreds of acres of land and a huge mansion one of the Vanderbilt's built years ago. There's also a spectacular hotel in Asheville ... Grove something I think ... where lots of celebrities, famous people, and several presidents have stayed. It's a Christmassy looking place and it's less than a day's drive from here. That might be interesting."

"It sounds like it has potential. Do you want to work on it?" Andy asked.

"Sure. I'll make some calls when we get back to the apartment. Christmas is only four weeks away, and I don't know what's still available, so we need to make some arrangements as soon as we can."

Edwin Wiley Grove, who everyone called E.W., was twelve years old when his father left their home in Whiteville, Tennessee, in 1862 to serve under Confederate General and first Grand Wizard of the Ku Klux Klan Nathan Bedford Forrest. E.W. finished school in Whiteville and then he moved ninety miles north to Paris, Tennessee, to clerk in a pharmacy, which he later bought from the founding partners in 1880. Not long after, his wife, Mary, and youngest daughter, Irma, died from malaria, and E.W. made it his personal mission to develop a cure.

In 1885, E.W. created Grove's Tasteless Chill Tonic, quinine suspended in a flavored syrup to make it more palatable than quinine alone. By 1889, E.W.'s tonic was in such high demand that his company outgrew its production capacity in Paris, Tennessee, and he moved it to St. Louis. It was said at the time that Grove's Tasteless Tonic was so popular that more bottles of it were sold than bottles of Coca-Cola. By 1900, the company had offices in London, Toronto, Rio de Janeiro, Buenos Aires, and Paris … France, not Tennessee … and E.W. Grove had become a very wealthy man.

E.W. suffered from recurrent bouts of bronchitis and his doctors suggested that the clean mountain air of western North Carolina would be good for him. That's how he first discovered Asheville and quickly fell in love with it. Later, on a trip to Detroit, E.W. met Fred Seely, a fellow pharmacist, and he invited Seely to visit him at the summer home in Asheville E.W. shared with his second wife, Gertrude, and their daughters, one of whom would eventually become Fred's wife.

E.W. and Fred realized that the tranquil environment in Asheville was an ideal setting for a luxury resort. In 1909, they bought four hundred acres of land on Sunset Mountain with a vision of constructing a grand hotel to serve as a relaxing and luxurious mountain retreat. At the time, Asheville was home to several sanitoriums for tuberculosis patients and E.W. believed that for Asheville to become a destination for the well-heeled to relax and recreate, it had to erase its image as a haven for those suffering from ill-health. He bought up many of the sanitoriums and the boarding houses that catered to tuberculosis patients and their families and he had them dismantled. Often, real estate deals he made included covenants that precluded construction of facilities for the treatment of tuberculosis patients. E.W. was so adamant about distancing his gilded inn from illness that when it opened, he mandated that the inn only use fresh dollar bills, wash all coins, and boil the silverware … twice.

E.W. wasn't satisfied with designs local architects prepared for his grand hotel and eventually he settled on a plan Fred drafted, even though Fred had no formal architectural training. Fred's design was modeled after Yellowstone National Park's Old Faithful Inn, except Fred relied more on stone than wood in his design. E.W. and Fred commissioned Roycroft craftsmen in New York to create the inn's furnishing and chose the best weavers in France to make its carpets.

Building the Grove Park Inn was a Herculean task. Four hundred workmen – many of whom had worked on the construction of George Vanderbilt's Biltmore Estate – toiled ten-hours a day, six days a week, lugging thousands of pounds of granite boulders and timbers up the mountain to the hotel site. The hotel was completed eleven months and twenty-seven days after Gertrude Grove tossed the first shovel of dirt at the groundbreaking ceremony on July 9, 1912. The Inn officially opened for business on July 12, 1913, and Secretary of State William Jennings Bryan traveled to Asheville from Washington to deliver the keynote address at the grand opening ceremony. In his speech, Secretary of State Bryan proclaimed that the resplendent Grove Park Inn "was built for the ages."

The Secretary's claim proved true as over the years the inn compiled a long list of distinguished guests. Harry Houdini, Will Rogers, Al Jolson, Henry Ford, Harvey Firestone, John D. Rockefeller, Thomas Edison, Albert Einstein, F. Scott and Zelda Fitzgerald, Alex Haley, Helen Keller, Jack Nicklaus, Mikhail Baryshnikov, Jerry Seinfeld, Margaret Mitchell, Don Cheadle, Jim Belushi, and George Gershwin, as well as Presidents William Howard Taft, Woodrow Wilson, Calvin Cooledge, Herbert Hoover, Franklin Delano Roosevelt, Dwight D. Eisenhower, Richard Nixon, Geroge H. W. Bush, Bill Clinton, and Barack Obama have all been guests of the Grove Park Inn. The inn served as an internment center for Axis power diplomats during World War II, and later as a rest and rehabilitation facility for American soldiers and sailors. The Philippine government operated in exile from the inn during the war leading some to say that the capital of the Philippines was at one time Asheville, North Carolina.

They hadn't been on the road for more than twenty minutes before Andy fell asleep in the passenger seat. It was going to take eight hours to drive to Asheville and Andy was still experiencing what the doctors euphemistically called "moderate discomfort," and he called "excruciating pain," so Kelli made sure he was thoroughly medicated before they left the apartment. She looked over at him asleep next to her and she smiled. She was happy that he was able to sleep, and she was grateful that he seemed to be on the mend, although he still had a long way to go.

The scars on the left side of Andy's face where the glass fragments had imbedded were still raised and red. His arm was still in a sling most of the time, but he could use it for short periods to perform simple tasks that didn't require any heavy lifting. The headaches were as intense as ever, but they didn't seem to occur as frequently as before, and their duration had decreased. Andy was beaten and battered, but he was alive and making slow but steady progress on his journey to recovery. Kelli remembered that day in August, just a little more than four months ago, when she saw the smoldering ruins of the embassy and wondered whether Andy was dead or alive. All things considered; they had been lucky, very lucky. Andy was fortunate to be among the four thousand who were injured that day rather than being one of the two-hundred and thirteen who perished.

Kelli enjoyed the picturesque view as she crossed over the high point at Sam's Gap and began the descent down I-26 towards Asheville. It had been overcast for most of the drive with occasional sprinkles of rain along the way, and Kelli detected what appeared to be a few flakes of snow as they passed through the highest elevation on their route. She wished Andy could see it too, but she decided to let him sleep a little longer since he looked so peaceful. After she passed Weaverville and Woodfin, she saw the French Broad River on the righthand side of the highway flowing north as she drove south. When the Asheville skyline emerged, she decided it was time to wake Andy up.

She tapped his leg. "Andy. Wake up honey. We're almost there."

Andy opened his eyes and then he yawned. He sat up in his seat, pushed his shoulders back slowly, and moved his neck from side to side to shake off the stiffness. He flinched a bit when he moved his left arm, a reminder that there were still months of rehab to go before it would get as close to normal as it was ever going to get.

"It's about time. We'd have been here an hour ago if you had let me drive."

"That's funny. I don't have any recollection of you offering to drive. And with all the medications you're on, I sure as hell wouldn't have been able to sleep with you behind the wheel. We'd probably be off in a ravine somewhere waiting for a tow truck to pull us out if you drove."

A moment later, I-26 merged into I-240 and they headed east along the edge of the city. They exited off the highway and turned left onto Charlotte Street.

"Hey look! It's a Fuddruckers. You're going to feel right at home here," Kelli said.

"To be honest, I could go for a burger and fries and a thick chocolate shake right now. All this sleeping has made me hungry."

"Well, you can forget that. We've got a dinner reservation tonight at seven at the hotel and I'm not going to let you spoil your appetite. Maybe after we get settled in our room we can go down to the bar and get a drink and a snack to tide you over until dinner."

Andy moved his left arm slowly and placed his left hand on Kelli's thigh. "Or we could skip the bar and stay in the room, and I could show you fifteen or twenty of the most exciting seconds you could ever hope to experience this holiday season."

"Oh really? You got a friend stashed in the trunk you didn't tell me about?" Kelli mused as she patted Andy's hand. "Sex with you would be like this drive; I'd have to do all the work and you'd just be along for the ride."

"Work you say? I don't know that I've ever considered it work, although in my head I do commend myself for doing a superior job when I'm able to make your toes curl up tight. When I have to yank the sheet out from the clutches of your cramped toes, I know I've put in a good day's work, and I got the job done to your satisfaction."

Kelli chuckled. "In your dreams, pal. In your dreams."

Kelli turned right onto Macon Avenue, drove up the hill, and wound her way along the narrow road to the entrance to the Grove Park Inn.

"Wow! This is quite impressive," she said as they drove around the circle to the front doors where two valets in matching uniforms came out to open their car doors.

"Welcome to the Grove Park Inn. Are you two checking in to stay with us?" one of the young men asked.

"Thank you," Andy replied. "Yes, we're the Halstroms and we're going to be spending Christmas with you."

"Excellent, sir. Reception is through the doors and to the right. If you two would like to head inside and get checked in, we'll unload your luggage, park your car, and deliver your bags up to your room shortly."

Andy and Kelli walked into the Great Hall, a massive room measuring one-hundred-and-twenty feet in length, eighty feet in width, and with twenty-four-foot-high ceilings. Fires roared in the two gigantic fireplaces, one at each end of the room, both twelve feet wide and six feet in height, big enough for most adults to stand up in, with andirons that weighed over five hundred pounds. Kelli slowly surveyed the Great Hall. A huge twenty-foot-tall Christmas tree twinkled in the middle of the room. Cedar and juniper garlands, red and green ribbons, and tinsel were out in abundance. Andy and Kelli said they wanted to go to some place Christmassy, and they'd found it at E.W. Grove's Grove Park Inn.

Their room was on the fourth floor of the Main Inn, one of the one-hundred-and-fifty original rooms completed in 1913 before two additional wings were added in the 1980s. The room had a king bed and a stunning view of the Blue Ridge Mountains off to the west. A few moments later there was a knock at the door and a valet wheeled in their bags and placed them

198

on luggage stands. He hesitated for several awkward seconds until Andy realized that the young man was waiting for a tip, and he reached for his wallet.

"Sorry about that," Andy said.

"No problem, sir. Thank you. I hope you folks enjoy your stay and I wish you a merry Christmas," the young man said as he departed.

Andy and Kelli freshened up, changed clothes, and then went down to the lobby. It was just past five o'clock and the lobby was bustling. There were dozens of rocking chairs at each of the fireplaces, and nearly all of them were filled with guests rocking contentedly and staring at the mesmerizing flames as they danced and crackled. Andy and Kelli found a small table near the Great Hall Bar and when the server came around, they ordered a bottle of chenin blanc and a warm pimento cheese appetizer. As they sipped their wine and nibbled on their snack, off in the distance the sun was about to set behind the Blue Ridge Mountains. The scattered clouds caused the dwindling sunlight to refract creating a reddish-pink glow that hovered just above the ridgeline.

Andy raised his glass. "To you my dear. This was an excellent idea. Here's to us and here's to a very merry Christmas."

Kelli clinked her glass against Andy's and then took a sip. "I'm glad we did this," she said and then paused a few second. "And I'm glad you're still here. There was a time back in Nairobi when I thought I'd lost you. It felt like the wind had been knocked out of me and I couldn't breathe. I didn't know how I'd survive without you. We really do have a lot to be thankful for this year. I love you so much." She wiped a tear from her eye and then leaned in and kissed Andy.

Christmas day was cold, clear, and breezy, and the high at the hotel remained below freezing. Andy and Kelli slept in and then ordered a late breakfast that was delivered to their room. They spent most of the afternoon in the lobby by the fireplace reading, although Andy's eyes were closed about as much as they were open. That evening, they dined in the Blue Ridge Room. They ordered a bottle of wine and Kelli went to the appetizer table and fixed them a plate of cheese, fresh baked slices of bread, olives, and cured ham to enjoy before the main course.

"Merry Christmas, honey," Andy said as he reached inside his jacket, pulled out a small, wrapped box, and passed it across the table to Kelli.

"I thought we were going to exchange gifts back in the room, so you're going to have to wait before I can give you your gift."

"The gift I can't wait to unwrap up in the room is you," he said with a wink and a smile.

"You talk a big game," she said with a laugh. "We'll see if you can play one later."

Kelli untied the ribbon, removed the wrapping, and opened the box. Inside was a Rolex Yacht-Master watch with a band of white and yellow gold.

"It's beautiful, but you shouldn't have. That's way too much money to spend on a watch when my old Seiko just keeps on ticking."

Andy reached across the table and took Kelli's hand.

"Since the incident, you've been by my side constantly and you've taken care of me. I couldn't do it without you. The whole thing has been hard on me, but I know it has been just as hard on you, and you've never wavered, and you've never ever given up on me, even at times when I wanted to give up on myself. I'll be forever indebted to the Army for sending me to Monterey because I might have never met you if it hadn't. I struck gold when I found you and giving you a little in return doesn't come close to showing you how much you mean to me and how grateful I am that you're my wife."

Kelli's eyes got moist. She stood up, took a step around the table, leaned down and took Andy's face in her hands, and kissed him.

"I love you. And listen, I feel every bit as lucky as you do that fate … or maybe it was the Army … brought us together. The lives we've led since we met, well, who could have predicted it? We've done things that people will never know about, and we've survived things that people could never begin to imagine. We're a team. Nothing will ever tear us apart."

Andy and Kelli remained in Washington for nearly two years as he continued to recover from his physical and psychological injuries. The vision in his left eye was permanently impaired. Andy described it as like looking through a tunnel where the edges of the circle are fuzzier than the center. Corrective lens helped, to an extent, but Andy was not fond of wearing glasses. The scars on the left side of Andy's face faded slowly, but they never disappeared entirely. He regained partial use of his left arm. He couldn't raise it past parallel with the ground and it had about two-thirds the strength of his right arm. Kelli told Andy that the limited use of his left arm reminded her of the senator from Arizona, John McCain, who suffered permanent damage to his arm and shoulder when he was shot down and held captive as a POW during the Vietnam War.

Andy's psychological injuries weren't as readily apparent, not even to Kelli. She knew that he suffered from nightmares from time to time and he would flinch when he was startled by an unexpected loud noise. She didn't know that several times a day he experienced bouts of

201

anxiety, often unexpectedly, that could last for a second or two or for a couple of minutes. Andy developed coping mechanisms to help him conceal his panic attacks. If he felt one coming on, he'd excuse himself and slip away to someplace quiet where he'd meditate until he regained his composure. If he was in a crowd and couldn't slip out, he'd think of a tranquil scene and he'd go there in his mind as outwardly he projected a façade of stability and composure to those around him. Often, he thought about the Christmas he and Kelli spent at the Grove Park Inn. A few days after Christmas, it snowed; not a lot, but enough so that everything rested under a blanket of pristine white powder. They drove west of Asheville and found a spot where they had a breathtaking view of layers of snow-covered mountains from a vantage point high up on a ridgeline. Andy escaped to that spot often in his mind when he felt a wave of anxiety about to wash over him.

Because of Andy's limitations, the Agency decided it was time to end his and Kelli's involvement in what those in the intelligence community call "wet ops." Practitioners in that field need rock-solid minds and a strong bodies, and Andy, because of the injuries he suffered in the bombing, no longer met those standards. Director Neal called them in and told them that they would no longer be used to conduct physical operations, but instead they would be called upon occasionally to collect and assess information and to consult on matters related to their areas of expertise. Andy and Kelli were disappointed, but they understood why the Agency made the decision. As they left Director Neal's office, Kelli said, "well, at least now we can use our credit card in the giftshop."

Andy and Kelli returned to their duties full-time at the State Department. Over the course of the next eighteen years, they served in diplomatic posts abroad with two stints in Washington in between. The taskings they received from the Agency grew few and far between, and they stopped all together after Director Neal retired in 2010.

Andy and Kelli first started discussing retirement shortly after Andy was diagnosed with Parkinson's disease in 2017. Kelli noticed a slight tremor in his hand when he extended his right arm, and she urged him to go see his doctor. When he did, Andy learned that he was in stage one of Parkinson's disease. The doctor said the disease usually progressed slowly and it could be a decade or more before Andy experienced significant medical problems like dementia or physical incapacity, and he could live well into his eighties, although he would likely be significantly impaired in his later years. The doctor started him on medication to control his symptoms and urged him to increase his physical activity and reduce his stress level. Andy was dejected at first – he'd worked hard to recover from the injuries he suffered in the bombing, and now this – but over time his attitude changed, and he faced it with the same determination he had displayed nearly two decades earlier as he fought to recover from his bomb-related injuries.

Andy and Kelli had fond memories of Asheville, and it soon rose to the top of the list of potential retirement spots. They made several trips to the Asheville area to look at existing homes and at vacant tracts. They toured several homes that were quite nice, but they weren't exactly the dream home they envisioned. Some were too big, and some were too small. Some had potential, but they'd need a lot of renovation. They knew that Andy still had some good years ahead of him health wise, but they were acutely aware that eventually he would start to experience physical limitations, so they wanted a house that could accommodate his needs as his health began its decline. They learned that the term for that is a house built for the occupants to "age in place." They also knew that they needed to be within a reasonable distance of medical care. They finally decided that their best option was to buy a lot close to or in town, and to have a house built on it tailored to their exact desires.

Carla Ellis, the woman who pretended to be C.I.D. Agent Valerie Bronson when Andy and Kelli were interrogated at the Language Institute in Monterey in 1981, called them early one Sunday morning in the summer of 2018. Carla had risen through the ranks at the Agency, and she was named Director of Operations when Carson Neal retired.

"I know you two were close with Carson and I thought you'd want to know that he and his wife were killed last night. The police say it looks like a botched carjacking or a robbery attempt. He and his wife were in their car in Northwest D.C., and they say they both died insfrom gunshot wounds to the head. They don't have any suspects at the moment, but they said it happened in an area where carjackings and armed robberies occur fairly often, and most of the time they're gang related."

Andy and Kelli were stunned. They had attended Director Neal's retirement ceremony in 2010, and they met him for lunch several times in the years since whenever they were in Washington, but they hadn't seen him in the eight months since they'd returned to the area after an overseas posting. He seemed to have been enjoying retirement. He'd bought a house on the Eastern Shore of Maryland, and he and his wife spent a lot of time there in addition to traveling extensively. Kelli had been meaning to give him a call to see how he was doing and to catch up, but now it was too late. Dealing with death had once been a part of Kelli's skill set and she was adept at compartmentalizing the emotions that go along with it, but it was different when it was someone she'd known for so long and respected so much. Andy was saddened by the news too, but it struck Kelli much harder. She went for a walk alone … and cried.

At about the same time Carla Ellis called Andy and Kelli, Khaled Abadi, the nephew of Hassan Abadi, sent a text message to his father who was Hassan's older brother. "Located the friend you told me about. Before he departed, he gave me information on two others I should visit. Will try to drop in on them before I return home."

Soon after Carson Neal's death, Andy and Kelli decided it was time for them to finalize their retirement plans and they settled on the summer of 2019 to bring their careers in government to a close. By then, they would have completed thirty-seven years of service at the State Department. Add in their time in the Army and they both would have served their country for more than forty years. Andy would be sixty-six at the time they retired, and Kelli would be sixty-five. They had already decided that they were going to retire and move to Asheville where they'd been looking at properties and meeting with home builders. Just one more year until they would officially become Ashevillians.

The land on the west side of Bull Creek where James and Hannah Craig settled in 1789 stayed in Craig family hands for two-hundred and twenty-six years. On June 22, 2015, one-hundred and sixty-nine acres of land known for generations as Craigsfield and then as Coggins Farm was sold to a developer for a little over four million dollars.

The developer originally planned to build a high-density development with nearly four hundred residential units plus commercial retail space. Residents in the Riceville area protested and more than three hundred of them signed a petition to stop the development. They argued that a high-density development would forever alter the rural, agricultural nature of the area and clog the already congested roadways. The developer fought it at first, but eventually conceded and amended the plan to a more modest ninety-nine parcels for single family homes situated on lots ranging in size from one to three acres. Locals still objected – they even organized a fundraising effort to try and buy the property from the developer – but the developer pressed on, and the Buncombe County Planning Board approved the amended plan. Soon thereafter, construction equipment rolled onto the land and Oakwood Farm was born.

The weekend after they learned of Carson Neal's death, while they were at home in D.C., Andy saw a house on an online site that looked interesting. It was described as a "mountain modern" design that incorporated wood and stone to give it a mountainy look, but with totally modern features like geothermal heat and air, on-demand hot water, solar power, and energy efficient sprayed-in foam insulation. The house was in a development called Oakwood Farm on the outskirts of east Asheville and just fifteen minutes or so from Mission Hospital. They had done some research and found that Mission Hospital – a nonprofit, community-based healthcare system centered in Asheville that served most of Western North Carolina – earned rave reviews from area residents and was considered one of the region's real treasures. A year earlier, the availability of healthcare wouldn't have been one of their primary considerations, but after Andy's diagnosis, it climbed to the top of their priority list. Andy showed the house to Kelli, and she liked what she saw. They decided they'd take a look at Oakwood Farm when they visited Asheville next weekend.

It was only ten minutes from the Grand Bohemian Hotel in Biltmore Village to Oakwood Farm. Andy pulled out of the hotel, crossed over the Swannanoa River, and turned right onto Swannanoa River Road. He made a left at the Veterans Affairs Hospital, passed under the Blue Ridge Parkway, and then turned right on Old Farm School Road. A few minutes later, they arrived at Oakwood Farm.

A man in a Jeep was waiting next to the mailboxes at the entrance to the development. When Andy and Kelli pulled up, he stuck his hand out the window and waved.

"Good morning! You folks must be the Halstroms. I'm Mike Nixon. Why don't you park over there and then jump in here with me and I'll show you around."

Oakwood Farm is a gated community, and Mike had to punch in a code number before the gate went up and allowed him to drive in.

"The gate's closed on weekends and at night, but it's open on weekdays so the builders and their crews can come and go without having to sit here and wait. When all of the construction is done, it'll probably be closed during the week too. It doesn't provide a whole lot of security, but at night and on weekends when people are more likely to be up to no good, it's somewhat of a deterrent and might cause them to keep moving and look for an easier target."

The first half mile or so was mostly flat and open, with very few trees. Mike said that part of the development was called The Meadow. There were four or five houses already built in that section and a couple more were under construction. Directly ahead and over to the right, the view of the mountains was gorgeous. Off in the distance, Lane Pinnacle was white and sparkling, and Andy said it looked like it had snowed, but Mike explained that it was just heavy frost on the trees that were sitting at over five thousand feet of elevation where the temperature was cooler.

He said the frost would burn off soon as the sun climbed higher, and the temperature rose. They passed the house Andy saw online, and he pointed it out to Kelli.

"A couple from Florida had that one built," Mike said. "My understanding is they'll split their time between here and their house in Florida. I'd say most folks plan to make Oakwood their permanent home, but there are a few snowbirds who'll only be here for part of the year. If you can afford it, I guess it's nice to be able to enjoy the mountains and the coast."

When Mike reached an intersection, he stopped. He said the area to the right was called The Creek and extended down to Bull Creek plus a few more acres on the east side of the stream. The rest of the property on the east side of the creek belonged to Warren Wilson College and contained miles of hiking trails that the college maintained. The area directly ahead was called The Hill. Oakwood Trail, the main road running through Oakwood Farm, extended all the way from the gate to the top of The Hill, a little over three-quarters of a mile in distance, where it ended at a cul-de-sac.

Mike drove on through the intersection, went up to the top of the hill, turned around in the cul-de-sac, and stopped. There were no leaves on the trees yet and the two-hundred and seventy-degree view from the top of the hill was impressive. You could see Lane Pinnacle and further off in the distance was the even taller Craggy Knob. A little closer in was Brushy Mountain, the place where the mother bear and her cub hibernated before they walked down to Thomas Williams's cabin beside Bee Tree Creek in 1783. And just down the hill a few hundred yards, even though it wasn't visible through the brush, was Bull Creek where Thomas and the mother bear died and their blood set in motion the process of turning an acorn into an oak tree, where James Craig was shot outside his grist mill in 1808, and where Tobias Wilson was nearly hung in 1879. Andy and Kelli didn't know it, but a lot of history took place within walking distance of the The Hill.

"Wow! This is gorgeous," Kelli said.

"It is," Andy added. "Could we build a house right here?"

Mike chuckled. "If it was up to me you could, but I suspect my boss wouldn't be too happy if I let you put up a house in the middle of this nice road he had built. The lots around the circle are all sold, but that one directly in front of us," Mike said as he pointed towards a thick stand of trees, "is still available. You'd need to take out some trees to put a house on it and that would really open it up and give you a great year-round view. As you can see, right now with the leaves off, the view is damn nice as it is. You're looking towards the east, so you'd wake up to some gorgeous sunrises on that lot. Let's get out and take a closer look at it."

Andy and Kelli walked the lot with Mike. It sloped a bit from front to back, but it wasn't nearly as steep as some of the other lots they'd seen that would have required spending a ton of money on retaining walls and fill dirt to create a spot that could accommodate a house. This one, Mike said, was perfectly suited for a house with a walk-out basement. It was a beautiful lot. It was an acre and a quarter, nearly square in shape, and framed by Oakwood Trail on the top and westerly side, and Oakhaven Way down at the bottom. There were several red oaks and white oaks, and a few were large and clearly quite old. There were also pines, maples, sourwoods, and a couple of hardy rhododendrons and mountain laurels, as well as several exposed boulders ladened with moss and lichen. Kelli thought to herself that it was a shame that some of those magnificent trees would have to come down to make room for a house, but she couldn't see any way around it. Kelli looked over at Andy and gave him a nod of approval. She could see them spending their retirement years right there on that spot.

"This isn't bad," Andy said to Mike, trying not to seem like he was overly interested and ripe for the picking. "I mean it's not exactly what we had in mind, but it would do and it's in a decent location where getting into town wouldn't take too long. What are you asking for it?"

"There are only a couple of lots in here that offer a view like this, so they go for a little more than the ones down in The Meadow. The elevation up here is close to twenty-five hundred feet, which is about three-hundred feet or so higher than down at the mailboxes where you parked, and that gives you these great views. Anyway, this lot's priced at two-hundred-and fifty thousand. It's the last of the view lots we've got left up on The Hill."

Andy nodded. "Okay. Well, let us think about it and I'll get back to you. We've looked at several other places we like, and we just need to decide which one suits us the best."

"That's fine, but I wouldn't wait too long. I've shown this lot a couple of times already and I've got another couple coming out tomorrow morning to take a look at it. If you decide this is the lot you want, let me know. And do it soon before it slips away from you, and you end up regretting it."

Mike drove Andy and Kelli back down to the mailboxes where they'd parked, dropped them off, and then drove away. It was just past noon, and Andy and Kelli were hungry, so they went to Native Kitchen and Social Pub in Swannanoa for lunch. Andy ordered a cheeseburger and fries, and Kelli ordered fish tacos, and they both ordered Lo-Pitch Hazy IPAs from Hi-Wire Brewing. They took their beers and walked out to the patio and found a table.

"Well, what do you think?" Kelli asked as she took a sip of her beer.

"I like it. I mean some of the others that we've looked at had views that were as good or maybe even a little bit better, but the one at Oakwood has a great view and it would be much easier to build on than the other ones that are on steeper slopes. That would save us some money that we could put into the house rather than into stone walls and dirt to create a spot to build on. There isn't much difference in the prices of the lots, so all things considered, I think the one at Oakwood is our best option. What do you think?"

"I agree. I like it a lot. Let's do it. Why don't you call Mike and tell him we'll take it before someone beats us to it," Kelli said as she picked up her beer mug and clinked it against Andy's.

Andy smiled and reached for his phone. The paperwork was signed on Monday morning and the lot on The Hill at Oakwood Farm was officially Andy's and Kelli's.

That afternoon, they drove out to the lot to take some pictures before they flew back to D.C. the next morning. They walked around, talked about where they might position their house, and tried to figure out how they could preserve as many of the trees as possible. There was a huge oak, thirty-two inches in diameter, near the bottom of the lot above Oakhaven Way that they especially wanted to keep. As they stood there talking about how they could situate the house and retain the stately oak, an older woman walked out of the woods on the other side of the road and approached them. Andy saw her first and waved.

"Hey there. How are you?" he asked just as he noticed that she had a pistol in a holster riding high up on her right hip.

"I was a damn-site better before you and your kind turned up here," she replied.

Kelli was taken aback by the woman's blunt statement. "I beg your pardon?"

"You heard me," the woman said curtly. "Coggins Farm was here for more than two hundred years, and then your kind came along and destroyed it. There used to be wildlife – bears, deer, turkeys, squirrels, box turtles – all around here until the bulldozers showed up and started knocking down the trees and digging up the dirt to make roads into what had been an unspoiled

211

sanctuary where wildlife thrived for centuries. For nearly forty years, I used to sit on my deck," she said as she pointed to a house several hundred yards away on a hill to the west, "and enjoy the peace and quiet. Now it's a bunch of fucking chainsaws and dump trucks and hammering from daylight to dark. Even if all of you assholes packed up and left tomorrow, it would take a hundred years or more before nature could repair all the damage you've done."

She rested her forearm on her pistol, looked at Andy and Kelli for a moment, and then spit on the ground. "Me and a bunch of the other locals – who hate you and your kind just as much as I do, by the way – fought the developer and tried to save this place, but he had deep pockets and paid off local officials and got his way. Thanks to you and your kind, traffic is worse, and our property values went up, so now we pay more in taxes and in return I get to spend the rest of my life having to look at you and the other outsiders who came here with your wads of cash and fucked us over. I pray every night that the whole lot of you will burn in hell for what you've done."

Andy's face turned beet red. "Ma'am, I owe you an apology. It seems I've given you the impression that I give a shit what you think," he said and then paused for a second before he added, "I don't. So why don't you haul your bitter old ass back up the hill and get the hell out of our faces. If you've got a beef with the developer, that's between you and him, but you've got no reason to be pissed off at us. And unless you're a descendent of the Cherokee, which I highly doubt, why don't you go apologize to them for fucking them over and ruining their land. They were here long before there was a … what did you call it? … a Coggins Farm. And how about your house? They had to move dirt and cut down trees to build your house, so don't come down here acting like I shit in your cornflakes when we're not doing anything you haven't already done yourself."

"Well, I've never …" the woman exclaimed before Andy cut her off and said, "and I can see why."

The woman stomped away. She paused at the edge of the woods, gave Andy and Kelli a middle finger wave, and then disappeared through the rhododendrons and back into the woods.

"Holy shit," Kelli said. "What have we gotten ourselves into? We haven't turned a shovel of dirt yet and already Annie Oakley is madder than a wet hen."

"I don't know. It seems we've made an enemy here before the ink is even dry on the contract. Can't say that bodes well for us enjoying the tranquil retirement we'd envisioned."

Khaled Abadi is the son on Mohammed Abadi and the nephew of Hassan Abadi. The Abadis were not extremely religious, and they were not officially part of the terrorist groups that sprang up in the Middle East when Mohammed and Hassan were young men. The Abadi brothers were motivated by money, not by martyrdom, and they saw the extremist groups as a pathway to wealth. Mohammed and Hassan started out small, providing forged documents and handling logistical arrangements for some of the upstart extremist groups. Over time, they expanded into furnishing guns, armament, ammunition, and explosives. As their enterprise grew, they started a legitimate venture that operated under the guise of an import-export business specializing in medical equipment and supplies, which provided cover for their more lucrative business in the illicit arms trade.

Khaled was born in 1987, four years after a truck bomb killed two-hundred and forty-one U.S. military personnel at their barracks in Beirut, Lebanon, and three years before his uncle Hassan went missing during a trip to Tripoli, Libya. Khaled was the first-born son of

213

Mohammed Abadi and his favorite wife. Khaled grew up in a posh compound on the outskirts of Riyadh, Saudi Arabia, where all of the members of the Abadi family lived. He studied at an English run school in Saudi Arabia, spent his senior year at a boarding school in England, and then attended George Washington University in D.C. where he earned a degree in international relations. He fell in love with one of his classmates, an attractive redhead from a wealthy family in Boston, and he wanted to stay in the U.S. when he graduated, but his father insisted that he return home to the family business, which put an end to his relationship with his American sweetheart.

Khaled was handsome with black hair, a dark complexion, and piercing eyes. He let his beard grow when he was at home or traveling in other middle eastern countries, but he shaved it off when he traveled to western countries. He spoke nearly perfect English with just a hint of an accent, and when his hair was cut and he was clean shaven, many mistook him for Hispanic. His mother harassed him constantly about being single at his age, and he had to work hard to avoid the events she tried to arrange to find him a bride. Khaled was handsome and from a well-to-do family, so there was no shortage of mothers with daughters who approached Khaled's mother with marriage proposals. Khaled found that the best way to avoid his mother's matrimonial schemes was to volunteer for as many business trips as he could. He knew that his mother was harassing his father more and more to try to get him to pressure Khaled to take a wife, and he wondered how much longer he could put off what seemed to be inevitable.

Khaled never wanted to go into the family business, but he felt an obligation and reluctantly returned home after college and dove in headfirst. His father started him off with relatively safe jobs, but as he gained experience, he took on more challenging and dangerous assignments. That included, from time to time, maiming or killing those who failed to pay up or otherwise interfered with the family's clandestine business. Khaled didn't like the enforcer tasks his father assigned him, and while he'd never admit it, he was scared the first few times his father sent him out with instructions to inflict physical pain or worse. He remembered how his hands shook the first time he decapitated a man in Yemen who had tried to squeeze the Abadis out of the local market by undercutting the prices they charged for explosives and refused to negotiate with them to try and resolve the dispute. But by 2018, Khaled could complete a gruesome job and then enjoy a nice dinner before going back to his hotel and falling sound asleep.

Mohammed Abadi never stopped searching for his brother after Hassan went missing in 1990. It consumed him at first, but as the years passed, he thought of it less and less. Inshallah – if God wills – he would someday find out what happened to Hassan. That day came in late 2016.

Mohammed didn't have direct business connections with the Russians, but he often supplied arms to groups that carried out attacks on those the Russians were happy to see suffer. So, when the Russians flipped a C.I.A. agent and obtained a trove of information, there was one piece that was of no use to them that they thought Mohammed would appreciate and remember when the time came, and they needed a favor from him.

Nikolai Novikov arranged to meet with Mohammed at the Abadi company offices in the heart of Riyadh. Mohammed and Nikolai had crossed paths on occasion over the years, and Mohammed knew that Nikolai had once been a senior official in the Russian intelligence agency the FSB and was still close with Russian President Vladimir Putin. Mohammed greeted Nikolai when he arrived in the lobby.

"Salam Alaykum, my friend," Mohammed said as he hugged Nikolai, kissed him on the cheek, and took his hand. "Please, come with me."

Mohammed and Nikolai sat down in plush leather chairs around a coffee table in Mohammed's palatial office, and soon a young man came in with a tray of hot tea and an assortment of sweets. They drank tea, ate pastries, smoked cigarettes, and talked about their families and their travels for nearly an hour before Mohammed finally asked Nikolai what had prompted his visit.

"I know that you've spent years looking for information about what happened to your brother, Hassan. I have acquired information that might be of interest to you in that regard. I have it from a very reliable source that your brother was killed by the Americans in Tripoli in 1990. It was carried out by the C.I.A. in retaliation for your brother supplying the explosives that killed their troops in Beirut in 1983. A senior C.I.A. official named Carson Neal directed the hit on Hassan, although he did not carry it out himself. He sent a team, a man and a woman I'm told, and perhaps others, to do the job. My source could not provide the names of those who killed your brother, but he said they were also C.I.A. and worked for this man Carson Neal. He said they disposed of your brother's body, so there is nothing of him left to be found I'm afraid. I don't know if that information is of use to you, but as your friend, I thought I should pass it along to you."

The Russians were right. Mohammed was grateful for the information, and he intended to use it to avenge his brother's death. Mohammed gave Khaled the task of finding Carson Neal, killing him, and tracking down and killing the man and woman and any others who might have been involved in the assassination of Hassan. Once that was done, Mohammed would have settled the debt that he owed his brother and the family.

"Hassan wasn't just my brother and my business partner; he was also my dearest friend. It is my solemn duty to him to avenge his death, and I am placing the family's honor in your hands, my son, and trusting you to set things right."

"I promise you, father, that I will find and kill those responsible for murdering Uncle Hassan. You have my word."

Khaled had spent four years in Washington when he was in college and he had been back a couple of times for short visits since then, so he knew the city well and was happy to go back, even under these difficult and perhaps dangerous circumstances.

Khaled looked on his college's online site and found a four-week, non-degree, continuing education program in international relations that was slated for the spring. He figured he could tack a few days on the front and back ends of that and get five weeks in the Washington area. That should give him plenty of time to carry out his mission and catch up with some of his college friends who were in D.C. He did a Google search and found an address for Carson Neal, and he printed it out with a map of the surrounding area. Now, it was just a matter of waiting for his journey to America.

Weeks later, Hassan parked outside a row of townhouses in Alexandria, Virginia, and within an hour, an African-American man came out, walked over to a BMW SUV, got in, and drove away. Khaled followed the BMW, which eventually pulled into the parking lot of a Home Depot on Pickett Street. When the driver got out and went inside the store, Khaled walked behind the BMW, looked around to make sure that no one was watching, got down on the concrete, slid under the car, and attached a small magnetic tracking device. He went back to his rental car and drove away.

On Saturday night, Carson Neal took his wife to Le Diplomate, a French restaurant in northwest Washington near Logan Circle, for dinner. He dropped her off at the door and then he parked the BMW in a garage a short distance away. Khaled followed their route on an app on his phone. When he saw that the BMW was stationary, he found a parking spot for his rental car a couple of blocks away. He slipped inside the parking garage, being especially careful to avoid the security cameras, and waited. About two hours later, Carson Neal and his wife walked into the garage. Carson opened the passenger side door for his wife, closed it when she was inside, and then he walked around to the driver's side. Just as he opened the door to get in, a man with a ski mask over his face stuck a gun in his back.

"Be quiet, don't do anything stupid, and get inside."

Carson got in and the man climbed into the back seat. Carson's wife screamed.

"Shut up!" the man said as he pointed the gun in her face. "Be quiet, look directly ahead, do as I say, and no one will get hurt."

"You can have my wallet. You can have my watch. Hell, I'll give you the keys to the car, just please, don't hurt us," Carson pleaded.

"I don't want your money or your car. What I want is some information. Give it to me and I'll get out of here and you can carry on with your evening," Khaled said and then paused for a few seconds. "I know that two people who worked for you at the C.I.A. murdered Hassan Abadi. I want to know who they are."

"I don't know what you're talking about," Carson said. "I wish I could help you, but you're mistaken. I can't give you what I don't have. You must have me confused with someone else. So please, take the car, take the money, take whatever you want, and please let us go."

Khaled took the butt of his gun and hit Carson's wife hard on the back of her head. She screamed, grabbed her head with her hands, and started to cry.

"Do you think I'm stupid? Don't try and bullshit me. I know that you ordered the hit on Hassan Abadi and that the man and woman who killed him worked for you. They're the ones I want, not you. So, I'm going to count to three and then I'm going to make your wife's headache go away by blowing her brains out unless you tell me who they are and whether others were involved in Hassan's murder. And don't try and make up some shit. I know where you live in Alexandria and if you lie to me, I assure you that the people I work for will hunt you down and kill you both, and they'll make sure you die slowly and painfully. Now I'm going to count to three and if you don't tell me who the man and woman are your wife's brains are going to be splattered on your windscreen," Khaled said as he placed his gun against the back of Mrs. Neal's head. "One, two, th…"

"Okay, okay, I'll tell you. Just please, put the gun down." Carson paused for a few seconds. "Their names are Andrew and Kelli … Andrew and Kelli Halstrom. They're husband and wife, and they live here in D.C."

"Were others involved in killing Hassan?"

"No. It was just the two of them. They carried it out alone. Now please, let us go."

"You better hope that's the truth," Khaled said as he screwed a silencer onto the barrel of his pistol. He aimed the gun at the back of Carson Neal's head and pulled the trigger, and then he turned the gun towards Mrs. Neal and fired again.

Khaled reached over to the front seat, took Carson's wallet, watch, and phone, and then grabbed Mrs. Neal's purse and removed the diamond ring from her finger. Hopefully, that would make it look like a robbery when the police came to investigate. He stepped out of the backseat of the BMW, removed his ski mask, and placed his gun inside his coat. He bent down, reached

under the rear bumper, removed the tracking device, and then he walked away. Andrew and Kelli

Halstrom, he thought to himself. Now he had to find them and finish the job.

Andy and Kelli were tired from their trip to Asheville, and they were glad to be back in

Washington. Andy stuck the key into the door of their apartment, but the door wasn't locked. He

looked at Kelli, held a finger to his lips, pointed at the door, and used two fingers to simulate

someone walking to let Kelli know there might be someone inside. She nodded indicating that

she understood. He motioned for her to stand to the right side of the door, and he moved to the

left side. He turned the knob and pushed the door so it would open slowly, then he reached inside

and flipped the switch to turn on the overhead lights. He peered inside and could see that the

apartment had been ransacked.

"I'm armed and I've called the police and they're on their way, so come out now with

your hands raised and you won't get hurt."

There was no response. Andy went in first with Kelli right behind him. They searched

both bedrooms, looked under the beds, and opened all the closets. No one was there. Kelli called

911 and reported that there had been a break-in at their apartment. As they waited for the police

to arrive, they looked to see what was missing. Kelli's jewelry box was gone. While she was

upset to have lost some valuable jewelry, she was glad that she had worn the Rolex watch Andy

gave her and her diamond engagement ring, and that she had taken a few other pieces of jewelry

with her on the trip to Asheville. Andy pressed on a small panel inside the bedroom closet and

the door to the hidden storage area he'd built opened. Inside was a lockbox that contained a hard drive, two pistols, passports, some cash, and a few other important documents. Fortunately, the intruder hadn't found the secret compartment. Andy closed it and made sure it was hidden behind some hanging clothes before the police arrived.

There was a knock at the door, and Kelli let two police officers in. They looked around the apartment and one took down information to put into their report. The senior officer said the fact that there were no signs of forced entry suggested that whoever broke in had some level of expertise. He said they would check with the building manager to see if there was any surveillance video, but he said Andy and Kelli shouldn't get their hopes up that there would be an arrest or that Kelli would ever see her missing jewelry again.

Andy and Kelli worked well past midnight cleaning up the mess in the apartment. It was almost two o'clock in the morning before they finally went to bed.

As Andy and Kelli were lying in bed trying to fall asleep, Khaled was finishing his breakfast in the first-class lounge at the airport in Frankfurt, Germany, as he waited for his flight to Riyadh to board. His father would be happy to hear the details on how he killed Carson Neal, but he would be disappointed that the man and woman responsible for killing Hassan were still out there and still drawing breath. Khaled knew that he would have to wait a bit before he could return to the U.S. and finish the job, and he'd need to find another pretext for a return trip. He thought he'd be going back to America in a matter of months to find Andy and Kelli and kill them. He was mistaken.

A few months after Khaled returned home, Saudi authorities raided the Abadi compound in the predawn hours. Khaled, his father, and several other members of the Abadi family were arrested and taken into custody. The Americans had captured a senior leader of a terrorist group in Afghanistan and turned him over to the Egyptians who applied what the Americans referred to as "enhanced interrogation techniques" and what most people call torture. Before he died of unnatural causes, the terrorist group leader gave up the Abadis as the source of the group's arms and explosives. The Americans demanded that the Saudi government hand over the Abadis so they could be tried in American courts, but the Saudis refused. Instead, they promised that they would hold the Abadis accountable in their own courts.

While the Saudis had been willing to turn a blind eye to the Abadi family's illicit business dealings for many years, pressure from the U.S. government to shut them down finally tipped the scales. Khaled, his father, and the others were convicted in the High Court of Riyadh and sentenced to prison where they would undergo "reeducation and deradicalization." Mohammed Abadi and some of the older members of the family received lengthy prison sentences while Khaled and some of the younger ones received shorter sentences.

A year into his prison sentence, Mohammed Abadi suffered a major heart attack, and he died a short time later. One of his final acts was to ask Khaled to reaffirm his vow to finish his mission and avenge the killing of Hassan. Khaled swore that he would keep his promise just as soon as he completed the four years left on his prison sentence.

On May 22, 1967, George Harding filed a patent application with the U.S. Patent and Trademark Office. George was an inventor. He worked as a top manager for General Motors in the 1930s and then became a senior official in the Department of War's Department of Strategic Metals during World War II where he was involved in the production of Liberty Ships. It was during his time in shipbuilding that he invented a portable toilet made of metal and wood that could be moved around shipyards as needed so that workers didn't waste time leaving the worksite to get to a stationary toilet every time nature called. After the war, George developed an interest in plastics. That led to his patent application for a portable toilet made of rigid plastic, that he called a "portable toilet cabana." On June 3, 1969, the Patent Office awarded George a patent on his creation and by the mid-70s the porta potty business was off and running.

Carl Freeman earned a decent living installing and servicing septic tanks. Like Mohammed Abadi, he also hoped that someday his son would take over the family business, but his son wanted nothing of it. The son was rebellious and barely made it through high school. He cut classes, smoked and drank a lot, chased girls, and got into some occasional skirmishes, which fortunately was back in the day when teens settled disputes with fists rather than firearms. When Carl's son was sixteen, the boy's grandmother remarked, "that boy's as wild as a buck," and the label stuck. From that point on, the boy was known as Buck Freeman.

Carl made Buck help him out with his septic tank business on weekends, afternoons, and during school breaks. Buck hated it and he wasn't bashful about letting his father know that he had no interest in the family business. As soon as he graduated from high school, Buck got a job working for a local construction company that built residential and light commercial buildings. Carl was so angry that Buck wouldn't work for him that he kicked his ungrateful son out of the house and the two didn't speak for over a year. The fact that it irritated his father made Buck enjoy his work as a carpenter even more. It was hard work, but Buck was good at it, and it paid well. By the time he was twenty-one, Buck was the lead on a framing crew and by twenty-five he was a project manager overseeing residential construction projects.

Buck met Eleanor Martin during the summer of 1978. Eleanor's parents were building a house, and they hired Buck's employer as their builder. Eleanor and her parents stopped by one afternoon to see how their house was coming along at the same time Buck was there checking in with the leader of the finishing crew. Buck was rolling up blueprints and preparing to put them away when the Martins arrived. The site supervisor greeted the Martins and led them over to the house to show them the work they'd done since the Martins last visited. Eleanor glanced over just as Buck looked up and they made eye contact. She smiled, turned, and then caught up with her parents.

The following week, Buck stopped at a doughnut shop to pick up coffee and doughnuts to take out to a crew at one of his job sites. While he was waiting on his order to be prepared, Eleanor walked in. Eleanor was twenty-three, three years younger than Buck, and had graduated from college the year before. She took a job as a management trainee at the local credit union, and she had stopped in the doughnut shop to buy doughnuts for a staff meeting later that morning. She was looking at a menu as she waited to place her order, and she didn't notice Buck as he walked over and stood next to her.

"Good morning. You're the young lady who was with the Martins last week when they came out and checked on the house they're building."

Eleanor looked up at Buck. "Yes, I am. They're my parents and they invited me to tag along with them. I'm Ellie Martin."

"Pleased to meet you, Ellie," Buck said as he extended his hand. "I'm Buck Freeman. I'm the project manager overseeing the houses going up in the development where your parents are building." Buck pointed at the menu and said, "I have to say, you don't strike me as the doughnut type. You look more like a yogurt or a fruit smoothie kind of girl."

Ellie chuckled. "No. I'll have a doughnut every now and then, but I don't make a habit of it. I'm a runner and I always feel like I need to put in a couple of extra miles whenever I eat a doughnut. I'm just picking these up for a meeting at work, but I may have to cheat and eat half of one; they're too good to pass up."

Ellie placed her order and then she and Buck continued talking as they both waited. After a few minutes, a person behind the counter called Buck's name, and passed him a large bag and a container of coffee.

"It was a pleasure to see you again, Ellie. I hope you enjoy your doughnuts."

"Thank you. You too."

Buck started to walk away, and then he turned back. "Ellie, I hope you don't think I'm being too forward, but I don't know when or if I'll ever bump into to you again, and this might be my one and only opportunity. Would you consider going out with me sometime, and if you have a boyfriend or something I'll understand, but I just wanted to ask while I have the chance."

"No, there's no boyfriend, or at least there hasn't been for some time. Sure. I'll go out with you. I'd like that."

Buck took out a pen and paper and wrote down Ellie's phone number. They went out a few nights later and they were married less than a year after that first date.

Buck and Carl had mended the rift between them by the time Buck married Ellie, but they grew even closer afterwards. In 1981, Buck and Ellie had a baby, a girl they named Amy Lynn, and Carl was a doting grandfather. One Sunday afternoon, when Buck and Ellie brought Amy Lynn over to visit her grandparents, Buck and Carl grabbed a couple of beers and walked out onto the deck and sat down in rocking chairs while the women stayed inside and played with the baby.

"So, how's work going? You still tied up with that development over on the river?"

"Yeah. We're probably about halfway through. They still have some unsold lots, so I'd say it'll be a couple more years before we finish building there and close it out."

"You still liking your job? I could always use you back here."

Buck laughed. "Come on, dad. You know I'm not coming back here to work for you. I like my job, but I know that I'll never be the one running the company. I want to do better for Ellie and Amy Lynn, and I've thought about starting my own construction company, but I don't know if I can come up with the money it would take to get started or whether I could make a go of it. The handful of builders in this area are all pretty well established and breaking into that market and getting a toehold could be tough. I'm not sure I could do it."

Carl took a drink from his beer and sat there in silence for a moment. "I've got an idea. You may not like it but hear me out. I've had several inquiries, mainly from builders, including the one you work for, about porta potties. You know what I'm talking about, those plastic outhouse things? No one in this area has them and I suppose it makes sense that people call me looking for them. You wouldn't have to worry about breaking into the market, you'd be establishing the market. And it's related to what I do, so I'd be happy to help you out, that is if you're interested."

Buck didn't think he was interested at first, but he thought about it some more and a few days later he went back to see his dad. He'd warmed up to the idea of running his own company and getting in on the ground floor of something before anyone else could stake a claim to the market. With some financial help and advice from his dad, Buck bought a truck and two dozen porta potties, and Thunder Huts was officially in business.

Within a year, Thunder Huts had grown to three trucks, a hundred and fifty porta potties, and five full-time employees. You couldn't drive past a building site or attend a big outdoor event without seeing Buck's green porta potties and the Thunder Huts logo featuring the image of an old outhouse and a lightning bolt. By the five-year point, Buck was the dominant player in the porta potty business in the tri-county area and his business was prospering. He built a big house with an in-ground pool for Ellie and Amy Lynn. He flew them and his mom and dad – first class – out to Jackson Hole, Wyoming, where he rented a magnificent chalet right next to the ski slope where they spent Christmas and New Years. Buck's friends good naturedly nicknamed him "The Shit King," which Ellie thought was funny until she realized that per the rules of royalty that made her "The Shit Queen."

By the early 1990s, organized crime had extended its reach out into the tri-county area. Buck didn't like making cash payments to the mob family that controlled his area, but over time he began to see the benefits of the "donations" he made every month. If a customer was late paying his bills, he might get a visit and a word of encouragement from some of the mob boys, and usually the bill was paid before the end of the day. A competitor from the next county over decided to try and cut into Buck's territory. The competitor bought an old building a quarter of a mile from Thunder Huts and was nearly finished renovating it when a fire that the fire marshal said was caused by a short in the electrical wiring burnt the building to the ground. Some men visited the competitor and told him that it would be a shame if he tried to rebuild and then suffered another tragic accident. The competitor decided that perhaps Buck's area wasn't right for him, and he stayed off Buck's turf.

In 2016, Buck and Ellie decided it was time they made plans for retirement. Buck would be turning sixty-five soon and Ellie was almost sixty-two. Buck had been running Thunder Huts for thirty-four years. He had turned down some generous offers to sell the business over the years, but now it was finally time to think seriously about cashing out and handing the reins to someone else. His daughter Amy Lynn was thirty-five and married. She and her husband had two small kids and lived on the west coast. They had no interest in moving east and certainly no interest in taking over Thunder Huts and ascending to the throne as the next Shit King and Queen of the tri-county region.

The competitor who had once tried to encroach into Buck's territory jumped at the chance to buy Thunder Huts, provided Buck's "friends" would go along with the deal; the competitor didn't want to buy the business only to see it go up in smoke due to another mysterious electrical issue. When the deal was done and all the bills and commissions were paid, Buck and Ellie walked away with nearly six million dollars in cash. Buck kept the property and the buildings where Thunder Huts was located, and the new owner of the company paid him ten thousand dollars a month in rent. Now that their financial future was secure, Buck and Ellie just had to decide where they wanted to spend their retirement years.

Buck and Ellie were among the first to buy property in Oakwood Farm and they were the first to build and move in. They built a craftsman style house with exposed beams, stained wood trim, and stone around the base of the house. It was two stories, over thirty-five-hundred square feet, with four bedrooms and three and a half baths. Behind the house, Buck added a woodshop with a guest room above it. From the rear deck of their house, they had a nice view of the mountains and the nearby ridge line. After nearly forty years of marriage and forty-five years of hard work, Buck felt like his life's dream had come true. He'd come a long way from his days as a rebellious teen begrudgingly working with his dad pumping putrid sludge out of septic tanks.

Now that she and Buck were retired and had more free time, Ellie dove back into running and soon she was fully immersed and addicted. She enjoyed the satisfaction of reaching the point where her legs ached and her lungs burned, and her mind and body screamed for her to quit, and then pushing through the pain to a state of euphoria when a flood of endorphins surged through her veins and produced a runner's high. She ran rain or shine, hot or cold, and she found that on the occasional days when she couldn't get in a run, she experienced a sense of melancholy and felt out of sorts. She enjoyed running through her new neighborhood and watching the progress on the houses that were spreading like kudzu across Oakwood Farm. She'd follow the road down to Bull Creek, cross over the foot bridge, and run along the Warren Wilson College trails. She had to pay close attention to her footing. The dirt trails were often wet and slick, and she had to traverse over tree roots and rocks. She found the challenges on the primitive trail more interesting and satisfying than running on the safe, smooth asphalt roads.

At first, Buck enjoyed spending time in his wood shop making tables, bowls, cutting boards, and boxes. He bought a lathe for his shop, but Ellie refused to let him use it until he took a class and learned how to operate it safely. Buck enrolled in a week-long woodturning class at the John C. Campbell Folk School, a school created in 1925 in Brasstown on the Cherokee and Clay County line to teach others the skills used commonly in everyday life in Appalachia. Buck enjoyed the course so much that he went back at least once a year for other courses. He bought a pop-up canopy with a canvas cover and a long folding table, and every couple of weeks he'd set up a booth at an arts and crafts fair and sell some of the wooden crafts he made in his shop. The money he took in barely covered his expenses, but he wasn't doing it to earn a living; he was doing it so he had something to do to occupy his time.

There were only so many hours Buck could spend cloistered away in his shop, and he needed to find something else to keep him busy. Soon, anytime a tree fell, a fence rail needed mending, or some briars needed to be pruned back, he was johnny on the spot. The work helped to keep him engaged, and he relished the praise he got from his neighbors for being so helpful. He was like a puppy who rolls over on its back for its owner to scratch its belly after it fetches a tennis ball; he got a sense of gratification from being praised for being such a good boy. Ellie let it slip to one of her neighbors that Buck had been known as The Shit King in their prior life, and word quickly spread, although no one ever called him that to his face. As the population of Oakwood Farm grew, everyone knew they didn't need to waste money on a handyman to perform manual labor when The Shit King would do it for free.

The whine of the chainsaw down the hill infuriated Meg Hawkins. She walked out onto her deck, and she could see two pickup trucks at the lot in Oakwood Farm where she had confronted Andy and Kelli back in the spring. She heard a snap, and then the sound of the chainsaw stopped, followed by a loud thud that echoed across the valley as a rail-straight poplar nearly a hundred feet tall tipped over and then smacked the ground hard. They were desecrating the land and destroying the habitat where deer and bears had roamed for centuries. Meg had half a mind to go inside and get her gun and go over there and run the bastards off, but the sheriff had already been out to see her twice after Mike Nixon complained that Meg was trespassing on Oakwood Farm property and frightening away potential buyers. The sheriff warned her that if she kept it up, he'd have no choice but to arrest her, and she wasn't keen on going to jail. "Fuck you," she yelled as loud as she could when it got quiet, and when the workmen looked up towards her, she gave them the finger with both hands, and then she walked back inside her house and poured herself another cup of coffee.

The builder that Andy and Kelli chose started clearing the spot where their house would be situated just before Halloween. A bulldozer pushed away the topsoil and then a backhoe dug a trench for the foundation. A crew came in and set forms in the trenches, and then a procession of cement mixers, their engines groaning from the strain as they trudged slowly up the hill, waited in line for a special truck with a pump to deliver the wet concrete slurry over to the worksite. The crew returned a few days later after the concrete had set and removed the forms. Andy and Kelli were ecstatic when they got a text from their builder with a picture of the foundation for what would eventually be their new house.

Winter was cold and wet, so work proceeded slowly. The framing crew didn't begin to construct the skeleton of the house until spring. The ZIP sheathing – green panels seven-sixteenth of an inch thick for the exterior walls and red panels five-eighths of an inch thick for the roof – were secured in place with nail guns and the seams were sealed up with wide strips of strong black tape. The constant pop-pop-pop of the nail guns was like fingernails on a blackboard to Meg Hawkins. She'd put up with the persistent disruption for two years and she knew she had two or three more years to go before all the lots in Oakwood Farm were filled with expensive houses for the rich outsiders who had invaded what had been her solitary space. From time to time, she thought about going over there late at night with a can of gasoline and a pack of matches and setting one of the houses on fire. She knew she'd enjoy sitting out on her deck with a nice glass of bourbon and watching one go up in flames, but she also knew that she'd be the prime suspect if that ever happened, and she didn't relish the thought of spending the final years of her life in a prison cell.

Andy and Kelli retired from the State Department in the summer of 2019. Their colleagues arranged a retirement luncheon for them at Founding Farmer DC on Pennsylvania Avenue a stone's throw from the White House. It was one of their favorite restaurants, not only because the food was delicious and they crafted their own spirits in their distillery, but because the restaurant prided itself on being environmentally friendly and supporting the local farming community. Kelli had her usual, a Spinach Bacon Blue Salad to which she added grilled shrimp and a glass of Viognier, and Andy decided to go for the gusto and ordered a New York Strip with spicy braised red cabbage and an Old Fashioned. Kelli got teary eyed when her colleagues got up and talked about how much they enjoyed working with her and how much they would miss her. Andy got a lump in his throat when it was his turn, and he had to work hard to make sure no one noticed. When lunch was over and they'd said their goodbyes, they collected up their retirement gifts and headed to their apartment. After more than forty years of public service, their working days were done.

Andy and Kelli rented a cottage in Chunns Cove and moved to Asheville in February of 2020. Chunns Cove Road dead ends on the south side of Town Mountain. While it's only five minutes from downtown Asheville, it's heavily wooded, sparsely populated, and creates the impression that it's a long way from civilization. The old cottage had been built by renowned architect Douglas Ellington who designed some of Asheville's most iconic buildings in the 1920s and 1930s. Ellington built himself a grand house in 1926 made of stone, wood timbers, and cast iron, and covered in ivy, and across the road he built a small wood cottage for a relative that featured a dark, wormy chestnut interior. At the time the cottage was built, wormy chestnut was considered throw away wood because it was damaged by worms and insects boring into it, but today, since chestnuts are nearly extinct, wormy chestnut, if you can find it, goes for more than twice times the price of oak.

The cottage was quirky. Subsequent owners expanded it and the additions that were attached to the original structure required stepping up or stepping down as you walked from room to room. Once a year, biologists from the North Carolina Wildlife Resources Commission visits Chunns Cove to capture, examine, and tag black bears as part of the state's effort to restore the once dwindling bear population. The area around the cottage was like a black bear thoroughfare, and in the fall when the bears are fattening up in preparation for the winter months, they were present in the yard several times a day loading up on berries from the kousa dogwood trees and acorns from the oaks.

The cottage was located on a narrow road called Bear Left and it was only a ten-minute drive from there to Oakwood Farm. It was a convenient temporary home for Andy and Kelli while their forever house was being built. Their builder texted them one afternoon and said that the next morning he'd have a crew on their lot to begin framing their house. Andy got up early and went to Hole Doughnuts in West Asheville for a baker's dozen and then to PennyCup Coffee in Haw Creek for a container of coffee to take out to the worksite. When he and Kelli arrived at their lot, three men and a woman were already at work carrying lumber from the stack near the road over to concrete foundation.

"Hey! Why don't you guys take a break and warm up with a cup of coffee and a doughnut," Andy yelled to the crew.

After the crew served themselves, Andy and Kelli poured cups of coffee, they each took a doughnut from the ones left in the box, and they sat down on the stack of lumber.

"Damn! That's delicious," Kelli said after she took a big bite out of her doughnut. "What flavor is this?"

"It's honeysuckle glazed," Andy responded. "The young lady at Hole – I think her name was Laurie – said the glaze is made from honeysuckle the owners picked last year."

"If you've already found Hole Doughnuts, I'd say you're off to a pretty good start here in Asheville," the woman on the framing crew said from her seat on the tailgate of the crew's truck.

Andy nodded. "One of our neighbors in Chunns Cove told us about it. This is my first one, but I guarantee you it won't be my last," Andy said as he took another bite. "By the way, do you think our house will be done by the Fourth of July?"

The leader of the framing crew – a man in his thirties with a long beard and his hair pulled back in a ponytail – laughed. "Sure, probably sooner. If you keep bringing us coffee and doughnuts in the morning and maybe a cooler full of IPAs at the end of the day, we can have it finished in two weeks."

A month later, the skeletal frame of the house was in place. Andy and Kelli tried to stay out of the way and not interfere with the work, and they vowed not to visit the site every day, but they broke their vow more often than they kept it. The builder said it would take another six to eight weeks to get the house dried-in, assuming the weather cooperated, and he said if everything went according to plan, the house might be done in time for them to celebrate Christmas in it.

That night, Andy and Kelli were eating dinner in the living room of their Bear Left cottage and watching ABC Evening News when David Muir announced that the White House had declared a national emergency due to the coronavirus that had recently emerged in America.

"Oh shit! This thing is getting serious."

Andy nodded in agreement. "Hopefully, it's not going to have an impact on finishing our house. They're working in open air, so I don't think it'll be a problem, but I suppose time will tell. And I guess we're lucky to be here in Asheville rather than back in D.C. Better to ride it out here in the mountains than to be packed in like sardines in the city. You wouldn't want to be stuck on the D.C. Metro at rush hour with a carload of people who might be infected with the virus."

Work on the house stopped for a couple of days, as did work on most everything else across the country. A few of the builder's craftsmen had concerns about the virus and chose not to come back to work, but the majority decided to return under new guidelines that required social distancing and the use of face masks while working in enclosed spaces. It became more difficult to get materials from suppliers as many of the manufacturers closed their shops or ran at reduced capacities. The house was finally dried-in by Memorial Day, the roof and siding were on by the Fourth of July, and the sheetrock was hung by the end of July.

As the devastating impact of COVID became more apparent, Andy and Kelli chose to isolate themselves as much as they could. They mostly stayed in Chunns Cove. They read books they had been meaning to read forever, but never seemed to find the time, and they ~~bingewatched~~binge-watched television shows that in normal times they probably never would have watched. They blazed through two seasons of Ozark – twenty episodes, each an hour-long – in five days, and they watched all nine seasons of Suits – one-hundred and thirty-four episodes, each one about forty-five minutes long – in less than a month. Andy confessed that if he ever left Kelli it would be for the sultry Donna Paulsen, the legal secretary to the main character in Suits, and Kelli said he'd get no push-back from her provided she got to run off with the main character, the dashing and debonaire Harvey Specter.

Kelli got back into running. Late one afternoon, she ran down Chunns Cove Road to Camp Allis Road and followed it until it ended over on the south side of Town Mountain where she turned around and started back home. Five minutes after she made the turn, as she rounded a corner, just ahead of her in the road were four black bears; a mother and her three cubs who were almost eight months old. Kelli stopped. The bears had flipped over a trash can, ripped open the garbage bags, and were munching on the scraps. The three cubs were totally focused on the trash spread out before them and oblivious to Kelli's presence. The mother bear, however, was vigilant and saw Kelli at the same time Kelli saw her. The mother bear took a step towards Kelli, raised up and then stomped the ground with her front legs, and let out a loud grunt. Kelli knew it was mama's way of saying, "back off, bitch!"

"Be nice now mama," Kelli said as she slowly took a few steps back while keeping a close eye on the bears. "I'm not going to hurt you or your babies."

Vance Gap Road is a narrow, dirt road carved into the side of Town Mountain. To Kelli's left was a steep incline and to her right was a sharp drop off, and briars and brush rendered both sides of the road inaccessible to anyone with bare legs. There was no way for Kelli to get back to the cottage except to go straight ahead. She waited several minutes thinking that the bears would eventually move on, but they didn't. She tried yelling at them, but it was to no avail. She thought that perhaps a car or truck would come along and scare the bears away, but none came. Finally, after nearly fifteen minutes of waiting and with no end to the standoff in sight, Kelli pulled out her phone and called Andy.

"Hey, I'm stuck, and I can't get home. Can you come get me?"

What?" Andy asked. "What do you mean you can't get home?"

"I'm out on Vance Gap and a family of black bears has taken up residence in the middle of the road and won't let me pass. Can you jump in the car and come get me?"

A few minutes later, Kelli heard the sound of a car approaching. It was Andy in their Subaru Outback, which seemed to be the unofficial car of choice for progressive Ashevillians. Andy blew the car horn and the bear cubs scurried off into the brush. Mama bear just stood there. She gave Andy a look that he interpreted to mean "fuck you, asshole," and then she slowly waddled off the road and over to the edge of the woods. Andy pulled forward and Kelli climbed into the passenger seat.

"Thank you," she said as he drove down to a fork in the road, turned around, and started back towards the cottage. About fifty feet past the spot where the bears had knocked over the trash can, Kelli said, "okay, you can stop here and let me out."

"What? You made me come out here so I could drive you what, fifty feet maybe?"

"Yes," she said as she leaned over and kissed him on the cheek. "I'll see you back at the cottage." Kelli climbed out of the car and resumed her run. When Andy drove past her, he rolled down his window and gave her the finger. She laughed and responded back with double birds.

Andy and Kelli didn't have an active social life before COVID rolled in and even less of one afterwards. Once a week, a neighbor in Chunns Cove who had a firepit would invite them and another couple over. Each couple brought their own food, beverages, and chairs, and they sat at least ten feet apart around the fire. Andy called them his "COVID Comrades" and he enjoyed the social interaction, as impersonal as it was. He wondered whether this was going to become the new normal and he worried about how the world might change if COVID kept spreading and growing worse. The death toll was climbing, and there didn't seem to be any light at the end of the tunnel. He thought how ironic it was that a year ago you'd get in trouble if you walked into a bank wearing a mask over your face and now you get in trouble if you walked in not wearing one. Neither he nor Kelli had ever used Zoom before, but now Zoom was their lifeline to the outside world. They soon adapted to doing things from their couch clad in sweatpants and slippers that used to require getting dressed in real clothes and driving to a face-to-face meeting.

On a warm afternoon in mid-September, Kelli went to Trader Joe's to do her weekly shopping. Because of COVID, an employee was stationed at the door to limit the number of customers who were allowed inside at one time. She had to wait in line for ten minutes before it was her turn to go in. Kelli was a decent cook, and her skills improved as she cooked more than she ever had before out of necessity during the pandemic. It occurred to her as she was shopping that they had saved money because of the virus. They used to eat out five or six times a week. Now, they ordered takeout every couple of weeks and did their own cooking the rest of the time.

She wondered if they would ever be able to return to their old lifestyle or perhaps some modified version of it. She finished her shopping, lugged her four reusable cloth shopping bags loaded to the brim with supplies out to the Subaru, and headed home. Even though she knew the way and had heard it many times before, she punched in "home" on the GPS just so she could hear the soothing female voice instruct her to "bear left on Bear Left." It made her smile every time she heard it.

After she unloaded the car, she decided to drive out to Oakwood Farm to check on the progress on the house since their last visit. Andy was on his laptop working on an op-ed he was planning to submit to the Asheville Citizen Times newspaper, so he said he wanted to stay there and keep working. Kelli got to the house at Oakwood Farm, pulled down the makeshift gravel driveway, parked, and went inside. In the early days of construction, progress was readily apparent every day; another wall was up, the roof was covered, there was flooring where there used to be planks across the floor joists. Now that they were doing more intricate finish work, progress wasn't as noticeable. It was clear that work had been done since the last time she was there, but if pressed, she couldn't identify exactly what they'd done.

Kelli locked up the house and walked back towards her car. A short distance away, she heard someone coughing. She looked over towards the road and saw Meg Hawkins, handgun on her hip, trudging up the hill. The coughing got louder and more violent.

"Ma'am, are you okay?" Kelli asked.

Meg stopped, coughed again, and said "mind your own damn business."

"I'm not trying to meddle in your business, but it sounds like you're under the weather. Can I help you or give you a ride home?"

"No, god damn it, I don't want a fucking ride," Meg said before she started coughing again and had to double over with her hands on her knees to steady herself. When her coughing finally subsided, she said, "listen honey, I know you mean well, but I don't need any help. I'll be fine on my own. But thank you for offering."

Meg continued walking towards the path that led up to her house, coughing every few seconds as she proceeded along slowly.

"I hope you feel better," Kelli shouted. Then she got into her car, started the engine, and drove back to the cottage at Bear Left.

When she got home, Kelli told Andy that she'd checked on their house and really couldn't see that the builder had done much since the last time they were there.

"As I was leaving, I saw Annie Oakley again. She sounded like she was going to cough up a lung and she looked like shit. I offered her a ride home, but she declined."

Andy smiled. "Did she tell you to go fuck yourself?"

239

Kelli smiled back. "Words to that effect."

The next morning, Andy was up first and made coffee for himself and for Kelli. He carried the cups to the bedroom where Kelli was slipping on her jeans. She thanked Andy for the coffee, took a sip, and said, "I know you're going to think I'm crazy for saying this, but I'm worried about Annie Oakley. I think we should go check on her."

Andy looked at here in disbelief. "Have you got a death wish? Are you just trying to create a reason for her to shoot us?"

"Come on, Andy, I'm being serious. I'm pretty sure she lives alone and I'm telling you, she was really sick when I saw her last night. If you don't want to go with me that's fine, you can stay here, and I'll go by myself."

"I'm not going to let you do that. I'll go with you. Do you even know how to get to her place? The only way to get there that I've seen is that footpath that leads up through the woods."

"I'm not sure how to get there, but I bet we can find the road on Google Maps."

Even though Annie Oakley's house was only a quarter of a mile away from where Andy and Kelli were building, it wasn't in Oakwood Farm. It was on Reed Road, which branched off from Old Farm School Road a half mile before Oakwood Farm. The GPS guided the way. The road was narrow and paved, and then turned to dirt a hundred yards before it reached Annie Oakley's house. The house was small and appeared to have been built several decades ago. It had cedar siding that hadn't been stained or sealed in years and a dark gray metal roof with streaks of brown from years of runoff and patches of moss in spots where moisture puddled. Andy turned off the engine and looked over at Kelli.

"Are you sure you want to do this?"

"Yeah. But listen, it might be better if I go knock on the door alone. The two of us together might set her off. But you be ready to get us out of here quick if she goes ballistic."

Kelli got out of the car and walked slowly towards the house.

"Hello. Are you home? It's me, the woman you saw last night. I just wanted to check and make sure you're okay." Kelli stepped up onto the deck, walked over to the door, and knocked.

"Hello. Are you okay?" There was no answer. Kelli listened closely, but she couldn't hear anyone moving inside the house. Kelli walked around the deck to a big picture window and looked inside. She saw Annie Oakley lying face down on the floor next to a couch and her pistol sitting not far away on an old beaten-up coffee table.

"Andy," she screamed. "Come here quick."

Andy jumped out of the car and ran towards the house. "What's wrong?" he asked when he got to the deck.

"She's face down on the floor and her pistol is on the coffee table. I don't know if she's dead or alive."

Andy looked in through the window and saw a woman's body stretched out on the floor. He knocked on the window. "Hey! Can you hear me?" The woman didn't move. Andy went to the door and tried to open it, but it was locked. There was a stack of firewood nearby, and Andy grabbed a log and used it to break the glass in the door. He reached careful through the broken pane, turned the deadbolt, opened the door, and he and Kelli went inside. Kelli got down on her knees next to Annie Oakley and checked for a pulse.

"She alive," Kelli said as she gently turned Meg over onto her back.

Andy pulled out his phone to call 911, but there was no cell signal. "Fuck! No service. Let's get her to the car and drive her to Mission Hospital."

Andy slid his arms under Annie Oakley's body and lifted her up. Kelli ran ahead of him to the car and opened the back door. Andy placed Annie Oakley gently on the back seat while Kelli ran around to the other side, climbed into the back, and placed the woman's head on her lap. Andy started the engine and drove as fast as he could to Mission Hospital.

Annie Oakley – whose real name is Meg Hawkins – had COVID. For a time, it seemed she was destined to become part of the growing number of COVID casualties in Buncombe County, but Meg was as tough as shoe leather, and while it was touch and go for nearly three weeks, she pulled through. Five weeks after Andy Halstrom carried her unconscious body into the emergency room at Mission Hospital, an attendant wheeled her out front and helped her into Kelli's Subaru for the ride home.

Kelli and Meg rode in silence until they were almost halfway to Meg's house. As they waited at a traffic light on Tunnel Road, Meg broke the silence.

"Thank you and your husband for looking out for me. I know I probably would have died had you not come out to the house to check on me. I don't have any friends of family, so my rotting corpse would have been stinking the place up by the time somebody came along and found me. I'm grateful to you."

Kelli reached over and patted Meg's hand. "You're welcome. Andy and I are just glad we could help and we're happy that you're okay and able to go home. That's what neighbors do; they look out for each other."

When they reached Meg's house, Kelli helped her inside and got her situated on the couch. Kelli walked out to the Subaru and returned with a cardboard box. "I doubt you're going to feel like cooking for a few days, so I made you some things that I'm going to put in your refrigerator. There are a couple of salads and some other dishes that you'll just need to heat up.

242

Hopefully that'll tide you over until you're back on your feet. And I'm leaving a note on your countertop with my cell phone number. If you need anything, just give me a call."

Meg's eyes got moist. "I don't know what to say. You've been so incredibly kind to me, even after I treated you and your husband like dog shit. I owe both of you an apology. I'm sorry about the way I behaved. I really do appreciate everything you've done for me. I mean it."

"Don't you worry about it. We're happy to help. But if you don't mind me asking, Meg, why are you so angry towards other people?"

Meg paused for a moment before she answered. "I wasn't always like this. Sharon and I moved here in 1983, and we had this house built. There was no such thing as same-sex marriage back in those days, but we felt as if we were every bit as married as those who had a big church wedding. Both of our families disowned us, and we didn't feel welcomed where we lived in Texas. People made rude comments and a couple of folks said we were going to burn in hell, but it was mainly the hateful looks we got almost every time we went out in public. That led us to Asheville. I mean we still got a few nasty looks every now and then, and an occasional hostile comment, but for the most part we felt accepted here, like we were regular people rather than some oddity or aberration. Sharon taught at the university, and I worked downtown at a book shop. And we had our little house out here in the woods away from civilization and everything was wonderful for a lot of years. We were happy, incredibly happy. We had developed a small, close-knit community of like-minded people, and everything was just great. We'd found a place where we fit in."

"Then, about the times word got out that Coggins Farm was going to be sold, Sharon was diagnosed with cancer. That was back when Mission Hospital was still a fabulous medical facility, and she got great care there, and she was doing well. She took an active role in the fight

243

to stop the developer from building Oakwood Farm, and I think that gave her something to focus on and a real purpose to her life."

"She was devastated when the county approved the development and then the developer rolled in and started take down trees and carving out roads. And then her cancer flared up again. I came home one evening, and I found a note there on the coffee table. It said she was tired and wanted to rest. That she was worn out from fighting and wanted to be at peace. She said she loved me, and she knew I'd be devasted, but it was her decision to end her life rather than letting her body and mind continue to deteriorate bit by bit. I found her in the bedroom. She'd taken almost a whole bottle of Vicodin."

"After Sharon died, I shutout the people who had been our friends. I blamed the developer and the people moving into Oakwood Farm for taking away Sharon's will to live. I remember the first time I met you and your husband, and he told me to haul my bitter old ass back up the hill. He was right; I'd become a bitter old ass. I had a lot of time to think about it the past few weeks while I was laying in that hospital bed. There's no one to blame for Sharon's decision to take her own life. I shouldn't have let my grief turn into anger, but that's what I did. I wanted to find someone to blame when really no one is to blame."

Kelli sat down next to Meg and took her hand. "I'm so sorry, Meg. You've been through a lot, but you're still here. Well, tomorrow's a new day. I've found that when you wake up in the morning, whether you tell yourself that it'll be a great day or it'll be a horrible day, when you go to bed that night, whichever one you chose probably came true. You've got good days ahead of you, if that's what you want."

Meg smiled. "Thank you."

A week after they took Meg Hawkins to the hospital, Andy came down with COVID too. For several days he had a fever, and he told Kelli that his throat felt like he had gargled with broken glass, but, as shitty as he felt, he didn't require hospitalization. Within a week, the symptoms began to subside, and after three weeks, he had fully recovered. Kelli was lucky and managed to dodge the COVID bullet despite being in close contact with both Andy and Meg when they were infected.

Nearly all the property owners at Oakwood Farm knew about Meg Hawkins; many of them had experienced her ornery disposition firsthand. It didn't take long for word to spread that Andy and Kelli had saved Meg's life. While folks at Oakwood Farm weren't particularly fond of Meg, they thought it was commendable that Andy and Kelli rescued her. Andy and Kelli hadn't even moved into the neighborhood yet and they were already considered heroes by many of their soon-to-be neighbors. That didn't make Buck Freeman happy.

All the lots in Oakwood Farm were sold, so the developer packed up and relinquished control over the community to the residents on January 1, 2020. Now that the residents were in charge, they had to choose who would serve on the board of directors of the Oakwood Farm Homeowners' Association.

Buck Freeman relished the opportunity to serve as what he considered to be the Mayor of Oakwood Farm. He and Ellie were close friends with some of the others who were among the first residents to move into the development. That included Bob and Denise Carlson and Karen Walters. Bob Carlson had been a radiologist in Buffalo for nearly four decades. Denise hated the harsh Buffalo winters, and Bob promised her that when he retired, they would move to a more temperate climate and escape the cold and the snow. Karen Walters and her husband Bill were both attorneys who founded their own firm – Walters Kirkpatrick & Simons PLLC – in Miami. They bought a lot in Oakwood Farm intending to build a few years later after they both retired when they planned to split their time between South Florida in the winter and the Asheville mountains in the summer. Not long after they closed on the lot, however, Bill suffered a stroke while golfing with two of the other partners and a client, and he died a few days later. Karen hadn't planned to retire for another four or five years, but after Bill's unexpected death, she reassessed her life and decided it was time for her to start a new chapter. The remaining partners in the law firm agreed to buy out the interest she and Bill held, and she sold their house in Miami and moved to Asheville for a new beginning.

Just before Christmas in 2019, Buck and Ellie invited Bob, Denise, and Karen over for drinks and hors d'oeuvres. It was supposed to be a holiday celebration, but for Buck it was the initial move in his scheme to take control of Oakwood Farm. After everyone had a few drinks and they were relaxed, Buck spoke up.

"Listen, we've got to elect a board soon to run the HOA. We were all among the first to build and move in here, and we know the neighborhood better than the newer arrivals. We've got a good thing going here and it would be a shame to let others we don't know all that well step in, take over, and screw things up. I think we ought to stick together and run for the board. What do you guys think?"

Denise agreed. "I think it's an excellent idea, but it's not something I want to do. You and Bob and Karen would make a great team, so I think it should be the three of you."

Bob nodded in agreement. "Makes sense to me. I'm game if Karen is."

"Count me in!" Karen said as she raised her glass of wine. "Let's do it!"

Buck smiled. "The board seats are for four years, so we'll be in charge until 2024. By then, most of the houses will be built, and we'll have molded Oakwood Farm the way we want to see it evolve. After that, who gives a shit? By then, all the board will need to do is make sure the grass gets cut and the potholes get filled. It's these early years when the community is taking shape that matters the most."

When nominations for the board opened, only one other resident put his hat in the ring. Mark Scott and his husband were relative newcomer to Oakwood Farm, and they weren't part of the early arrival clique. Over the course of a few weeks, Buck spoke with most of Oakwood Farm's residents, and he made it clear that he "had nothing against the gays, but I'm not sure we need that kind running our neighborhood." Mark Scott finished a distant fourth in the voting. Buck was chosen as president – or as he preferred to think of it, "The Mayor" – Bob became the vice-president, and Karen assumed the duties as secretary and treasurer. The Oakwood Farm Homeowners' Association was officially up and running.

Andy realized that they hadn't checked the mail in nearly a week. He told Kelli that he was going to walk down to the Chunns Cove mailboxes, and he would be back shortly. It was late October and there was a chill in the air. Andy grabbed a jacket and a knit cap from the hallway closest, and then he slipped on his hiking shoes. The leaves had turned beautiful shades of red, orange, and yellow, and when the wind blew, they showered down on Andy as he strolled down the hill. He thought to himself how nice it was not to have to rake leaves. Instead, he periodically got out a blower and blew them away from the cottage and into the woods where they could decompose and nourish the soil. When he reached the bottom on the hill, he used his

247

key, unlocked the mailbox, and pulled out a handful of mail, most of it junk; sale flyers and political postcards from candidates running in the November election. He turned the key and locked the mailbox, and then he started back up the hill to the cottage.

"Did we get anything important?" Kelli inquired when Andy walked in.

"Not really. It's mostly just crap. There's a bunch of election stuff. I see that none of the candidates are talking about what they plan to do if they win, instead it's all dire warnings about what assholes their opponents are. I'll be glad when the damn thing's over. I'm sick of the attack ads and the doom and gloom scare tactics."

Kelli laughed. "Well, some of those assholes are going to end up winning, and then it won't be long until the whole process starts over again. It's like one election cycle just rolls right over into the next one and it just never stops."

Andy opened an envelope, pulled out a single-page letter, and read over it quickly. "Well, that's a crock of shit," he said in disgust.

"What?" Kelli asked.

"It's a letter from the fucking HOA saying they're fining us five-hundred-dollars because our builder cut down too many trees on our lot. They cleared the trees over a year ago, and we're just now getting fined? Someone from the board has been up on the lot numerous times while we've been building, and they've never said a damn word about the trees. The letter's signed by Buck Freeman. I'm going to call him and see what the hell's going on here."

Andy called Buck, and they arranged to meet at the lot the next afternoon.

Andy was already there when Buck drove up the hill in his truck and parked by the side of the road.

"Afternoon, Andy," Buck said as he extended his hand.

"Hey Buck. How are you?"

"Doing fine. Your house is really coming along. When do you think they'll be finished?"

"They say we'll be in it before Christmas, but I'll believe it when I see it. COVID's created supply chain problems, and some of our appliances are still on backorder. They keep checking, but Haywood Appliance says they're having a hard time getting definitive information from the manufacturers on expected delivery dates. The county's not going to give us a certificate of occupancy until we get the appliances installed, so we'll just have to wait and see how it goes. I'm keeping my fingers crossed."

"Well, you're not alone. Some of the other folks who're building are getting held up too waiting on windows and doors and roofing and such. It's a shame those idiots up in Washington have damn near shut down the whole fucking country over this coronavirus horseshit. It's a load of nonsense if you ask me."

Andy didn't know Buck well, and he started to respond to his spurious claims about COVID, but then he realized that he knew Buck well enough to know that engaging him in a debate on whether the pandemic was real or a hoax would be about as productive as arguing with a tree stump, so he let it go. Andy reached into his coat and pulled out the letter he'd received from the HOA.

"I wanted to talk with you about this," he said as he showed Buck the letter. "Our builder cleared the lot last October and now, a year later, we're just getting notified that he took out too many trees and we're getting fined?"

Buck nodded. "Yeah. You're allowed to cut down trees that are within the perimeter of where the house will be situated, and you can take out twenty percent of the trees outside the perimeter that are four to eight inches in diameter and ten percent of the trees greater than eight inches in diameter. I don't have a problem with the trees they cut down where your house is sitting or the smaller trees they took out, but they cut down more than ten percent of the trees outside the perimeter that we're eight inches or bigger. If you want, I can show you the stumps where the trees were."

"Please do," Andy responded.

Buck and Andy walked around the lot. Buck pulled out a tape measure at several spots where trees had been cut down almost flush with the ground and he measured their diameter.

"Look here. You can see that this is more than eight inches, actually it's eight and a quarter."

"I see that," Andy said, "but aren't you supposed to measure a tree at chest height rather than down there flush with the ground?"

"Well, the tree's gone, so I can't measure it at chest height. All I can do is measure what's left."

"You're telling me that a tree that's eight and a quarter inches at its base would be over eight inches at this height," Andy said as he held his hand flat in front of his chest. "What have you got that proves that?"

"Well," Buck replied, "what have you got that proves it was less than eight inches?"

"You're going to fine me five-hundred-dollars when you can't prove that some of these trees were over eight inches at chest height and then you want to put the burden on me to disprove it? Do you really think that's fair?"

"Well, hero, fair or not, that's the way it is. As the letter says, you have thirty days from the date of the letter to pay the fine, and if you don't, we'll slap an additional fine on you every day until it is paid. I don't give a damn one way or the others, it's not my monkey and it's not my circus. It's yours, pal."

"That's bullshit," Andy snapped back angrily.

"You ain't seen nothing yet, hero. Shit, we're just getting started," Buck said as he chuckled, turned, and started walking back to his truck.

"Fuck you, you prick!" Andy yelled.

"The only one who's going to get fucked is you, asshole," Buck responded, and then he got in his truck and drove away. He gave Andy the finger as he went by.

Andy appealed the fine to the HOA board. He supported his appeal with a letter from a certified arborist who said a poplar, an oak, or a pine that was eight and a quarter inches at the ground would almost certainly be less than eight inches in diameter at chest height, which is a height of four and half to five feet above the ground. The board voted to deny the appeal and told Andy that if the fine was not paid within two weeks, they would impose additional fines and if necessary, they'd slap a lien on his property. That made Buck Freeman happy.

Andy and Kelli were pleasantly surprised when their builder's prediction came true, and their house was finished before Christmas. They had already picked out most of the furniture and just a few days after the house was ready a truck from Tyson Furniture pulled up and two men went to work carrying pieces off the truck and to the bedrooms, living room, and dining room. Over the months, Andy and Kelli had visited over two dozen art galleries and purchased works from Olga Dorenko, Philip DeAngelo, and Jonas Gerard for their walls. They bought handblown sculpted glass from Lexington Glassware and custom metal and wood artwork from Mark Woodham's studio in Burnsville. They worked daily well into the night to get everything placed and hung, and the house was beginning to take shape, but still something was missing, and Andy knew exactly what it was.

The next morning, Andy told Kelli to get in the car, there was somewhere they needed to go. When she asked where, he said "just trust me."

It was just a couple of days until Christmas, but there were still a lot of cars in the parking area at Sandy Hollar Farms in Leicester when Andy and Kelli pulled in.

"The thing we're missing at our house is a Christmas tree," Andy said as he turned off the ignition. "I imagine the best ones have already been chopped down and taken, but it looks like there's still some decent ones left for us to pick from."

Kelli smiled. "You're right. Let's go find our tree."

And an hour and a half later, they pulled into their driveway with an eight-foot-tall Frazier fir tied down securely on the roof of the Subaru. They carried it inside and Kelli brought out a box containing lights and ornaments, and they spent the next hour decorating the tree. When they turned off the lights in the room that evening after it got dark and plugged in the lights on the tree, they both stood there in silence marveling at the warmth and beauty it added.

It was cold and windy on Christmas Eve. Kelli ladled chili into bowls as Andy opened a bottle of merlot, poured two glasses, and set them at their places on the live-edge dining table. He walked over and added another log to the fire just as Kelli set the bowls down and then took a seat. When Andy got to the table and sat down, Kelli raised her glass.

"Here's to our first Christmas in our new home. I can't believe that we're finally here and settled. It's perfect."

"And here's too many more Christmases to follow," Andy said as he clinked his glass against Kelli's.

By the time they finished eating, snow had started to fall, tiny flakes coming down lightly at first, but then much heavier as the night went on. The next morning was bright and sunny. The snow had stopped falling, but not before leaving a three-inch white covering on the ground and on the branches of the trees. Kelli looked out the big picture window in the living room. To the east, Lane Pinnacle and Craggy Knob were resplendent as the rising sun made the white capped pines and rhododendrons glisten. Andy walked in with two cups of coffee and handed one to Kelli. Andy placed his arm over her shoulder as he stood next to her and admired Mother Nature's beauty. Andy pulled Kelli tight against his side.

"Our first Christmas in our new house is a White Christmas. I think that's a good omen."

Kelli looked up at Andy and then kissed him on the cheek. "'Tis indeed."

As 2021 began, it had been nearly four years since Andy was diagnosed with Parkinson's. The medications his doctors prescribed seemed to help mitigate his symptoms and most days a casual observer wouldn't see any signs that Andy suffered from the disease. Every couple of weeks he would have a day or two here and there where he had a noticeable tremor in his right hand and right foot, his legs were stiff and made it difficult to stand or walk, and he had trouble falling asleep and was restless in bed. Fortunately, the worst of the symptoms would end in forty-eight hours or so and then he would have a string of good days where he felt fine again. Still, Andy knew that there were more bad days on the horizon and that inevitably his symptoms would progress and get worse. Regardless, he was thankful that Parkinson's was taking it slow and allowing him to enjoy at least the early part of retirement in relatively good health. He was going to take advantage of the good days he had left and enjoy as much of the outdoors as he could for as long as he could.

Hippocrates – considered to be the father of mind-body medicine – said that "the natural healing force within each one of us is the greatest force in getting well." The Cherokee believe that health is tied to living in a harmonious, stable, and reciprocal relationship with nature, what they called "Duyukta," the path of harmony and balance. Andy hadn't put any real thought into it, but he was practicing what Hippocrates and the Cherokee preached. The best medicine he was receiving was right outside his window … those beautiful Blue Ridge Mountains.

Ellie Freeman and Karen Walters ran together nearly every day on the paved roads in Oakwood Farm and the dirt trails on the Warren Wilson College property on the other side of Bull Creek. Several times a week, Kelli would cross paths with them when they were all out on a run at the same time. At first, she waved and said hello, but after it became apparent that they were deliberately snubbing her, she gave up. Ellie and Karen always dressed in ~~colorcoordinated~~color coordinated running attire and in full makeup with their hair pulled back in matching scrunchies. Many Oakwood Farm residents who weren't part of Ellie's and Karen's early arrival clique referred to them as the Desperate Housewives because of their haute pretentiousness. Andy referred to them as "the shrews" because of their ugly dispositions.

Ellie was a competitive runner when she was younger, and she ran on her high school and college track teams. She didn't run much after she married Buck and soon gave birth to Amy Lynn, but she still managed to do an occasional half-marathon when she was younger and ~~tenkilometer~~ten-kilometer events as she got older, and she always placed well among the women in her age group.

254

Karen was never a competitive runner, but she and her late husband used to jog occasionally, and they participated in a few five-kilometer charity runs. After Bill died, Karen decided she needed to be more health conscious, and she made a vow to get into better shape. She started running almost every day. She was happy when she was able to connect with Ellie after they both moved into their new homes, and they were among the first of the early arrivals in Oakwood Farm. They were kindred spirits, and they enjoyed their daily runs that were equal parts of exercise and of gossip.

Kelli had never done anything to provoke Ellie and earn her ire. Instead, Ellie's resentment was the product of jealousy. Ellie considered herself to be attractive, particularly for a woman her age, but she knew that she couldn't hold a candle to Kelli whose natural beauty needed no enhancement. One evening when Ellie and Buck were having drinks with Bob and Denise Carlson, Ellie overheard Bob and Buck talking as Bob was uncorking a bottle of wine.

"I saw the new girl, Kelli Halstrom, out running this morning in a pair of those skin-tight pants that leave little to the imagination," Bob said. "Good God almighty, that's one incredible piece of ass."

Buck chuckled. "I know what you mean. I've admired that view as well. I sure as hell wouldn't kick her out of bed for eating crackers."

That did not make Ellie Freeman happy.

On a cold January morning, Kelli was well into the endorphin-fueled stage of a run when she rounded a corner on one of the Warren Wilson trails and saw Ellie and Karen up ahead of her. A few times before she had come up behind them, made a concerted effort to catch up to them and pass them, and then left them trailing behind eating her dust. She knew she shouldn't be proud of the pleasure she got out of beating them, but she enjoyed it, nonetheless. Kelli picked up her pace and overtook the pugnacious duo just before they reached the bridge that crossed over Bull Creek and back onto Oakwood Farm. As she went past them and then merged back into the center of the trail, she heard Ellie mutter "bitch!" Kelli slowed down, stopped, and turned around. Ellie and Karen stopped too, about ten feet away.

"You know Ellie, you're a bitter, pathetic, coward who'll talk trash behind peoples' backs, but you're too chickenshit to do it to their faces."

Ellie folded her arms across her chest, tilted her head to one side, and looked directly at Kelli. "I'll call you a bitch to your back or to your face, it doesn't matter to me. You and your husband roll in here and you think you're better than the rest of us. Well, we were here first, and we don't have to put up with your high and mighty bullshit. So, I suggest you run on home to your weak, pathetic husband and stay the hell out of my way if you know what's good for you."

Kelli laughed. "I know it can't be easy for you being married to The Shit King, and if you were a halfway decent human being, I'd pity you, but you're not, so I don't. You're just a hateful old hag who can only make yourself feel better about your own miserable existence by trying to drag down others. So, you just hate on if that's what it takes for you to get you through your shitty day. Your hate doesn't put a dent in my happiness. Oh, and I hope you enjoy the view of my ass, because that's the only view you'll ever have." Kelli turned and resumed her run.

"You're going to regret that, you arrogant bitch!" Ellie yelled. Kelli raised her right arm and extended her middle finger, and she didn't look back.

A week later, Ellie was out by herself on a run when she saw Kelli run across the bridge and over onto the Warren Wilson trails. She knew that in about a half-hour Kelli would be back at the bridge to cross back over into Oakwood Farm and head home. Ellie walked down to Bull Creek to the bridge. She went down to the edge of the creek, picked up a river rock about the size of a softball, walked a short distance off the trail, and hid behind a big oak tree that stood next to a long row of rhododendrons. She sat down on a big rock and waited for Kelli to return. "I'll teach that bitch a lesson," she thought to herself. "You don't fuck with Ellie Freeman."

It seemed to Ellie like a long time passed, but eventually she caught a glimpse of Kelli as she rounded a corner and headed in her direction. Ellie stood up, grasped the rock with her right hand, and raised it to a throwing position. As Kelli came off the bridge and went past Ellie, Ellie brought her arm back and was about to hurl the rock at Kelli, when she felt a sharp poke in her back and heard Meg Hawkins say, "if you do that, it'll be the last damn thing you ever do on this earth. Drop it!"

Ellie turned around and saw Meg less than three feet away with a pistol in her right hand. Ellie swung her arm and tried to strike Meg on the side of her head with the rock just as Meg pulled the trigger. Ellie fell to her knees, dropped the rock, and slumped over on the ground. Kelli heard the gunshot and stopped. She looked back and saw Meg with the pistol in her hand and Ellie down on the ground. She turned and ran back towards them.

"Oh my God! What happened?"

"She was about to hit you in the back of the head with that rock," Meg said as she pointed at the rock on the ground with the pistol she was still holding in her right hand. "I told her to stop, and then she took a swing at me with it, so I shot her."

Kelli got down on her knees and rolled Ellie over onto her back. She was still breathing. Blood poured from a wound to her lower abdomen. Kelli rolled Ellie over on her side to look for an exit wound, but there was none. Kelli took off her jacket and pressed it against the wound to slow down the blood flowing profusely from the wound. "I'm going to stay here with her. There's no cell service down here, so you go to the first house you see and call 911."

"Why in the hell would I do that?" Meg asked. "She could have killed you and she tried to kill me. I say we drag her ass into the brush and leave her out here where she belongs. No one will be the wiser and they sure as hell won't miss her."

"Are you serious? I'm sure other people heard the gunshot, and they'll come to see what happened."

"No, they won't," Meg said. "The Park Service has a firing range not far from here, so people are accustomed to hearing gunshots. They won't think a thing about it."

"Well, when she doesn't show up at home, Buck will start looking for her, and there's no way they won't find her eventually. I doubt you want to go to jail for murder and I sure as hell don't won't to go to jail for being an accessory to murder, so go call 911 ... now!"

An ambulance pulled up on the other side of Bull Creek a short time later followed by three sheriff's deputies. The EMTs took over from Kelli, placed Ellie on a stretcher, carried her over the bridge to the ambulance, and raced off to Mission Hospital with lights flashing and the siren blaring. The commotion attracted a gaggle of onlookers, and the deputies cordoned off the area to keep them back. The sheriff arrived and spoke with Kelli and Meg. Meg explained that she was out for a walk when she saw Kelli running towards the bridge and then she noticed Ellie come along, pick up a rock, and hide in the rhododendrons. She suspected Ellie was up to no good and was planning to do something bad to Kelli, so she circled around behind Ellie to try and stop her if that proved to be the case. When she saw Ellie raise the rock to throw it at Kelli, she pulled out her gun and told Ellie to stop. When Ellie swung the rock at her and tried to strike her in the head, she fired the gun. The sheriff said he was going to take Kelli and Meg to his office to get formal statements, but it sounded like a case of self-defense.

The district attorney agreed with the sheriff, and Meg wasn't charged in the shooting of Ellie Freeman. The bullet Meg fired passed through part of Ellie's intestines and lodged in a hip bone that was partially shattered. The surgeons had to remove a portion of Ellie's intestines as well as the remnants of the bullet and some bone fragments. Ellie was in the hospital for nearly three weeks, but she survived. Because of her injuries, she was never able to run again. Before she left the hospital, the sheriff questioned Ellie about what happened that day. Ellie invoked her Fifth Amendment rights and declined to answer any questions. The District Attorney considered bringing charges against Ellie for her attempt to either kill or injure Kelli and her assault on Meg, but Kelli persuaded him to let it go. "She's paid a hefty price for what she did. She doesn't need to go to prison too. Just let it be."

Word spread around Oakwood Farm about Ellie's attempt to attack Kelli and Kelli saving Ellie's life. Kelli had now saved the lives of two people, and she had earned the admiration of many of her Oakwood Farm neighbors, with the exception of the early arrivals clique. Buck Freeman was grateful that Kelli saved Ellie from bleeding to death, but he resented how she and her husband were admired by their neighbors while Ellie's actions had tarnished their own reputations. He had thoughts of moving away and getting a fresh start somewhere new, but then he decided that he wasn't going to be run out of his own neighborhood by a couple of late arriving do-gooders. He figured that the animosity towards him and Ellie in the Oakwood Farm community would dissipate with the passage of time, and he was willing to ride it out, but still it ate at him.

Not long after, Andy was going through a stack of mail when he found a letter from the Oakwood Farm HOA informing him that they were fining him one hundred dollars for failing to bring his trash can in from the curb on trash day. Buck Freeman's signature was on the bottom of the letter.

By the summer of 2023, there were only six lots in Oakwood Farm where construction hadn't begun or been completed. More than three-quarters of the homes were finished and occupied, and over a dozen more were in various stages of construction. As more and more residents moved in, the influence of the early arrivals clique began to dissipate.

Bob and Denise Carlson's daughter had a baby, and Bob and Denise decided to move back to Upstate New York. It seems proximity to a grandchild outweighed Denise's aversion to the cold Buffalo winters. As a result, Bob stepped down from the board and the property owners elected a relative newcomer – Maggie Leith, a woman in her forties who was a cybersecurity analyst for defense contractor Booz Allen – to take his place. Maggie was cordial with Buck during board meetings, but she didn't trust him, and she didn't let him run roughshod over Oakwood Farm like he had before.

The relationship between Karen Walters and Ellie Freeman went ice cold after Ellie's attempt to attack Kelli Halstrom. Running was the cornerstone of their friendship, and now that Ellie was physically unable to run, their link was broken. Karen continued running and even started to wave and say hello when she and Kelli crossed paths. Karen was impressed by Maggie Leith's intelligence and tenacity, and when there was a disagreement between Buck and Maggie on board matters, more often than not, Karen sided with Maggie. That did not make Buck Freeman happy.

Andy and Kelli settled into a comfortable routine. They volunteered regularly at MANNA Foodbank where they helped to package donated food and load it into trucks for delivery to food pantries that assist families in need across Western North Carolina. They joined the Leadership Asheville Forum and attended the monthly luncheons where they heard speakers talk about various issues impacting the local area. A neighbor invited Kelli to join her for a yoga class at the Asheville Yoga Center, and she was hooked almost immediately. Kelli tried to get Andy to join her, but he refused saying he'd only go if he got to do goat yoga. Andy joined the Blue Ridge Bicycle Club and did rides of fifty miles or more most weekends when his health allowed it. He'd always been a road biker, but some of the other riders persuaded him to join them on a mountain bike ride and it wasn't long until a new Trek Rail 9.7 mountain bike was hanging in the garage alongside his Cervelo Soloist road bike. Andy and Kelli developed a closeknit group of friends, mostly retirees about their own age, and they took turns hosting dinner parties, arranging nights out at local restaurants and concert venues, and planning hikes. Life for Andy and Kelli was going along quite well ... until it wasn't.

It had been more than six years since Andy's Parkinson's diagnosis. His symptoms had remained relatively minor, sporadic, and brief in duration, and the disease had little impact on his normal day-to-day life. But starting in the spring of 2023, he noticed that the tremors that affected his right side were now showing up on his left side as well. Standing up and walking was getting more difficult, and at times he was unsteady on his feet and would have to grab hold of a wall or the back of a chair to avoid stumbling. His good days were growing fewer and the span between them and his bad days was beginning to shrink. By Labor Day, he was rarely able to hike, bike, or perform manual labor at home or at the food bank.

Kelli continued to run nearly every day, but she curtailed some of her other outside activities so she could be at home with Andy out of fear that he might fall and hurt himself. She had known that a time would come when his condition would worsen, but still, she wasn't really prepared for it. When she was alone and Andy couldn't see her, she often cried. She tried to be stoic and strong for Andy's sake, but deep down she worried about him and what the future held for them both.

Khaled Abadi was released from prison in November 2023. He was happy to be back at home, and he was especially happy to be eating his mother's cooking once again. The day he was released, his mother organized a big family gathering and prepared a feast to celebrate his return home. Seeing his sisters, aunts, and cousins reminded him just how important his family was to him, and it reminded him of the pledge he made to his father in prison right before Mohammed died. It was his duty to avenge his uncle's death and uphold his family's honor.

Khaled did some research and found that the Halstroms had moved from D.C. and were now living in Asheville, North Carolina. He discovered that getting back to the United States was going to be more difficult now that he had a conviction and a prison sentence on his record. He couldn't travel as freely as he had before. Honoring his commitment to his father was going to take some time to plan and execute.

In early 2024, one of Khaled's friends agreed to help him get to Bahrain. When the time came, they left Riyadh and drove towards the border. That evening, as they approached the King Fahd Causeway connecting the two countries, they pulled off the road. Khalid hid in a compartment beneath the backseat and his friend climbed into the driver's seat and pulled back out onto the highway.

"Salam alaykum," the friend said to the Bahraini border guard.

"Alaykum assalaam," the guard responded as he took the friend's passport and examined it. "What is the purpose of your visit to our country?" he inquired as he handed the passport back through the open window.

"I'm attending the Grand Prix this weekend. I'm hoping I get to see Verstappen start the F1 season off with a win."

The guard smiled. "Not me, I'm a Leclerc fan. I'm tired of Verstappen winning all the time. Somebody else deserves a turn at the top. 2024 is going to be Leclerc's year, you wait and see. Normally I'd say enjoy the race, but since you're a Verstappen fan, I wouldn't mean it."

"I understand," the driver said with a smile. "Well, hopefully when the race is over at least one of us will be happy." He put his passport away, place the car in gear, and drove into Bahrain.

Mohammed Abadi had an old friend in Bahrain who was renowned for his skill in forging documents. Khaled hoped his father's friend could help him procure the papers he needed to get to Asheville. He was relieved when he got to the address and found that the old man was still alive and still living in the same house where he lived more than a decade ago when he and Mohammed worked together. Khaled told him that he needed an American passport and an American driver's license. He said he was going to shave off his beard and cut his hair, and he was going to present himself as Hispanic. The old man said he could produce both documents, but it would take time and money. He told Khaled to come back the next day after he shaved and got a haircut, and he would take photographs to use in the documents. They agreed that Khaled would pay him ten thousand dollars – half then and the other half when the documents were ready – and that Khaled would return in two weeks to pick up the documents.

Khaled was impatient and wanted to get on with his mission as soon as possible, but after five years in a Saudi prison, he enjoyed having time to rest and relax in Bahrain. Bahrain is more unconstrained and permissive than Riyadh. Alcohol flowed freely as did young, shapely women, mostly from Russia. Khaled did his best to make up for the five years he'd missed enjoying both while he was in prison. When the time came, he returned to pick up the documents. Just as his father had told him, the old man proved to be exceptionally talented. The passport and the driver's license were perfect. Khaled Abadi was now Javier Diaz from Fort Lauderdale, Florida.

Khaled traveled from Bahrain to Dubai, and from Dubai to Toronto, Canada. In Toronto, he rented a car to drive into the United States. When he stopped at the border, the U.S. agent barely looked at his passport before waving him through. Khaled stopped off for a night in D.C. where he visited a storage locker to retrieve the gear he needed for his mission. The next morning, he turned in the rental car he got in Toronto, and he rented another car from a different rental car agency.

Khaled reached Asheville that afternoon and checked into the Embassy Suites hotel on Haywood Street. It was unseasonably warm for March, so that night, he walked down Montford Avenue in just jeans and a button-up shirt to Nine Mile for dinner. He sat at the bar and surveyed the menu. He asked the server for a recommendation, and she suggested the Kingston 12; sauteed shrimp in a red curry and coconut sauce. Khaled ordered it and a Montford IPA that was brewed there on site. As he sipped his beer and waited for his meal, he took out his phone, pulled up Google Maps, and found directions to Oakwood Farm. He'd drive out there tomorrow to get the lay of the land and then he would devise a plan to do what he came there to do.

The next day was Thursday, so the gate at Oakwood Farm was open when Khaled arrived at the entrance. He drove slowly through the neighborhood trying to pass for someone who was out looking at real estate, what the locals contemptuously call a "looky-loo." He drove up the hill on Oakwood Trail. He had to stop for a minute while a large cement mixer struggled to back into the makeshift driveway at a lot where a house was under construction. A short distance ahead, Buck Freeman's truck was pulled off on the righthand side of the road next to Oakhaven Way, and Buck was standing at the tailgate pouring gas from a red plastic container into his chainsaw. Sections of a large poplar tree were lying next to the road, and from the fresh sawdust on the road, Khaled assumed the tree had fallen and Buck was clearing it from the road. Buck looked up as the car approached and waved as it went past. Khaled smiled and waved back. Buck thought to himself, "just what we need in the neighborhood, a Mexican."

Khaled saw a house on the right near the top of the hill that matched the address for Andy and Kelli Halstrom. He went past it, made a wide turn in the cul-de-sac, and drove slowly back by as he examined the landscape. It was not an ideal location for someone who wanted to murder two people and make a safe getaway. The only way to reach the house by car was on Oakwood Trail and the only way out was to take the same road all the way back through the neighborhood to the gate and onto Old Farm School Road. If the gate was closed, a vehicle was stopped in the road, or some obstruction made the road impassable, he would be trapped with no way out. The house was three-quarters of a mile from the main road, it was near the top of a hill, and it was surrounded by thick vegetation that include briars, so walking in and then fleeing on foot after the deed was done would be challenging, but it was probably a safer choice than driving in where there was only one way for him to leave. At least on foot, Khaled figured he would have more options to choose from if alternatives became necessary as he made his escape.

As he made his way down Oakwood Trail, Khaled turned left at the intersection and followed the road down to Bull Creek. As he was turning his car around, he saw a woman on a foot bridge run across the creek and disappear into the woods. He thought to himself that if there was a trail on the other side of the creek that provided access to Oakwood Farm, and it wasn't too far from the house, that might be the best way for him to get in and out and remain undetected. He pulled Google Maps up on his phone and centered in on his current location. As he expanded the view, he saw that Riceville Road wasn't far away and the satellite image seemed to suggest that there were several trails through the woods that led from Riceville Road to Oakwood Farm. He decided it was worth taking a few minutes to check it out. He drove away unaware that the woman he saw run across the bridge and disappear into the woods was Kelli Halstrom.

Khaled drove up Riceville Road past the North Carolina Outward Bound School. A quarter of a mile later, he saw a dirt parking area on the left side of the road directly across from Berea Baptist Church, and next to it was an entrance into the Warren Wilson College trails. He parked his car and got out. Based on what he could see on Google Maps, from there back to Oakwood Farm was less than half a mile in a straight line, although it appeared the trails meandered through the woods. It looked like it was the same distance whether he went left or right, so he chose the trail on the right. He walked for about five minutes and then he reached a fork in the trail. As he checked the map on his phone to try and determine which fork to take, he heard feet pounding the ground and the sound was growing closer. He looked up and saw the woman he had seen earlier on the bridge running towards him. When she was about ten feet from him, she stopped.

"You look like you're lost. Do you need some help?"

Khaled smiled. "Yes, thank you. I'm down here looking at real estate and I was just over in Oakwood Farm. I saw that there were trails nearby and it's such a nice day that I thought I'd check them out. I was trying to find the way down to the creek and to the bridge that goes over to Oakwood Farm."

"Well, either one of the trails will get you there. The fork on the left is a little shorter distance, but as long as you keep making your way downhill, you'll eventually run into Bull Creek, and if you follow it downstream, it will take you past the bridge. You can't miss it."

Khaled stuck his phone into his pocket. "Thanks. Like you, I enjoy running, particularly cross-country. I thought that if I ended up buying property in Oakwood Farm these trails might be good running trails."

"I run out here almost every day, and my husband I walk the trails a couple of mornings each week. It can get a little slippery when it rains, and there are tree roots and rocks in some spots, so you have to watch your step, but it's pretty out here and it's peaceful. I hardly ever see anyone on the trails, although sometimes I come across a bear or a deer. So, do you think you might buy property in Oakwood Farm?"

"I don't know. Right now, I'm just scoping things out, but I like what I've seen. My wife and I can both telework, so we've been thinking about getting out of the city and this area seems to offer a lot of the things we're looking for."

"This is a lovely area. What city would you be moving from?"

"D.C. We've lived there ever since we graduated from Georgetown, but we're getting tired of the noise and the traffic, and we want to start a family, and a place like Asheville really appeals to us."

"Wow!" Kelli exclaimed. "My husband and I moved here from D.C., and for many of the reasons you just described. We love it here, and I bet you and your wife would too. I'm Kelli, Kelli Halstrom by the way," she said as she extended her hand.

"I'm Javier Diaz," Khaled said as he shook Kelli's hand and tried to act nonchalant. "It's a pleasure to meet you."

"It's a pleasure to meet you too, Javier. Well, listen, I'd better get back to my run. Good luck with your property search. Maybe I'll see you again someday out here on the trails or in Oakwood Farm."

"You just might," Javier responded, then nodded, and started walking down the trail on the left. He smiled as he thought about how lucky he had been to run into Kelli Halstrom on his first morning in Asheville and to learn that she runs alone in the woods almost every day and walks with her husband there several times a week. This job, he thought to himself, could end up being quicker and easier than he'd expected.

After Buck finished taking care of the tree that had fallen and partially blocked the road, he saw a large poplar nearby that was dead and had the potential to fall as well. It was a nice day, and it was still early, so he decided he'd go ahead and take the dead tree down before it eventually fell on its own. He walked up the embankment, chainsaw in hand, and examined the tree. He decided to try and drop it next to the road, but not in the road, where he'd have room to cut it into manageable sections that he could handle alone. He cut a V-shaped wedge out of the left side of the tree and then he started to make a back cut towards the wedge from the right side, when suddenly the tree fell straight down to the ground and began to topple back towards him. Buck dropped the chainsaw and tried to run down the embankment towards the road, but he stumbled and fell flat on his back, and a second later the tree came crashing down across the tops of his legs and pinned him to the ground leaving him with his feet facing uphill and his head facing downhill.

The pain was intense, and Buck screamed. He felt moisture, and at first, he thought it was blood, but then he realized he'd pissed and shit himself. He was embarrassed at first, but he soon realized that soiling himself was the least of his problems. The tree was heavy, and he was in an awkward position on the bank with his head down below his feet. He tried a couple of times to push the tree off his legs, but it was a futile effort. He looked around for a rock or a stick that he could use to try and dig some of the dirt out from around his legs so he could perhaps slide out from under the tree, but the only stick within his reach was brittle and it broke as soon as he tried to dig. He hoped someone would come along soon to help him, but there were only a few houses up above him on the hill and it might be a long time before anyone drove by.

Buck's phone was in the back pocket of his jeans, but because the weight of the tree was across the upper part of his legs, he couldn't reach it. Several minutes passed. Buck tried to wiggle his toes to assess the extent of his injuries. He couldn't see his feet because the tree obstructed his view, but it felt to him like his toes wiggled, which he thought was a good sign.

"Damn," he thought to himself, "why doesn't someone drive by?" A few seconds later, he heard the tap, tap, tap of feet pounding on the pavement, and the sound kept getting louder. He turned his head and looked down the hill, and he saw Kelli Halstrom running up the road towards him. His first thought was "why does it have to be her?" but then he realized that in his situation he couldn't be choosy.

"Help!" Buck yelled. Kelli was focused on the road in front of her and hadn't noticed Buck's truck parked on the grass beside the road ahead of her or him pinned beneath the tree on the bank on the right. She glanced in the direction of the cry for help, and she saw someone wave an arm. She switched from a jog to a full-on run, and she raced towards Buck.

"Oh my God, Buck! Are you alright?" she asked.

"I don't think anything's broken, but I'm not sure. I just can't get this damned thing off of me. My chainsaw is over there by that stump. If you can get it and cut this thing into smaller pieces, I can get out from under it."

Kelli looked up the hill and saw the chainsaw lying on the ground by a tree stump a few feet away. She retrieved it and explained to Buck that she'd never used a chainsaw before, so he walked her through the steps on how to start it and to how to make the cuts that would divide the tree into smaller, lighter sections. She pulled the cord twice and the engine fired. She made a cut through the tree about two feet above Buck's legs and then she moved down below him and started a second cut. As she was cutting, a Waste Pro garbage truck came up the hill and stopped in the road next to Buck's truck. Two men climbed out and ran up the hill. When Kelli completed the second cut, they lifted what was left of the tree off Buck's legs. Buck sat up and wiggled his toes. Despite the pain, he managed to smile.

"Do you think you can get up," Kelli asked.

"I don't know, but let's give it a try," Buck responded.

The two men stood behind Buck, grabbed him under his arms, and helped him up to his feet. He tried to take a step, but he stumbled, and the two men had to catch him to prevent him from falling.

"Shit!" Buck screamed. "I've got a terrible pain in my hip, and I think I've either sprained or broken my ankle."

"I can call 911 and have them send an ambulance," one of the men said.

"Or we can put you in your truck and I can drive you to Mission Hospital," Kelli interjected. "That'll be faster than waiting on an ambulance to get here."

Buck agreed, and the two men helped him down the embankment and into the passenger side of his truck. Kelli ran to the other side and climbed in behind the wheel. "Thanks fellas, I appreciate it," Buck said to the two men as Kelli started the engine and drove away.

The adrenaline from the excitement Kelli experienced began to wear off before they reached Old Farm School Road. Kelli didn't want to add insult to injury, so she didn't say anything to Buck, but the stench from the shit in Buck's pants was about to make her wretch and she rolled down her window all the way to let in some fresh air.

Kelli pulled into the emergency entrance at Mission Hospital, jumped out of the truck, and ran inside. A moment later, she came back out followed by two men pulling a stretcher. They got Buck out of the truck and onto the stretcher, and they wheeled him inside. Kelli moved the truck to a parking space and then she went inside to the ER lobby. She called Andy and told him what had happened. Andy grabbed his keys, headed down to Buck's house, told Ellie about the accident, and drove her to the hospital. About thirty minutes after they arrived, a doctor came out to speak with Ellie. She said Buck had a fractured hip and a broken ankle, but there were no serious internal injuries. He was headed up to surgery and he would be in the hospital for a few days, but he should make a full recovery. Ellie hugged the doctor and broke down in tears. When she released her grip on the doctor, she turned to Kelli. "Thank you," she said as she wrapped her arms around Kelli and squeezed her tight.

As the two men from Waste Pro who had helped rescue Buck continued their rounds, they told some of the other Oakwood Farm residents about the accident. When one of them asked if Buck was seriously injured, one of the Waste Pro men said it didn't appear that he was hurt too bad, and added, "but he did shit himself." Once again, word spread around Oakwood

Farm that Kelli Halstrom had saved someone, and this time it was Buck Freeman. Word also spread that The Shit King shit himself. When Buck Freeman heard about it, he was not happy.

Khaled woke up Friday morning and walked to the window of his hotel room. The mountains to the west were barely visible through the clouds and the street below was wet as a light rain fell. By the time he got dressed and went down to the lobby, the rain was coming down in sheets and ran down the street like a raging creek trying to escape its banks. No one was going to be out for a walk or a run in this weather. Khaled got a cup of coffee and went back up to his room to figure out what he could do to kill some time. He took out his phone and Googled movies that were playing in the local area. He was happy to see that Dune Part Two was on at the Regal Theater in Biltmore Park. He had seen Dune Part One and liked it, so if he had time to kill, that was about as good a way as any to do it. He looked online for restaurants close to the theater, and he decided he'd go to Tupelo Honey on Hendersonville Road for dinner and then catch the seven-thirty show. He knew that when the rain stopped it was going to be muddy on the Warren Wilson College trails, so he decided that if the rain let up in the afternoon, he'd walk over to Mast General Store and buy jeans and a pair of waterproof hiking boots. Until then, he'd just lay on the bed and read and later he'd go down to the hotel's gym for a workout, and he hoped that the weather would be more favorable tomorrow.

Andy woke up before Kelli and walked slowly and quietly to the kitchen to make coffee. He looked out the window to the east and saw red and yellow bands of light over the tops of the mountains as the sun started to rise. In about a month, leaves would begin to fill in the trees and the grass would start to turn green, and already the daffodils were poking their heads out of the ground. Four white-tailed deer moved slowly through the trees below the back of the house nibbling on whatever patches of green they could find. Andy just stood there and took it all in, and he thought to himself how lucky he was.

Kelli walked into the kitchen. "Good morning," she said as she stretched her arms back behind her head and yawned. "I didn't even hear you get up. Have you been up long?"

"No," Andy responded as he handed her a cup of coffee. "I've only been up long enough to make coffee and to admire the deer that passed through our backyard a few minutes ago. Looks like the rain has moved on through and it's going to be a nice day."

They walked to the living room. Andy settled into his chair and Kelli sat down on the sofa and pulled her legs up beneath her to keep them warm. They sipped their coffee, they both Wordled – Kelli solved it in three attempts and poked fun at Andy because it took him five tries – and then they spent the next hour on their iPads reading the news.

"It doesn't look like the mess in the Middle East is getting better anytime soon. I've got to say I'm glad we're out of the game. I know this is keeping a lot of folks up at night back at Langley."

Kelli nodded. "Yeah, I agree. To be honest, there are times when I miss it and I wonder what we'd be doing if we were still there, but that passes pretty quickly and I'm happy to be here where it's safe and it's quiet, and our biggest problem is trying to figure out which of our neighbor's dogs keeps shitting in our yard."

Andy smiled. "I think I know which one of those little bastards is poop-bombing us. I'm tempted to scoop up a pile or two, put it in a paper bag, drop it on Maggie's front porch, set it on fire, and then ring her doorbell and run away and watch her stomp it. Maybe then she'd get the

273

message and start cleaning up after Claude. Others don't seem to have a problem picking up after their dogs, so I don't understand why she won't do it."

"Oh, come on now. You don't know for sure that it's Claude. And I think Maggie is just clueless about it and has no idea what a nuisance it is. Just let it go. Besides, if you got caught and sent to prison, I don't know where lighting dog shit on fire on someone's porch rates in the prison pecking order – not very high, I'd guess – and I'd hate for you to get picked on by the other inmates who are probably doing time for murders and bank robberies."

Andy laughed. "I make no promises."

"Fine," Kelli said as she closed her iPad. "I'm going to go brush my teeth and change out of these pajamas. If you're feeling up to it, would you be interested in going for a walk down on the trail in a little bit?"

"Sure. I'm actually feeling pretty good today, and I definitely could use some exercise. With all that rain we got yesterday, the trail's going to be muddy, so I'd put on something you won't mind getting dirty."

"Yep. Let's give it a little time to warm up before we go, so let's shoot for ten o'clock."

When Khaled pulled into the parking area across from Berea Baptist Church at a little past nine, he was pleased to see that no other cars were there. He got out, looked around, and zipped his jacket up all the way around his neck. It wasn't especially cold for March, but the front that passed through and pushed out the rain left behind a stiff breeze that made it feel colder than what the car's thermometer indicated it really was. He had to step over a puddle to get to the entrance to the trails and he hadn't walked far when he had to move off to the right side of the path and onto the pine needles to stay above a muddy stretch that went on for twenty feet or more. He followed the trail until it ran into Bull Creek, which was running higher and faster than the last time he was there, and then he took the path to the left and kept going until he reached the foot bridge that crossed over the creek to Oakwood Farm. He looked down at the mud next to the first step up onto the bridge and saw no evidence of any footprints, which indicated to him that no one had passed that way since the rain stopped. He saw a huge oak tree and a thick stand of rhododendrons on the other side of the creek not far from the bridge, and he decided that would be a good place to conceal himself while he waited to see if the Halstroms were taking a walk that day. It was nine-forty. He thought that he'd give them a few hours and if they didn't show up by then, he'd go back to the hotel and try again tomorrow. He found a big rock amongst the rhododendrons – the same one that Ellie Freeman sat on several months earlier as she waited on Kelli to come by – and he plopped down on it to wait.

A few minutes before ten, Andy walked out into the garage, pulled his oldest pair of hiking shoes down off the shelf, and slipped them on. Kelli joined him a minute later, laced up her boots, and grabbed a pair of hiking poles.

"The trail's going to be slippery from the rain, so I'm taking my hiking poles. Do you want yours?" she asked.

"That's not a bad idea. Better to have'em and not need'em than to need'em and not have'em," he responded.

They closed the garage behind them, walked up their driveway, turned left, and then started making their way down the hill.

"Damn!" Kelli exclaimed. "The wind is making it feel a lot colder than I thought it was going to be."

"You want to go back and get a warmer coat?" Andy asked.

"No. I expect I'll warm up as we keep moving."

"Okay, but I know how you are. You always underdress and then you complain that you're cold. I don't want to get down to the creek and then you ask me if you can have my jacket."

Kelli smiled. "I think I'll be fine ... and if not, I'm sure you'll be chivalrous and help out a damsel in distress."

Andy shook his head. "Don't count on it.

It was a quarter past ten when Andy and Kelli left the pavement and started down the dirt path towards the bridge over Bull Creek and onto the Warren Wilson trails. Khaled saw them as they were approaching the bridge. He reached inside his jacket, pulled out a nine-millimeter pistol, and screwed a silencer onto the barrel. He stood up and positioned himself behind the oak tree to wait until they were on the bridge and past him so he could move in behind them and get on with the job. He heard their footsteps as they walked on the wooden bridge. A few more seconds and it would be done, and he would have fulfilled the promise he made to his father ... or so he thought.

"Hey Andy!" a man yelled from a short distance away. Khaled peered around the tree. There was a house visible through the trees about two hundred yards upstream and set back some distance from the creek. A man was walking from the house down towards the creek and waving his arms.

"Hey Andy!" Andy and Kelli stopped on the bridge and turned in the man's direction. The man kept walking towards them and then he stopped alongside the creek about twenty yards from the bridge. "I'm going to French Broad Stone to see about getting a load of rocks delivered

276

so I can build a firepit behind my place down here by the creek. I know that you mentioned a while back that you were thinking about building a firepit at your place too. Are you interested in going in on a load with me while they'll be delivering out this way?"

"I appreciate you asking, John, but I'm going to pass. The guy that did our landscaping came over about two weeks ago and he's preparing a quote on what he'd charge to build one for us. It's a bigger job than I feel like I can handle by myself. We're probably going to wait until the end of the summer before we pull the trigger on it since cold weather is just about over for this season."

"No worries. Just thought I'd ask. I'm lucky. I've got a buddy who owns a Bobcat that he's going to loan me, so I won't have to try and manhandle the big rocks. I'm hoping French Broad can get them delivered soon. I'd like to get the work done before the weather gets hot.

Anyway, you guys enjoy your walk. And be careful. I'm sure the trails are as slippery as owl shit after all that rain we got yesterday."

"Thanks John. Have a good day ... and tell Pam we said hey."

The man turned around and started walking back towards his house. Andy and Kelli proceeded across the bridge and away from where Khaled was hiding, headed up the trail, and then disappeared into the woods. Khaled stood motionless behind the oak tree. Even with the sound of the wind and the creek's rushing water creating some background noise, it was just too risky to shoot now with the man still close enough to potentially hear the shots, even with a silencer on the pistol. The man was walking towards his house and there was only one way for Andy and Kelli to get back across to Oakwood Farm at the end of their walk, so Khaled decided to wait until they returned and there was no one around before he did the deed. He walked back over to the rock in the rhododendrons and sat down. With any luck at all, he thought to himself,

277

he could do what he came there to do and still make it to lunch before noon. He hadn't eaten anything that morning and now he was hungry, but first, there were two people he needed to kill.

Andy and Kelli chose the path along the east side of the creek and followed it upstream. They walked up a slight rise, turned left, and walked over next to the creek where some old stonework remained from a dam the Asheville Farm School for boys built in 1910 to produce electricity for the school. A flood in 1916 washed the dam away, twenty-six years before the school merged with the Dorland-Bell School for girls to create what is now the co-ed Warren Wilson College. All that was left of the dam was the stonework, which stood about fifteen feet tall at its highest points on both sides of the creek. Many mistakenly believed that what remained were the remnants of the grist mill James Craig built and where he was shot two hundred and sixteen years earlier, but Craig's mill was a little further up the creek, and today there's not a trace of it left.

Andy and Kelli stood still for several seconds, listening to the sound of the creek rushing by and taking in the natural beauty of the place.

Kelli reached over and took Andy's hand in hers. "I know we've stood here dozens of times before, but the peace and tranquility of this place never gets old, does it?"

Andy smiled and squeezed Kelli's hand. "No, it doesn't." Andy paused for a moment. "I don't have any regrets about the lives we led when we were younger. A lot of people who know us now would never believe the things we did back then, but what we did made them and the world safer, even though they'll never know it. I don't think about it often, but when I do, I can't help but think how lucky we are to have lived through it all and to have never gotten caught. We were quite the team back in the day."

"Were? We're still quite the team," Kelli answered. "I try not to look back too often, but sometimes I can't help it, even though it's pointless. We can't change the past, even if we wanted to, and I don't want to. Who knows how things might be different now had we not done what we did, and I can't imagine that the world would be better off with the bad people in it that we disappeared. I wouldn't want to do it again – hell, I'm too damn old for that kind of stuff now – but I don't have any regrets about the things we did."

Andy smiled. "Sure, you're older, but you're still the most beautiful woman I've ever seen. You're like the Rolex on your wrist; you just get more precious as time goes by. I'm older too, but even with my Parkinson's starting to get worse, this is the happiest I've ever been. I've got you. We've got a beautiful house. We live in these beautiful mountains. We've earned a little peace and tranquility, and I intend to enjoy it for as long as I can. Anyway, enough of that maudlin shit. Let's get moving."

Khaled was cold and growing impatient. He tried to tune it out by thinking about where he'd go for lunch after he killed the Halstroms. He enjoyed the dinner he had at Tupelo Honey in South Asheville the night before, so he thought that maybe he'd try the original Tupelo Honey across from Pritchard Park in downtown Asheville for lunch. He'd never had chicken and waffles before until last night, and he might have chicken and waffles again for lunch; they were delicious. The minutes continued to roll by slowly and Khaled started to think that maybe Andy and Kelli had taken another route that crossed over the creek somewhere else, and they wouldn't be coming back his way after all. He was only going to give it a few minutes more before he packed it in and left, and then he spotted them as they came over the rise and continued walking in his direction. It was showtime.

As Andy and Kelli stepped off the bridge and walked past the rhododendrons, Khaled stepped out for behind the oak tree, raised his pistol, and said, "Hello there." Andy and Kelli stopped, turned around, and froze in their tracks.

"I've been waiting for you; in fact, I've been waiting for you for almost six years, and at last we finally meet."

"Javier?" Kelli inquired. "What's going on? What are you doing?"

"I'm sorry, Kelli, but I'm not Javier. My real name is Khaled Abadi. My uncle was Hassan Abadi. You'll remember him because you murdered him almost twenty-five years ago. My father was Mohammed Abadi. You never met him I assume, or he would have killed you himself. My father died a few years ago, but before he died, he made me promise that I would kill the people responsible for murdering his brother, my uncle. I took care of your old boss, Carson Neal, some time ago, and then I started looking for you. Thanks to your government and mine, I got sidelined for a long time, but now I'm here and I'm going to finish the job in honor of my father and my uncle."

Andy's training kicked in and his mind raced as he searched for a way out. He needed to buy some time to try and devise an escape from their predicament. "Hassan Adobe? We've never met anyone named Hassan Adobe. You've got us mixed up with somebody else. You're making a huge mistake here."

"There's no mistake … and it's Abadi, Hassan Abadi. I know it was you because your old boss gave you up right before I killed him and his wife. In fact, right after I killed them, I tracked you down and I went to your apartment in D.C. planning to kill the two of you too, but you weren't there. That was lucky for you it seems. You've ended up living a few years longer than you would have."

Andy knew that time was running out and still he saw no means of escaping, so he did the only thing that came to mind: He yelled "run Kelli!" as he hurled himself at Khaled. There was a muffled bang. Andy's initial thought was how quiet the gun was when it fired, and he gave Khaled credit for having a high-quality professional-grade silencer. His next thought was that something wet was running down his chest … and then he dropped to his knees.

"Come back here, now!" Khaled yelled at Kelli who had only managed to take a couple of steps. "I'll shoot you in the back and then I'll make sure he suffers in agony if you don't stop. Now, turn around and walk back towards me."

Kelli raised her hands, turned around, and walked back in Khaled's direction. "Are you okay?" she asked as she tried to reach down to Andy.

"Don't touch him. Stay right there." Khaled raised his pistol and pointed it at Kelli. "I could have killed you first, Andrew, but that wouldn't have been much fun for me. I wanted you to live to see your wife's brains splattered on the ground before you. I want you to suffer and experience the grief of losing someone you love the way my father suffered after you murdered his brother."

Andy held his right hand over the hole in his left shoulder to try and slow the bleeding. He figured he was about to die, so there was no reason to hold back. "Your father was a piece of shit just like your uncle was. They were responsible for thousands of innocent people dying, including American service members. Oh, and you should know that your uncle died like a whiny little bitch and the only good thing I can say about him is that after we killed him, his body fed the fish as chunks of him sank down to the bottom of the ocean. We did the world a favor taking out that scumbag."

Khaled pointed the gun at Andy's head. "Fu …" was as much of "fuck you" as Khaled managed to get out before a gust of wind blew especially hard and there was a loud cracking sound overhead. Khaled looked up just as a huge section of the oak tree broke off and came crashing down. It struck him on the head and then it landed across his chest and pinned him to the ground.

Kelli walked over to Khaled. He had a serious gash in his scalp, and was bleeding profusely, but he was still alive. "I … can't … breath," he said in a weak murmur as he labored for a breath. "Get … this … off … me … please."

"Fuck you," Kelli said, and then she sat down on the section of tree that stretched across Khaled's chest and she added her weight to it. Her feet were planted on the ground on either side of Khaled's head, and she looked down at his eyes as he looked up at her in desperation. She never blinked or broke eye contact as Khaled struggled to pull in a breath, and she didn't move until she saw his pupils enlarge and his gaze go blank, and the last glimmer of life passed out of his body.

Kelli stood up and turned to Andy. "How are you?"

Andy pulled his hand away from the wound and looked at it. "It hurts like a son of a bitch, but I don't think it's too bad. It looks like it went clean through and missed my collarbone. I just need to get the bleeding under control. I guess I should be grateful the asshole shot me on my bad side and spared my good side. Just like in the bombing, it seems my left side always get the worst of it."

"Are you able to stand up and walk?"

"I think so." Kelli helped Andy up to his feet. Just as she released her grip on him, Andy pointed up in the oak tree and said "look!" Kelli turned around and looked up. Two black bears –

a mother and a young cub – were making their way slowly down the tree. Andy and Kelli backed away a few feet and watched. When the bears reached the ground, the mother bear stood motionless for a moment and looked at Andy and Kelli. Then she turned and walked over to Khaled's body. She sniffed his remains and then she let out a loud snort. She looked at Andy and Kelli again, and then she seem to nod her head. The mother bear looked over at her cub, grunted, and the two bears walked across Bull Creek and disappeared into the woods.

"Holy shit! What in the hell was that?" Andy asked.

"I don't know," Kelli said. "Do you think the bears caused that section of the tree to fall, or was it that big gust of wind?"

"The hell if I know. Whichever one it was, I'm grateful. It saved our lives. Now what do we do with him?" Andy asked as he motioned towards Khaled's body.

Kelli glanced over at Khaled. If we report it, it's going to raise a lot of questions and if they figure out who he is then they'll figure out who we are and blow our cover. For now, why don't we see if we can get the tree off of him. If we can, we can hide the body in those rhododendrons, and I'll call Carla Ellis and see how the agency wants to handle this."

Andy found a tree branch and was able to use it and his good arm to create enough leverage to lift the section of tree up enough for Kelli to pull Khaled's body out from beneath it. Together, they dragged the body into the rhododendrons and then covered it with tree branches and leaves. Then they headed home. Andy was getting weak from the blood he lost. He had to put his good arm over Kelli's shoulder for support as they went up the hill towards their house. A neighbor who was out for a walk crossed paths with them and asked if Andy was okay. Andy said he slipped and fell while he and Kelli were walking on the trails near the swimming hole down by the Swannanoa River on the other side of Old Farm School Road and Kelli said she was

283

going to get him home and let him lay down and rest. The neighbor wished them well, and continued walking.

Kelli called Carla Ellis and told her what happened. Carla was surprised to learn that Khaled Abadi was responsible for the murders of Carson Neal and his wife, but it all made sense. She said the agency would dispatch a team to Asheville to dispose of Khaled's body and the team would include a medic who could patch up Andy's wound. Kelli told Carla about the wind blowing, the section of the oak tree falling, and the bears climbing down from the tree. Carla responded, "well, ain't that some shit. Just be thankful that luck was on your side." As they were finishing the telephone call, Carla added, "By the way. I'm planning to retire at the end of the year. I hear good things about Asheville. Maybe I'll join you two down there someday."

A Gulfstream jet landed at Asheville Regional Airport that afternoon and three people carrying big black cases climbed out. They loaded the cases into the back of a van, and they drove away. A short time later, the van pulled into Oakwood Farm and headed up the hill to Andy and Kelli Halstrom's house. A physician's assistant examined Andy's wound, cleaned it, and stitched it up. He said there didn't appear to be any permanent damage, but it was going to take some time before Andy healed up. He told Andy to keep a close eye on it and if there were any complications they'd get him up to D.C. for additional treatment.

Kelli rode with the other two agents over to the parking area across from Berea Baptist Church where they found a car they assumed was Khaled's. They followed the trail down to the creek and the patch of rhododendrons where Khaled's body was hidden. They removed tools from their cases and used them to dismember Khaled's body and they stuffed the pieces into heavy plastic bags. It had been years since Kelli was involved in wet ops, but she hadn't forgotten the tricks of the trade. The three of them carried the bags back up to the parking area

284

where they loaded them into the van. When they were done, one of the agents drove Khaled's rental car to an area behind an old shopping center on Tunnel Road that's known to be an area where drug use and drug deals are commonplace. The other agent drove Kelli home, picked up the physician's assistant, and then headed to Tunnel Road to retrieve the other team member. They were back in the air by nine-thirty that evening and arrived in D.C. with their cargo before midnight.

Javier Diaz's rental car was found abandoned in a parking lot in West Asheville the following week. The C.I.A. agent who abandoned it left the doors unlocked and it appeared that it had been used as a shooting gallery based on the drug paraphernalia the police found inside. Paperwork discovered in the console showed that the car was rented to Javier Diaz from Fort Lauderdale, Florida. That was the same name that had been reported to the police by a clerk at Embassy Suites after a guest failed to checkout and didn't return to retrieve his belongings. The Asheville Police Department officially listed Javier Diaz as a missing person, and he remains in that status.

Andy's wound was fully healed by the end of the summer. Fortunately, his Parkinson's symptoms stabilized and even improved a bit, and his good days began to outnumber the bad ones again. Kelli went back to running. Every time she ran down at the creek, she glanced over at the oak tree and thought about the day she and Andy almost died. A mother bear and her cub were regular visitors in Andy and Kelli's yard that season. They were certain they were the same bears that came down the oak tree after a section of it fell on Khaled. The authorities say you're not supposed to feed the bears. Andy and Kelli made an exception, and extra nuts and berries were on their grocery list that summer and fall when they went shopping. When mom and the cub would finish eating and start to amble off towards the woods, Andy and Kelli swore it seemed like the mother bear would look back at them and nod her head as if to say, "thanks my friends."

From time to time, Andy and Kelli talk about the day Khaled Abadi tried to kill them and how they would have died there next to Bull Creek had nature not intervened. They've never been able to decide whether the bears or the wind saved their lives. Truth be told, it was neither one. The sovereign oak acted alone.

Everything in nature is connected; if you harm one thing, you harm everything.

– Cherokee Proverb

Made in the USA
Columbia, SC
16 December 2024

49353673R00157